I'M ALIVE!

I'M ALIVE!

AN AUTOBIOGRAPHY

Cecil Williams

HARPER & ROW, PUBLISHERS

SAN FRANCISCO

Cambridge London
Hagerstown   Mexico City
Philadelphia   São Paulo
New York *1817* Sydney

FIRST EDITION

Designed by Jim Mennick

Library of Congress Cataloging in Publication Data

Williams, Cecil, 1929–
    I'M ALIVE!

    1. Williams, Cecil, 1929–   2. Methodist Church–Clergy–Biography.
3. Clergy–United States–Biography   I. Title.
BX8495.W638A33   1980   287 [B]   79–1783
ISBN 0-06-250950-0

---

80 81 82 83 84 10 9 8 7 6 5 4 3 2 1

This book is dedicated to my children, Kim and Albert.

For nine years I have been trying to give birth to this book. It happened with two people who pushed for its life:

DAVE RICHMOND, the writer, who seized the soul of my story and gave it life on the page;

JANICE MIRIKITANI, the editor, whose insight and perception helped shape the book.

Thanks to Harper & Row and Clayton Carlson for taking the risk.

I'M ALIVE!

ONE

WHEN I was ten years old, my train came to kill me. The voices warned of the train's intention, but they really didn't have to. I knew what the train was after, and for months that wore like years I felt and believed I would die in the darkness.

Before the night of the train, I loved that time each day when the sun darkened to a burnt orange and night began its approach. Then the family and community gathered on our porch to share the end of the day, our house being an unofficial public meeting place in the black section of a West Texas town called San Angelo.

The second youngest of six children—five boys and a girl—I felt I was different. From the beginning, everyone called me "Rev," a shortened label of the ministry that was both serious and playful. It was the highest praise and heaviest pressure that such a churchgoing family could place on the head of one of its sons, and we were very churchgoing. Like many black families whose options seemed beyond their control, we went to church not only on Sunday but nearly every other day as well. And if our black church could not grant us redemption on earth, at least it provided a frame of reference, a safe meeting place, and a context in which to view our lives. And deaths. The promise of death was a cornerstone of all such churches in black communities across the country. Freedom, liberation, and salvation, we were told, would be ours after life, not during it. In a sense, our church was a call to death, a place to get fitted for those golden slippers that would walk us up to heaven. Despite its insistence on death as a reward to the faithful, all through my young life the church seemed to me the one community institution that could galvanize people. My nickname, an informal ordainment, was the origin of anxiety as well as pride, even if I was unaware of such complex combinations at the age of ten.

My mother was the primary person in my life, but there was also Papa Jack. Mother was a source of love, tenderness, strength, and promise. Papa Jack was a measure of pride, defiance, and courage.

My maternal grandfather, Papa Jack was withered, stooped, and shrunken by age. He was very dark, with a deceptive frailty exaggerated by his use of a cane. But Papa Jack, nearing his eighties, employed his cane and age as badges of honor, not testimonials to his mortality. He was a free-cussin', hard-drinkin' man who survived the legal drought in Tom Green County by installing a still in the cellar of our Auntie's house next door. Hidden from all but the knowledgeable, the cellar not only housed a still but also gave us refuge from the tornadoes and sandstorms that raged through San Angelo.

Once a slave, Papa Jack migrated to the Southwest and worked as a cowboy. He always wore a cowboy hat, even when asleep. Each morning he gave us a glimpse of life on the trail. He never had anything but oatmeal and thick black coffee, ate and drank only from plates and cups of tin, and, to top it all off, ate his oatmeal with a knife. Relaxed in his porch chair, he kept the community children engrossed for hours with his cowboy tales. He told us how he herded cattle up the Chisholm Trail before the railroads came. He told us how U.S. soldiers rampaged through Indian villages slitting open the bellies of pregnant women, and how angry that made him. He told us how he escaped from Indians and gangs of white folks. Sometimes he even let us touch the bullets.

Papa Jack walked around with three bullets in his body, two in a leg and one in an arm, and occasionally he fiddled with the slugs as he talked. Each bullet had its own story.

"This a white man's bullet here," he would say, fingering one of the lead nuggets. "Dirty bastard."

I loved his stories, but I loved even more the way Papa Jack stood up to the white man.

It was the late 1930s. Blacks were niggers in substance even if we were "Nigra" or "colored" in name. There were three kinds of public restrooms in those days; "Men," "Women," and "Colored." When times were hard, as they somehow often seemed to be, insurance men, bill collectors, and other agents of a white world I didn't even pretend to fully understand came by the house.

I was very young, but I could still see it in their eyes and self-satisfied strut. It all suggested that the white world had given them the power to do any damn thing they pleased. It was not so much that we—the family and community—were scorned by these men. It was more the way they tried to show us that we were completely without value. Hatred, at least, is a form of recognition. These men didn't even give us that.

They often came in pairs and walked up the street as if they held its deed in their pockets. We were usually in front when they came. Without even acknowledging our existence, they strode up the stairs to the front door. Most of the time they knocked. Sometimes they just walked right in.

"Auntie!" They belittled my mother as they demanded her presence. Mother, a woman who could balance ten of them on the scales of humanity, was being insulted as "Auntie" once again. But I was only a small boy. What could I do about it?

"Auntie," one of them would say as his partner stood by. "Now, Auntie, y'know how good we been to you. We always tryin' to help y'all out. Y'know that, doncha?"

Mother wouldn't answer them.

"But you really fallin' behind here. We gotta get some payment today, Auntie, or you and your folks'll be in a little trouble. You understand, doncha, Auntie? A little bit o' trouble."

Despite the infirmities of age, Papa Jack would rise from his porch chair and march toward the white men, menacingly waving his cane.

"Git outta here!" Papa Jack's voice still had an intensity that showed he meant what he said. "Goddamn white bastards! Git on outta here! We'll get you the damn money when we can!"

Amazed that Papa Jack would cuss out white folks like that, the two men would look at each other in astonishment. But they knew he wasn't playing.

"Now you git the hell outta this house! Git yo' ass offa this porch, git yo' ass outta this yard, git yo' ass away from here or I'll beat the shit outta you with this cane!"

As the strangers retreated, sometimes in a panicked rush and other times in a forced stroll, I was alive with something beyond even pride. Papa Jack, a black man so old he had to walk with a cane, had declared himself to a world that considered him beneath respect. If they didn't do anything else, Papa Jack's declarations proved to us how wrong those white men and their world were. Maybe that was enough.

That wasn't Papa Jack's only lesson, though. Once a group of white students from the University of Texas sought out Papa Jack as part of a report on slavery. He had them sit on the porch with him. A group of young children were in the yard when the students began asking Papa Jack about his experiences with slavery. What hit me was how slowly the answers came from a man not known for reflecting too much on anything. It was as if the answers were so deep inside him, so far from his mouth and the moment that he had to travel a long way down to collect them, bring them up, and show them to the students.

It was mid-afternoon and the heat beat down on the yard with punishing force. Even the shade offered no relief. Papa Jack wiped his arm across his forehead, got up, and disappeared into the house. When he returned he carried a soiled folder full of photographs, the details of which I could not see. Papa Jack studied each picture at great length. Removing each one from the folder, he held them to the sunlight and looked at them in silence. When he finally came to the last picture, he stared at it even longer than he had the rest. After a while he raised his right arm, extended his index finger, and in a broad sweep pointed to all of us children bundled around his feet. He spoke to us without pity or resignation. He spoke to us only with a tight-jawed dignity, the authority of his experience as a slave, the anger and resolve which that experience had fed him. He said,

"Papa's an exslave. Now you all be exslaves too."

I've always remembered those words, even though I didn't understand what my grandfather meant as he spoke them.

Two months later Papa Jack died. He wanted to die in the house, surrounded by those he loved. One night he fell asleep in his cowboy hat and never woke up. It was the fall of 1938. I was nine years old.

Lizzie Best, Papa Jack's wife, had died in 1935. Half American Indian, she moved calmly but surely through our lives uttering only a few words of English. She had a deep, unshakable serenity that flowed silently into the free and even rebellious movements of her husband. I didn't attend her funeral. None of the children did. In those days children were not supposed to experience the ceremonies of the living in remembrance of the dead. But Papa Jack's case was an exception. We all went. It was my first funeral. And my first visit to a cemetery.

The service was at our church, which was Wesley Methodist. A handful of the mourners were white, and that's what I remember most about the funeral. It was the first time I saw blacks and whites come together like that. For all his fire and defiance, indeed perhaps because of it, Papa Jack had connections with the white community that no other black person had. I recognized most of the whites at the funeral because I'd seen them come by the house to talk with Papa Jack. The town fire chief was one of them. He came by a lot.

It was a sad but prideful funeral, with lots of crying, singing, and testifying. Different people sprang from the pews to eulogize Papa Jack. Even a few whites testified. All of them cried. Mother wept too, of course, but I sensed she'd found something with which to steel herself against the death of her father. After the service we emerged from the church. The sun was shining, and the sky was a clear, fragile blue. But it was very cold. I wrapped my arms around my body and walked with some of the children to a waiting car. It wasn't ours. We didn't own a car. A man from the community drove, and a woman sat beside him. The children sat in the back during the long, quiet ride. Finally we arrived at a large gate on the outskirts of town.

"Well, here we are," the woman announced with a sigh.

I didn't know what to expect, so I didn't say anything and let my expectations take shape as we moved along. I just looked out the window, another passenger on a slow train. This was the place of the dead, the place of ultimate and absolute equality, although I didn't think of it in those terms.

The road ran along the cemetery perimeter. On the right was

a fence and beyond it the last reaches of San Angelo. On the left were the cemetery grounds, lush, peaceful, and beautiful. The grass was velvet, pampered like the smooth and precious skin of a living thing. The graves were neatly arranged like rows of a strange crop. The tombstones were slate, gray, white, and brown. Some were large and some were small, some were ornate and some were simple. They jutted from the earth like hunks of clean bone. Wreaths and bouquets popped up among the rows, and small beds of flowers were planted meticulously in spots. There was a manicured grace to it all, a certain care and pride, as though the living, even and especially in their grief, were prepared to accept the reality of death while determined to affirm the dignity of life. I was impressed, and glad the cemetery looked as it did. If anybody deserved to rest this way, Papa Jack did. Lost in my observations, I heard the woman speak.

"We in the white section now."

The white section. Then there must be a black section too, I thought. I should have known, but I comforted myself with the hope that since the white section looked so fine, the black section couldn't be too bad. I imagined the black section would not be as fancy, that maybe there wouldn't be quite as many flowers and the grass wouldn't be quite as smooth. We rolled along that road for a long time. The view didn't change much. The cemetery still looked beautiful and dignified to me. Then we came to a huge swath of dirt nearly fifty yards wide. It looked like a road except that it was much too big.

"That's it over there," the woman said, pointing across the river of dirt. "The Negro section."

We got out of the car. The place looked like a bumpy pasture. I saw three white men leaning on shovels and standing by a big hole, dirt piled high on the side. Another white man, dressed a little better than the gravediggers, scurried about impatiently. Suddenly, for no apparent reason, he wheeled and pointed to a car in our procession that was nudging the edge of the white section's pastoral ground.

"Hey, you!" he hollered at the driver. "That car's too close, boy. You better move that thing over here!"

The driver did as he was told. Then I understood. The dirt

was meant to separate the two sections of the cemetery, insurance against roving bands of black corpses.

The black section was not lush, peaceful, or beautiful. Arrogant weeds burst through the soil at will. Uncut grass smothered the graves. There were no wreaths and bouquets, only a few round wire skeletons where flowers once hung. We didn't wish such desolation on our dead. It was only that we didn't have the money and the caretakers didn't care. The graveyard was like a forgotten dumping ground. I grew sad and ashamed.

Burial plots were marked by weathered two-by-fours. Graves were identified by a small piece of notepaper wedged between a metal backplate and a clear plastic cover attached to the top of a two-foot metal stake jabbed into the ground. The stakes were weak. Some had toppled to the ground and littered the dreary landscape. The burial plots varied in size, some accommodating two graves, some four, some a few more. But there was a limit to the number of gravesites a single black family could buy, assuming they had the money, so there was no guarantee that all members of a family would be buried together.

Led by the preacher, we walked over to our family's plot. I saw right away that the only tombstone in the yard lay in our plot. It belonged to my uncle, Albert Best. The army had provided the tombstone because Uncle Albert had served in World War I. He died of tuberculosis soon after. Papa Jack was to be buried alongside his wife. I looked at my grandmother's grave, my eyes climbing the metal stake to the plastic and paper. I saw, with shock and dismay, that the paper was blank. Her name had faded away. Dead only three years, and already her name was invisible. Everyone noticed.

The preacher got so worked up he damn near delivered another sermon, but I didn't hear what he said. I kept staring at my grandmother's grave, at Papa Jack's grave, at the white section across the dirt, and back again to the blank paper.

When Papa Jack's grave was full and the ceremony done, people began to talk. They spoke about their loved ones dying, how Lizzie's name had vanished, how bad the cemetery looked, how much they had to pay to get into it anyway. The first one to move was an elderly woman who wore an old black hat and a dark blue coat that was probably the closest to black that she had. She'd stood on the edge of the gathering without saying a word. I know she came to church a lot, but I don't remember her name.

"I wonder," she said in almost a whisper and to nobody in particular. "Lord, I wonder." Her voice grew louder, but she wasn't talking to any of us. "Lord, I wonder where, wonder if I can . . ."

She jerked away from us erratically and stalked down the narrow path toward the other graves, waving one arm in front of her. With a determination fed by fear or fury or maybe both, she marched on. As she grew smaller in the distance, I still heard noises escape from her throat. They didn't sound like words to me.

The others understood what they had to do, and one by one peeled away to search among the graves. I saw them trudge from plot to plot, beseeching the empty pieces of paper as if through sheer will they could make inked letters appear where there was nothing. Soon they were scattered across the yard, struggling to remember.

Suddenly a cry froze the late afternoon. I saw the woman in the dark blue coat twenty yards away, crumpled in a heap on the dirty ground. She was on her knees, her hands balled tightly into fists that pressed themselves into the hollows of her eyes. She cried loudly and deeply, and didn't care who heard or saw her. Her man lay among the anonymous graves. But there was nothing left to tell her where.

"Lord have mercy, they done took him away," she moaned. "I can't find him nowhere."

People rushed to comfort her. I stayed back. They managed to help her to her feet and walk her toward the cars. Her steps were sure but slow, each as painful as it was inevitable. I still heard her sobs.

I'd seen enough, and looked to find Mother and Daddy. They were standing, his arm around her, by Papa Jack's grave. When I got close enough, I heard Mother crying. It was unlike any cry from her since Papa Jack's death. She had cried when he died, and she had cried at his funeral. She grieved at his death and cried at her loss. But her sorrow was soothed because she knew he was a good man who lived fully and with as much dignity as he could create and command. They'd loved one another as father and daughter, and that had been enough to see her through. But now she shuddered as she cried. The tears came from a place Papa Jack's death had not touched. I didn't think they were all tears of sorrow.

"What's wrong, baby? Everything's gonna be all right." Daddy tried to console her. "What's the matter, baby?"

"I done my cryin' for Papa. Now I'm cryin' for where he's got to be buried, where all of us are buried."

She took Daddy's elbow as they stood looking at the others. "Come on," she whispered. Daddy nodded.

I tagged behind as they went to help the people wandering through the cemetery, staring at graves whose names had faded away.

Papa Jack's death called on me often as the heat of my tenth summer gave way to the cooling of autumn, and while I didn't fully realize its impact on me at least I was able to identify it as a significant event. Yet there was something even deeper that I felt only as an unspoken, unnamed anxiety.

Each year I'd been elected president of my school class, and among my peers I had the most to say about how we spent our time. If only within the framework of young black children growing up in dust-blown West Texas, I was already a leader. Many of the adults, including Mother most of all, indicated with their praise that somehow I would escape the boundaries of San Angelo and clear the barriers that restricted our community. Could I do it? And was I supposed to in some way take the rest of them with me? I never considered such questions directly, but they hung on the corners of all the encouragement and prophecy. They shadowed my family and community name, "Rev," even though they were never uttered.

I was completely at ease within my own community, at home among those who cared for and supported me. Although they continually forced me to confront my own future and potential, they never questioned my humanity. They accepted me. Within our own community, all of us could be exactly who we were. Outside the community, however, I was not acceptable. It puzzled, angered, and frightened me. In the larger world, I knew, even at ten, that I was an unacceptable person. I was rejected. Even if I was unable to embrace it, my blackness was something I acknowledged as reality. Time after time I had to say the words to my brothers, sister, and friends.

"No, they ain't gonna let us do it, they ain't gonna let us in. This ain't our place here, let's get on home."

At times, though, I found something that enabled me to get past the blanket rejection imposed on me by the world in which I found myself. I rejected that world's definition of me and other people.

In order to go to town, we had to ride a rattling old bus. Blacks automatically went to the back. The white bus driver never gave us a second glance. Throughout my early childhood, I followed the other kids to the back, realizing exactly what it signified. I can't say what made me do it, but one day I broke away. I was the last one to get on the bus that day. The rest of the kids went straight to the back, but I stopped just behind the driver's seat. Choking back my fear, I wrapped my hand around a metal pole.

"Hey, mistuh, is it fun drivin' this bus?" I said.

The driver looked at me suspiciously, seeing me through the eyes of the world—a little nigger kid who knew better. Yet I suppose I seemed innocent and sincere enough in my question about his mundane profession.

"Well, boy, guess it ain't all bad," he said gruffly.

I could hardly wait for him to finish. I had to go on.

"Bet it gets pretty hot sometime, don't it?"

I knew it was a safe question. Sweat was trickling down his neck and collecting on his pink and freckled upper chest.

"Yeah. Sometimes."

His answer was as abrupt as it could be, but at least it was an answer and not a command that I go to the rear. I kept right on talking. In time, he began asking me questions.

"You one of the Williams boys, ain't you?"

"Yessuh, I'm Cecil Williams. They my brothers there," I said, waving cautiously toward the back. Before I knew it, the old bus creaked to a stop. I waited for the other children to come forward, then we jumped down to the street.

Not going to the back of the bus was a personal victory, but it was about the best I could do to challenge the world and in a small way change my life in it.

Most of the time we bought our groceries in the black community, where white merchants sold inferior goods at inflated prices and maintained a solid grip on us through a batch of credit slips that ate away at Daddy's meager pay before he ever got it. One day, though, we had a little extra grocery money, so Mother decided to walk a half mile to a store in the white section that had better food and a wider selection. Despite the humiliation and rejection we had to endure, we thought it worthwhile to go there.

Mother was a very attractive, light-skinned woman, and Reedy, the family's infant son, had bright blue eyes and a fair complexion. This was the store where a white woman marched up to Mother while she held Reedy in her arms, and angrily demanded, "Who you been foolin' with, nigger?"

We had to wait a long time in line that day, as usual. All the white customers got served first, even if they came in after we did. They stepped in front of us as if we weren't even there. I guess we were supposed to feel honored that they let us in there in the first place. The clerk finally waited on us, we paid and left.

Two street cops awaited us outside. They looked large and ominous to me, especially since we were on their ground. I'd learned that the white police treated us differently in their community. When they confronted us there, they were eager to display their power. They degraded and taunted us, particularly when other white folks were observing the confrontation. In the black community, it wasn't quite the same. There they behaved with something nearer civility, maybe because they were outnumbered and in alien territory. Or maybe because there was no one watching who admired their power and reveled in its execution. But right in front of the white grocery store none of that mattered. We were on their turf.

"Hold it, Auntie," one of them barked. He was the bigger of the two, burly and mean. Legs spread wide, he stood with his thumbs tucked between his belly and belt. Nodding with contempt, he stared at Mother. There was the taste of a leer in his voice.

"Come on over here," he commanded.

Mother said nothing. We walked the short distance to him. A crowd was already starting to form. They could smell what was about to happen. There wasn't another black face anywhere.

"Lemme see your stuff," he said, the leer unmistakable now. "We wanna see what you got in them bags."

"What for?" Mother replied, as politely as she could under the circumstances.

"Never mind, Auntie, just do it."

"Why?"

"Ain't you got no sense at all? We wanna see if they all yours. Some y'all steal."

In a signal to the crowd, his partner guffawed. Titters began bouncing off the air. They were laughing at us. They did that every chance they got.

"We'll do what you say, officer, but can't we go 'round to the side? I don't want my children—"

"—Dammit, nigger woman! You gon' do it right here, right now. We told you what to do and now you gon' do it! You and them little niggers of yours get to work!"

We fell to our knees and began reaching into the bags, pulling groceries out item by item. The cops checked every one against our receipt. The crowd loved it.

"We watchin' you niggers. You ain't gettin' away with nothin'," one white boy sneered.

The big cop shot him a hard look. It was the cop's show, and he didn't want anyone to forget it. I tried to ignore the laughter, but I couldn't. We were a joke, something to liven up a dull Texas afternoon. Finally the cops seemed satisfied.

"Guess y'all are okay," the burly cop grumbled, disappointed that the exchange was almost over but gratified at its reinforcement of his power. "Pick up your mess and get back where y'all belong."

Groceries were rolling all over the street. We had to crawl to retrieve them.

"One thing," the cop said. "We gon' watch y'all next time you come around. You niggers can't get away with nothin' here."

That was the final humiliation. Mother glared at the cop.

"You're not ever gonna get me to take my groceries out the bag for you again! None of us steals. If my groceries come out again, you gonna have to take 'em out yourself!"

The cop looked at Mother with surprise and contempt, his bitter eyes handling her heaving breasts. He wanted her all the more then. He took her the only way he could.

"Why you nigger bitch!" he spat. "Don't you tell me! You'll take 'em out if I tell you to!"

His words cut through the howls and jeers. He paused to let them penetrate Mother first and the children next, then jammed his face up to hers.

"And you damn well know it, too," he hissed.

At that moment I would've done anything in the world to have been able to stand up to that cop. My eyes riveted on his gun, a wooden-handled .45 that hung from his waist. It looked as long as my arm and too heavy to hold with any confidence, but right then I wanted a .45 of my own more than anything. I wanted to feel its wood against my palm. I wanted to feel it tremble in my small and shaky hands. I wanted to hear the power of its roar. I wanted to smell the certainty of its cordite fumes. I wanted to see that big white cop grope for his guts, lurch forward, and fall. I wanted to feel proud.

But he had the gun, I didn't. It was the only time in my life I ever wanted to shoot a white person. But I couldn't shoot him. I couldn't do anything. We picked up the bags and headed for home. We were two blocks away before my ears no longer heard the laughter. The laughter still echoes in my mind today.

The insults and laughter haunted us. The white world rejected Mother and Daddy just as it rejected me, and in its attack raised a question and posed an answer that lay near the root of my unspoken and unnamed anxiety in the season of the train: If Mother and Daddy were in no position to challenge the rejection head on, if the adults who had amassed wisdom and strength through their life in the world were nevertheless rejected by it, then on whose shoulders did the responsibility for change rest?

Sometimes we talked about the laughter and the voices when we got home.

"Just let it go. It ain't our time yet."

Daddy said that to me so many times. He was a gentle, kind, and passive man who, although he didn't accept it, never challenged the nature of the world. I mistook his compassion and strategy of survival for a weakness, which I despised. I didn't despise him, but he was not the man I wished him to be. I never talked back to him, but I couldn't accept his conclusion that it wasn't our time. Many years passed before I began to understand him and what he did for us as we grew up.

The family and community presented me with a reality almost schizophrenic in the equally strong forces of its diametric opposites. I was needed, wanted, and loved among those people. Yet those same black people of various ages, sizes, descriptions, temperaments, and degrees of hope and despair were in a sense the embodiment of my own responsibility. They made me realize that my responsibility did not end with myself, but extended out into the world. The community was simultaneously a haven from the outside world and a constant call for me to confront the brutal rejection it imposed on all of us. The train came when I was in the midst of the community. But it called on only me.

The day the train came for me, the Sunday sky was settling into a dusky brown as the people began trickling toward the gallery, which was what we called our two front porches. They came alone and in small groups, each person surveying the wooden planks for a comfortable spot. Those twilight gatherings were the ultimate expression of our community's existence, which was why I enjoyed them so much.

The conversations were often joyful and humorous. Everyone participated, including the children. Sometimes we talked about the rejection, but it was never with the resignation of Daddy's "it ain't our time." When we talked about the white folks and their world, it was with an emotional humor that both affirmed and released a sense of power denied us beyond our border. Our power, in fact, lay in emotional response, and if we were denied its opportunity in the larger world, we compensated by letting loose around the porch as the day wound down. Someone would recount a put-down. Then someone else would say:

"But did you see how ugly that old sucker was?"

Our own laughter began.

"Lawd have mercy, that man was ug-lay!"

14

The laughter grew.

"Know he ain't got no dogs at home. Shit, he too ugly to keep a dog!"

We laughed our way through it so many times. We laughed at the reality because maybe we couldn't survive it any other way.

There was a feeling of peace during those nightly meetings, a fine sense of completion and redemption. We'd survived another day, and as nightfall promised itself we came together on our porch to share and celebrate that survival.

I don't remember that night, but I experience it again and again as the train comes for me today.

The fading sky is becoming streaked with long, thin clouds that look to me like the shadows of fingers. Less than a mile from the house, the railroad tracks cut through San Angelo. At 9 o'clock the regular train chugs rhythmically along on its way out of town.

A breeze blows among the trees and bushes. Leaves whisper. Dust dances in circles. Darkness has overtaken the world. The coarse wood of the porch feels hard against my butt. I squirm, wrap my arms around my bended knees, and stare out into the night.

Mother and others are joking. At first I hear their laughter, but never their words. I only look ahead into the darkness, grasped by its vastness. I crane my neck to look straight up, past the moon and stars, trying to spot the limit of the darkness. There is none. I feel the darkness as a cave or hole with all of us at the bottom, as though we are buried. There is no limit, no top, no light. Then I hear it.

Somewhere in the endless darkness I hear the long, sweet, low, mournful whistle of a train. I know that no train ever passes through San Angelo after 9 o'clock. But I also know, just as surely, that now a whistle blows like a slow, funereal song.

I say nothing. In the middle of the people, I stand and listen. For an instant I wonder if they hear the train. I don't ask.

The people, porch, and house disappear. I am alone with only the train and the darkness. The darkness has two parts; the actual darkness of the night, and a deeper, more powerful darkness that makes me feel helpless. The two arms of darkness have conspired with the train. They planned it all so I cannot escape. The train will pick me up and take me away, far back into the darkness.

I can't see or touch it, yet somehow I know it's much nearer now. No time to think. Something tears through me, rushing to all my extremities, ripping my limbs in different directions, pulling me out of my body. In a moment, my life, my being, will no longer be mine. This is the terror that grips me. Very soon the train will wrest me from where I stand, and I will not be able to fight it. The whistle is no longer a dirge. It screams in loud, staccato bursts. Somewhere in the darkness I'm sure I hear the sound of my name. The sound, the train, the darkness tug at my ankles. My body twitches. I turn full circle, hurriedly trying to catch a glimpse of my train before it comes down on me. Finally I see it—no train I've ever seen before. It devours everything. I want it to shrink so I can see light and space around it, but it will not. A dark train. A lurking yet galloping shadow with a life all its own. My senses desert me; time and space mean nothing anymore. The train rushes headlong toward me yet takes so unbearably long to reach me. It comes and fades. When it fades, it doesn't disappear. When it comes, it commands me. I can't turn it back. Why aren't the others listening? Surely they must hear it too. Why aren't they talking about it? Surely they must see it. Their silence says the train comes only for me. The train holds me in its tremendous power. And the others are blind to it. The others don't even know.

"They!"

I scream and fling my arms away from my body. They aren't my arms. They thrash about like fish yanked from water.

The sound of my scream terrifies everyone else almost as much as it terrifies me. For them, the scream destroys the peaceful stillness of the night. For me, it only enlarges the limits of my horror. It doesn't stop the train. As loud and as strong as my screams become, the roar of the train is stronger.

"They!"

"Who?"

Their voices come to me as if from across a canyon.

"They comin' to get me!"

I pant, sweat, scream, and move in a circle. Some of them must be trying to comfort and reason with me. I can't hear them anymore. They are here, yet they are not. How can they be here? I can't stop screaming.

"No!"

Maybe if I say it loud enough. If I can only hear the sound of my own voice, maybe then. What is real? At times I think I know, and then I want to cling to it. As the train prepares to pull me back, I know. I'm falling over the edge of a steep cliff, and the people, the porch, the house, the yard, the sound of my voice are roots of trees springing through the rocks. Desperately I lunge for them to stop myself from falling. But the presence of the train and darkness suck at me like a tornado and pull me toward their center. Nothing is as strong.

"No!"

I have no power. If they take me away, I know I won't come back.

We're here, Cecil.

The people's mouths are moving. They are not the ones who say what I hear.

We're here to take you with us.

Voices apart from flesh. The only voices I hear. The voices of aliens.

Come on, Cecil.

They don't need to scream. Their existence is their strength. The hands that are not mine jump for my ears.

Cecil.

"Who are you?"

Cecil.

"I can't hear you. Get away from me!"

There ain't nothin' you can do.

"I don't wanna go with you!"

There ain't nothin' you can do.

"No!"

Look, Cecil, look.

"No!"

Look, Cecil. Now!

They can't get me if I look away. I wrench my head toward the black and bottomless sky. The moon, a bright yellow bulb, dangles. So real, round, and shining. Does it know where heaven is? Way up there the moon can save me, help me get away.

Even as my eyes climb, the moon begins to lose its shape. Edges dissolve. All the moon is melting, dripping down the windows of the night. So fast, so long. I see the moon's blood creeping and falling down like rain. It's gonna rain on us all. Soon.

"The moon! It's rainin'! Can't y'all see it? It's gonna get me! It's gonna get you too! Run!"

Drops splash on my bare arm. My flesh bubbles. My body drenched in the drippings of the moon. My hands unable to move fast enough to wipe it all away. More horrible than the train and darkness. Were the voices right? Ain't there nothin' I can do?

"It's all right."

The voices of the community swim between the blood to reach my ears. Like a chant. Maybe it's the voice of only one person, and maybe that person said it only once. But I hear it as a chant. It is good.

"It's all right, it's all right . . ."

I need to hear them so badly. The canyon grows smaller. I see them clearly. I need to be touched.

"It's all right, Rev. Mother's here, it's all right now."

Her fingers on my dripping skin. Is it the blood of the moon, or is it only sweat? Mother's fingers help me choose. Her voice, soothing, comforting, loving, soft.

I'm wet, but it isn't raining any longer. My flesh slows to a crawl. The presence of the train, the darkness, the voices has not left me. But the terror draws back into the night without me. I know they watch me still. They're probably talking among themselves, but I don't hear them. I see my sister cry. Others cry too. I hear the silence of shock and disbelief. I feel Mother and others talk to me in rhythmic whispers, horrified to see the one on whom they bestowed so much being shattered. They don't know how close I came. They don't know what to do, so they only do all that they can. Not one of them ran from me as I became something I had not been before. I see them all around me now, clustered in a ragged circle making promises to the night. I am being lifted, hoisted onto uncounted shoulders. It's cooler now.

"Let's get him inside."

The voice of a man.

18

"We goin' inside to lay down."

Mother's whisper. I ride on the shoulders of the community, bumping and swaying into the house. Like a ghost hanging back on the fringe of the crowd, darkness follows. They lay me on the bed. I lie still.

"The light!" I yell.

Someone pulls the cord, and the room is suddenly bathed in light. The light is a flood rushing into every corner. It washes down the ceiling and it washes down the walls. It battles all the shadows. It helps me yet it is no answer. I long to see the sunlight. I need to see the light of day.

Mother undresses me. Again her fingers on my skin, up and down my arms and legs, soft and sure in their repetitive duty. They stroke me and caress me, and they drive the moon away. Flesh stops jumping. I shiver because I'm soaked with sweat. Soon even that stops. All the while, she talks to me.

The children have been shuttled outside, but the adults in the room tell me it's all right. They can't hide their fear and wonder, but I feel they're afraid for me, not afraid of me. With their very presence, they tell me I am not alone tonight.

"Tell me what happened, Cecil."

The voice pulls me from my drifting. It's Dr. Wyatt, one of the community's two physicians. His face is stern but kind. He's very close to our family. It must be very late.

"Tell me about it."

As I do, I get frightened all over again. My eyes widen and my speech stumbles. It is very hard.

"That's enough for now." Dr. Wyatt and Mother turn to go.

"Leave the light on!" I call after them.

They talk in the hall. Mother's voice is soft and low, Dr. Wyatt's deep and businesslike. I think I hear the sound of weeping.

I am very tired. Sleep is coming, and I am not afraid. I don't feel the darkness, but I know it's out there in all its disguises. I know how it feels to struggle against the darkness. I know how it feels to lose to it. Where does the darkness come from? Will it come for me again? And how then will I fight it? What power do I have? The questions are too much, and sleep too strong a temptation. The night is done. As sleep begins to take me, I think only of how much I want the dawn to come.

19

TWO

THE light found me waiting for it. I met it alone. Mother and Daddy, who shared their room with Reedy, had gone off to sleep. My sister Titter had her own room in the back of the house. My other brothers—Bro, Jack, and Dusty—stayed in the room with me, but they too were still asleep.

Serenity lay across the morning in a small gesture of reassurance, yet I felt out of touch, as though somewhere a soft melody were playing that I couldn't quite hear. I'd spent much of the night anticipating the comfort of the morning. Darkness and light had already become two different worlds. My struggle with the darkness had given the dawn a new identity for me. I welcomed it as a friend, and felt it as I never had before.

The first light came through a screen door that stood next to my bed and was open to the world as a solid door could never be. The world truly entered the house through that screen door, on the back of the wind, in the rays of light and the company of sounds and smells. There was a wooden door, too, but during the night I'd flung it open as if to hurry daybreak on. I felt tired but redeemed, a runner who'd finished one of many races.

As I lay there, I thought of how we used to race back home across the railroad tracks that sliced through San Angelo with the mute authority of an international border. South of the tracks lay the white community and downtown business district. North of them was home. On our frequent forays into the white community, we liked to think of ourselves as strangers in a strange land, a pack of nervous soldiers behind enemy lines. Sneaking along the alien streets carried a certain actual danger and an even more fanciful excitement, but its single most powerful attraction was to set up the run for home through what we called Freedom Path, the most powerful symbol of those complex days in Texas.

To the casual observer, Freedom Path was nothing but a short and narrow dirt passage flanked on one side by a cotton gin housed in a metal shed and on the other by a low wire fence. We called it Freedom Path because it abutted the dusty railroad tracks beyond which our homes and families welcomed our return. When we emerged from the white community and set foot on Freedom Path, we knew we'd made it once again. No harm would come to us there.

Freedom Path afforded me an escape so fleeting and confined it deepened my sense of restriction, as though it were a tunnel that only connected one prison to another. And I, a mere child, did not understand that illusory freedom, the slavish belief in escape, is the worst prison of all.

One hot summer afternoon, I'd left my shoes at home because they'd become too small. Last in line, I had raced through Freedom Path in the awakening twilight. Then slivers of glass bit my naked feet, pain shook me; my blood ran down into the dirt. Looking back down the path toward the white community, I had wanted to scream as loudly as I could. Instead, of course, I had only mumbled,

"One of these days I'm not going to run no more."

A futile gesture indeed, as real as my blood drying in the dust. I wanted the world to hear me. I wanted the white folks to hear me, but they were nowhere to be seen. I wanted the black folks to hear me too, but they were all inside their homes. Even the other children had already vanished across the tracks.

I wanted to make a stand against the glass in the dust and yell my anger at those who put it there. I wanted to hold my life in my own hands, feel it throbbing and kicking as an infant in the womb and know beyond all knowledge that I had the power to determine its direction. I would define myself.

At that moment, I had expected a miracle, which was not unusual for me. My life then was full of hopes for a miracle and longings for a vision, expectations inspired by constant exposure to biblical myths and the prophetic figures ghosting through them, a validation of my status as the chosen one. But on my new Freedom Path I saw miracle on my own terms. Miracles were not events to be witnessed apart—miracles were decisions made by men, women, even children. If I had the power to decide, that would be my miracle.

We suffered so much in the world, deathly afraid and eternally powerless. Defined by our very suffering. In the boundless space, filled only by a sensibility of self-determination and the possibilities it raised, I imagined taking on the power of Moses, the ability first of all to lead myself from Egypt, and I wanted everyone else to follow down my Freedom Path. Then everything would be all right.

I wanted to be like Moses, but I felt like Job. I wanted to make a stand, but I was afraid. I wanted divine intervention, but I felt so alone. I wanted an ordered existence, but I was in chaos. I wanted acceptance, but I was rejected. *I wanted to take Freedom Path with me wherever I went.*

Racism was strong in San Angelo, a town divided by my Freedom Path, but rarely bloody and hardly ever fatal, at least not overtly. Blacks and Chicanos tried to avoid the local hospital because too many came back dead from the colored ward in the building's basement, but there was nothing as harsh as lynchings or nightriders. I think that was because the nonwhites, who accounted for no more than a third of the population, were enough in the minority so as not to pose a serious threat to the whites. Later on I was to learn how different things were in East Texas, not to mention the Deep South. I think if I had lived in East Texas I might have died a very young man.

San Angelo was a curious place. With a population of 27,000, it was the largest settlement for a good hundred miles in any direction. There were maybe 6,000 blacks and 3,000 Chicanos. Neither urban nor rural, San Angelo worked hard to maintain a delicate balance between two flattering self-images. It boasted of being "The Wool Capital of the World" and owed much of its livelihood to the ranches and grazing lands along its edges. Yet there were not as many dirty boots and weathered hats downtown as one might have expected. That was because San

Angelo also liked to think of itself as poised on the brink of a cosmopolitan breakthrough, prepared to earn the designation of "city" in the best sense of the term. The whites controlled the economy and ran the city. Jobs for blacks were limited to the downtown hotels or to working for whites as cooks, janitors, and domestics. There was one black dentist and two black doctors. The only other black professionals were the teachers and the preachers.

The black community was poor and in some spots squalid, but it was by no means a shantytown. The wooden houses were invariably old, and most were built for large families. There were few commercial establishments of any kind, except down at Sharp End with its whorehouse, beer parlors, barber shops and cafes. As if to counteract Sharp End's lures, there were more churches in the community than any other kind of non-residential building. And there was something intangible going on in that black community, as instinctive to us as it was incomprehensible to the whites across the tracks. A tribal feeling existed among the people, a common bond forged from the often stark realities of our existence. The rejection we faced in the outside world made our collective retreat so much more real and intense that each drop of our lives, each response, each emotion became magnified and, in a curious but undeniable way, free. In many instances, there was no joy unless there was intense joy, no anger unless there was intense anger, no sorrow unless there was intense sorrow. The freedom to be human denied us beyond the tracks became a freedom unchained in the community of our own. We knew we had only ourselves. San Angelo embodied a paradox that I think America has yet to fully understand: Those most oppressed were in some ways the most free, and those most dehumanized were in some ways the most human.

The community was like a huge organism with the power to care for and repair itself, and rarely required or received assistance from any outside forces, including science and medicine. When one portion of the community became ill or damaged, those portions nearest it, immediately and without invitation, rushed to heal the sick. The people possessed the instinct to regenerate their community. There was the fabric of a village, perhaps the villages of our ancestors, in the way we lived, an ingrained awareness that we were each bound to one another by something more substantial than the proximity of our houses or the accidents of geography. News traveled fast. If anyone got sick, the community knew in a matter of hours. Then the healing began. The community took charge only because the sick could not, and the people never asked or suggested a return for their favors, because they were certain the return would come when it was needed.

In the morning light, I thought of the night I'd survived and the one that lay waiting for me fourteen hours away. My brother Dusty, lying next to me, began to stir and stretch. With gladness and trepidation, I waited. He sat up, rubbed his eyes, and turned to me. Of all the children, Dusty was closest to me, close enough to share the same bed. We were even born on the same day of the year, although he was two years older than I. He was something of a loner, perhaps a "problem child," but he was close to me. His given name was Claudius, but because of his reddish-brown skin we called him Dusty. There was curiosity and wonder in his eyes, but nothing like rejection.

"Hey, Rev," he said.

"Hey."

"You okay?"

"Little tired, I guess, but yeah, I'm okay."

"I'm sure glad to hear you say that, 'cause boy you was really performin' last night."

"Yeah, guess I was a little bit."

"A little bit!?" An incredulous voice with laughter in its middle erupted from the other bed. "A little bit?" it said again, more amazed than the first time. "Nigggggguh, shit! If that was a little bit I'd hate to see you get serious. Do it again and I'm gonna take you downtown and turn you loose on the white folks. Shit, Rev, you'd have 'em runnin' they asses off!"

I laughed for the first time since the sun had set the night before. We all laughed.

The voice belonged to Brother Jack, the second oldest of the four brothers in the room, who shared a bed with Bro. Dark like Bro, Jack was a jester and layabout who had the knack for finding a shade tree whenever there was work to be done. He constantly instigated trouble, primarily for his own amusement, but he was clever enough to avoid the turmoil of his creation.

"Okay, brother, that's enough."

Bro was the oldest, and when he commanded we obeyed. He was big and black, larger than any thirteen-year-old we'd ever seen. He was no dictator, not even a benevolent one, but as if to complement his size and stature he labored under such a sense of responsibility and had such a serious demeanor that in many ways he seemed an adult before his time. His given name was Earl, after our father, and when Daddy was away working or looking for work, Bro automatically became the man of the house. It was a role he assumed with a quiet, controlled ferocity. We hardly ever played with him because he was always off taking care of responsibilities that had been put on his shoulders, but we respected him and his wishes.

"Let's let Rev be," he said.

The room fell silent, but our raucous laughter had already had an effect. A robed figure stood in our doorway.

We never called her "Mama," because that was too undignified. For us she was a "Mother," not a "Mama." Her name was Sylvia, a rather short woman of about five-foot-three whose 140 pounds gave her an appearance of robust health. Her skin was light, her brown eyes so bright they were almost green. Her long black hair hung to the middle of her back. She definitely had black features but at times could've passed for a Chicana or even a white woman. She was an unusual-looking woman, the kind anyone would look at twice, but her presence transcended even her appearance. She was the sometimes flexible but ultimately unquestionable authority in our lives. I always felt confident that, whatever the situation, Mother could take care of it if necessary.

She slumped a bit in the doorway but not enough to obliterate her projection of strength. Her eyes were puffed. It looked as though she'd weathered a long night too.

"What in the world is happenin' in here?" she asked sharply.

Our mumbled replies were incoherent but enough to put her at ease.

"All right," she said with the trace of a smile. "I want you all to get dressed and go to the kitchen for your breakfast."

We all moved.

"No, Rev," she cut in. She looked at me strangely then, with deep affection and a slight tremor of fear. "Stay in bed, I want to talk with you."

She sat next to me on the bed and, as though she could truly protect me, put her arm around my small shoulders. I heard only the sound of our breathing. She kissed me on the cheek, her lips dry but tender. Her forehead rested in my hair. We were alone in the bright comfort of the morning.

"Are you feelin' better this morning?"

"Yes, Mother, I think so."

"Can you talk to Dr. Wyatt?"

"Yes . . ."

" 'Cause he's comin' by here after a while."

"Yes, ma'am."

"Son, you know Mother loves you, and I'm gonna be right here when you need me. Mother's gonna take care of you."

It was exactly what I needed to hear, and she knew it. It made me strong enough to ask my question.

"Is it gonna be all right?"

"Oh yes, Rev, we gonna make it all right . . . with the Lord's help. I'm prayin' for you, son. All of us are."

There was nothing she could give me that was stronger or more profound than her love—and her prayers. In Mother's life, indeed in the lives of most of us, there was nothing as valuable, as human, as much a part of one's being as one's prayers, one's relationship with God. When she gave me her prayers, she gave me everything she had. I took great comfort from it, yet I wondered. Would God really answer those prayers and help me defeat the aliens, the same God who might have uncaged the aliens to begin with? In the eyes of many, I was already a ten-year-old reverend, but I had more questions of God than I had the strength to ask. And, like the aliens only I had come to know, God was supposed to be everywhere.

Mother kissed my forehead and clutched me to her. I smelled the musky fragrance and felt the tranquil moisture of her skin. She rose from the bed and left me alone.

As morning passed, I grew more comfortable, certain that the daylight was my ally. I was in control. The only thing I had to fear was the coming of nightfall. Adding to my comfort was the constant stream of friends who came to see how I was doing. Dr. Wyatt came in around noon, wearing his benign smile. Mother was with him.

"Well, looks like you're gettin' along just fine today," he said to me.

"Yessuh."

"Anything hurt you, your head or anything?"

"No."

"Eyes, ears, anything bother you at all?"

"No, suh."

Dr. Wyatt seemed as much in the dark as I was. He didn't even bother dipping into his bag. He just looked at me for what seemed to be a while, then said:

"I'm just an ordinary doctor, son, and there ain't an awful lot I can tell you. What you had last night was a nervous breakdown, and there's no medicine I can give you for it. Now I want you to stay in bed and rest. Can you do that for me?"

"Yessuh."

Nervous breakdown. The words told me nothing. If there was no medicine, was there no cure? I felt the edge of that frantic, sinking sensation I'd fought in the darkness; I felt alone in my struggle against the aliens. Was I going to be deserted and desperate, like J.B.? I was isolated against my aliens, just as the family and community were isolated against their aliens in the outside world. How could any of us fully understand a "nervous breakdown"? And could any of us summon the courage to battle such an enemy, especially when we were compelled to compare it to J.B.?

I remembered all too well what an enemy J.B. had had. It was night. I was eight years old. Dusty and I had crouched by the bedroom window and peeped through the high row of hedges that ran along the side of our house. We had felt secure behind them because we could see out and it was difficult for anybody to see in.

"See anything?" Dusty whispered.

My eyes groped through the silent darkness.

"Naw, ain't nothin' out there."

Then we heard him. When J.B. screamed, everything else stopped. A young man who lived with his parents in the most rundown house in the block, J.B. often stalked his yard like a wounded animal. Realizing he was mad, we all kept our distance, particularly at night when he began to scream. That night, as Dusty and I huddled near the window, the screams seemed to tear open the darkness and rush toward us.

"No more!" the scream said.

It sounded to me like a desperate thrust in the night.

"Shit, that nigger's really crazy tonight," Jack muttered.

"Hell naw!" J.B. yelled.

A sickly fear began mixing with my sweat. I think we were all dazed and afraid. His screams nourished a horror that sprouted through the soil of our community, and no one was sure what to do about it. People began gathering along the dirt street, but none made a move toward J.B.'s house. Still, somehow none of us could turn away.

"You children stay inside," Mother commanded.

Outside, the adults stood suspended between running to aid the community madman and the pulsating terror of what that might do to them, torn between his screams and the silent voices in each of their heads. Light flickered through J.B's window, but we couldn't see what was happening because he was back in the kitchen.

"See what I got?" he screamed. "I'm gon' get you tonight!"

Each word exploded like a fresh bullet, and in the naked anger and pain trudged the hollow sound of defeat and surrender, as though total destruction had been embraced, finally, as the noblest choice of all. J.B. was alone in the house except for his mother. Her voice tried vainly to grab hold of something solid.

"No!" she cried. "Please, honey, don't!"

"Get back!" J.B. screamed, perhaps at her but maybe at something else. "There ain't nothin' you can do, goddammit!"

I swore I heard a sawing sound and then something like the tearing of sheepskin. Little by little his black skin was being sliced. There must have been the beginning of a wet, red chain around his neck that gradually became wider and deeper as the dull knife hacked its way through the outer layers of skin and flesh to ravage the veins hanging in the cavern of his throat. With each jerk of the knife, J.B. screamed his defiance and defeat, struggling to shape every sound into words. He staggered from the kitchen to the front window and let the shadows of his act play upon the window shades. J.B. and his mother sang a mad duet and unshackled a tension that made life and death so real it paralyzed us all.

At first his words were wild but clear, but as the knife ripped deeper they became muffled and distorted by gurgles and sputters. After a long time, the horrible gurgling seized control. His screams faded into moans and then an overwhelming silence that only deepened the sound of his mother's solitary crying. Finally, after it was over and he was dead, a few adults went across the street. The next day they talked about it a lot. Some of them said J.B. wanted all of us to bear his pain.

So I had already seen madness, and what it could do, when the train came and the aliens spoke to me.

As the aliens strengthened their grip around me, I came to dread the night even more. Every night they came for me, bringing with them the promise of death. Human forms that shimmered like ripples of heat and never seemed to touch the ground closed in on me. They spoke in croaks and hisses. Their weapons—knives, clubs, torches, and other instruments—got as close as they could without touching my skin. Some nights the weapons came alone, urged on by voices that had no bodies. More than anything else, I knew I was going to die.

It went on night after night, week after week. I kept the light on at night, and still they came. I read for hours, but inevitably a passage on the page called them forth. I buried my head beneath the covers, and still they found me there. I tried to push away the darkness, but it would not move for me. I tried to scream away the darkness, but it only came nearer.

"Calm down, Rev."

Mother spoke softly to me, touching my skin and sitting where moments before there had been nothing but darkness. The voices of the community always wrestled me away from the aliens, but only after I'd experienced the lure and power of death's call. A family member faithfully sat with me every night, but it was never enough to ward off the aliens. In some ways, I came to depend on the family and community because they always helped save me. Yet I also saw them as powerless in the face of darkness. My reality was not theirs. Neither were my delusions.

The aliens often came while people were gathered around my bed. The light flickered as though it were alive. When people took over, the aliens vanished, only to return in seconds.

"Come with us," they snarled, their fingers around my throat, their cold steel on my cheek, their fire licking my bedclothes. Like a river running home to the sea, they pulled at me. It had gone on for so long.

"Take me," I mumbled to myself, knowing they would hear. "If you want me, dammit, then take me now."

I stood at the window in the middle of the night and gazed at the cold black sky. I thought of it as a cloak I wanted to rip aside to reach what lay hidden behind it. I had no power of my own, and could think of only one more place to turn.

Oh God! Why you doin' me this way? I been good, Lawd.

Divine intervention, a lonely appeal to his pity . . . and his power. I saw it as my only hope.

What you tryin' to do to me, Lawd? Please don't treat me this way. Don't let the devil get me. Feel like I'm gonna die, scared all the time. Please don't let me die.

The night answered me with utter silence. There wasn't even the sound of wind, and it was dark as ever. I climbed back into bed. The sheets were like a frozen stream. I rubbed my hands together, then my legs. A long while passed, but in time the heat of my body melted the icy sheets and I was warm again.

My initial fear that the family and community might shun me had proven wrong. They nurtured me as best they could, and not a day went by without a throng of community people dropping by to see about me. But they couldn't silence those voices either, despite the love, caring, comfort, and prayer.

I paced the floor trying to push the darkness from the room, but it was like a blob of thick liquid. I felt I was underwater. The darkness stretched as far as I could see, beyond the perimeters of my vision and experience to a point that defied my comprehension. I heard footsteps crunching up the path to our front door.

"Oh God," I mumbled in fear and supplication. For a moment there was nothing, then bumps and murmurs in the hall outside the room. On the strength of instinct, I dove for the bed.

Mother and Daddy stood silently by the door, but something was wrong. They wafted toward me, and when they reached the foot of my bed a shiver rippled through me. Their eyes were like burning coals. Their teeth looked more like bones. They looked like Mother and Daddy, but they were not.

"Who's gonna do it?" Daddy asked. His voice echoed like sound from the pit of a deep chasm.

"I am," Mother replied. Her words were slow and unearthly, dripping from her lips like mud and molasses.

"You sure? I will if you want."

"No, I want to."

"Go ahead, then."

"Thank you, baby. You watch me now."

Mother shoved an open palm in Daddy's direction. His hand ducked inside his robe and returned with a butcher knife, which he slapped into her palm.

"Mother! Daddy! What—"

Her hand sliced through the air to cut me off.

"Relax, boy, and it'll all be over," she cooed.

I saw a gleam in her eye.

"No!" I screamed like J.B. I screamed like I never had before, a scream that pounded throughout my body and seemed to shake the entire room.

She straddled me, pinning me to the mattress, and clasped both her hands around the handle of the knife. I wanted desperately to squirm and break away, but she was too strong and the power too much. I wanted to escape, but my mind wrapped me in horror. I lay on the bed with my arms extended and no control over my body. I saw her raise the knife above her head and look to the ceiling. I saw her shoulders twitch. My heart strained to bust through my ribs. Blood roared through my veins as if it knew a secret place to hide. I saw Mother's arms swing toward me. I heard her grunt with effort. I saw the blur and glint of the silver blade hurtling through the darkness for my naked throat. I saw Mother plunge it down, down, down.

It was dark and moist where I was. On all sides I heard the sound of rushing water and the slow, hypnotic pounding of a drum. I was overcome with a feeling of peace and security.

"It's all over now."

All was calm and quiet, yet I sensed the peace was a lie because, despite the indications of comfort and security, I knew I couldn't move.

"It's all over, come on now."

The sound of words played on the water. I saw them sparkle, and groped for them with what strength and emotion I had left. The peace and security collapsed into fear. I wanted so badly to break free.

"Listen to me, son, listen to me."

The words had tendons and ligaments of their own. They were sounds formed of flesh that grabbed hold of me and yanked me from the damp floor of my corrupt Eden. I felt myself being swiftly lifted as the rushing water crashed down on me. Trauma and pain tore through me. I closed my eyes and let the floodwater and fleshwords battle one another. First a brutal chill jolted my skin, then the roar of water began to fade. I was exhausted.

"It's all right."

I opened my eyes. Mother's form hovered above me, blacking out everything.

"No!" I screamed. "Don't!"

"Rev, Rev," she whispered. Her cheeks were wet. There was nothing in her hands. My fingers lunged for my throat. There was no blood.

"Mother!" I blurted. "Oh, Mother, I'm scared!"

I sat up, threw my arms around her shoulders, and cried.

I felt better in the morning, as usual. It was Sunday, and there was always an extra feeling of joy and excitement then. They brought me eggs and biscuits dripping with syrup. Someone had even scrounged up a fatty piece of pork for me. I ate it all. The day moved on, and with it came a flow of people through the house, especially in the afternoon after church let out. As always on a Sunday, the kitchen was the center of activity. The sizzle of frying grease and aroma of succulent chicken over-whelmed the house. Around 4 o'clock Mother brought a steam-ing plate to me. Her face beamed as she set it on the bed.

"I know you're gonna like this," she said with a dose of pride. "You eat this, and I'll be back after a while. We're all in the kitchen if you need anything."

She stopped at the door on her way out.

"We all love you, Rev."

"I know," I said softly.

When she left, all I felt was alone.

I look at the plate of chicken, rice, gravy, and greens, and yearn for the time, so long ago now, when I eagerly awaited my Sunday supper, which I devoured with the grunting enthusiasm of a satisfied child. I'm just being stupid now. There won't be any more days like that. The chicken, crisp, brown, and juicy, lies on my plate like the dead meat it is. Funny how we eat dead things to stay alive.

I throw open the wooden door and look out through the screen. The sky is the color of dishwater, with veins of rust running through it. A chicken squawks. There are no other sounds. Nothing moves. The trees in the yard stand like sen-tries. Soon it will be dark. I've got voices of my own that can tell me things. Now, before dark, I need to hear them.

"Tell me, 'cause I don't know what to do anymore," I say.

They comin' tonight, y'know. Gettin' closer each time.

"Yeah, I know."

Give up, nigger! That's the easiest way. Hell, that's the onliest way. Even God wants you to give up.

"Wait a minute! You don't know that."

Can't you see it ain't your decision no more? It's your time to die, that's all.

There is great pity in the voice. And how can I refute its argument?

I think it the moment of final truth, but then a new voice I've never heard before speaks to me.

"You ain't got to listen to this stuff," it says.

"What?"

He gonna steer you wrong, boy, the old voice warns.

"I listened to you and now I'm gonna hear this."

"*I know you remember Papa Jack,*" the new voice says. "*On that real hot day? He was sittin' with those white men and he had those pictures.*"

"Yeah. He didn't say too much."

"*No, but remember what he told y'all at the end?*"

"He said, 'You all be exslaves too.' "

"*Yes! Don't you understand? Nigger, listen to me! We're talking about your life. Your feelings, your life. Nobody around here wants you dead. They got so much faith in you.*"

"I know, but it ain't easy."

"*It ain't never easy! Listen to that other voice if you want to hear about easy. Death is always easy to choose. Bein' a slave, callin' on God. Always easy, so damn easy.*"

The old voice returns with a cool arrogance as though lecturing a wayward child. I stand locked in position while my voices battle over me.

Damn right it's easy, the old voice says. *And it's for the best.*

"*The best way to be nothing. I'm tellin' him how to fight and break through,*" says the new voice.

What kind of life is that for a nigger?

"*The only kind there is.*"

Is Papa Jack's grave clean? If the aliens get me, will I still have a name? What about God? He didn't show his power even when I begged for it.

"Oh God . . . God . . . God. I called your name so much! Revren Carruthers told me to call and you would answer. Mother and Daddy told me to pray long and hard and you would deliver me from the devil. They all said you would help me.

"I ain't gonna beg you, Lord. I'm mad and scared—scared you're gonna get angry at me. I'm mad at you, Lord, 'cause you keep gettin' in the way. I'm turning you loose, Lord. I'm takin' it out of your hands."

I'm risking everything. For the first of what will be many times, I know how it feels.

"I'm mad and tired—tired of giving in, and mad, Lord, mad 'cause I've got only myself. I ain't gonna let that bad voice make me do the things I've been doin'. I'm gonna fight that bad voice myself, and I ain't givin' in no more. You hear me, Lord? I ain't givin' in."

THREE

"REV!" Mother called out as she rushed across the room toward me. "Is anything wrong?"

She'd heard me talking with my voices and God. I turned to face her when she called my name. She wore a flowered dress of vivid colors. At points each color stood out sharply. At other places they all blended together. I hadn't noticed it before.

"No, ma'am, everything's all right."

It was a lie.

"Who were you talkin' to?" she asked. "It's not dark yet."

I was splitting apart.

"Uh, no one—ain't nothin' wrong, Mother."

Dragging me in one direction was the same fear that had hunted me for months, the fear that I was worthless and powerless. I was certain that God would punish me for what I'd just yelled at him. And the voice was right about one thing—the aliens were on their way.

Simultaneously pulling me in a new direction was the growing realization that the battle was just between the aliens and me, and that I would have to take a great risk to survive them. I wasn't at all sure that I could stand my ground against them, alone. Nothing was for sure.

My head lay buried in the pillow. Suspended between sleep and wakefulness, I finally sensed the aliens' arrival. At first I neither heard nor saw them, but I felt them slip silently into the room like a magnetic force. I had no choice but to raise up and look. Two of them stood at the foot of my bed. One was a little white boy, no more than ten or twelve, dressed up in his Sunday best. He had dark blonde hair, a chubby, almost cherubic face, and skin so fresh and pure it appeared polished. The other was an old white man in a somber black suit who held a candle in one hand and a big revolver in the other. The candle wax was more lifelike than his skin, which was drawn tightly across his sharp and bony features like a rubber mask. I'd never seen either one before. As I sat staring, their power began lapping at my feet. Invisible fingers clutched and pulled me down. I was slipping into darkness.

In my mind I stood on the edge of a deep hole in the earth, peering down into its infinite blackness. The high sky was dark with clouds. A storm was coming. I saw nothing in the barren landscape that could tell me what to do.

"Be still," the man said in a rumble that rose from the floor.

"There won't be any more after this," the boy said in the man's voice. "Over yonder there ain't no misery."

His eyes took aim at my chest. A smile punched a hole in his face. I heard the man's revolver click.

"It's over now," he said.

They were leeches, and blood was being drained from my body. Shards of light pierced my eyes. My hands were going to tremble, my voice was going to scream. The aliens were stronger than ever, and I was alone. Was it worth it to do something? Was I worth it? I'd never faced such questions in the aliens' presence. I had to decide. The gun stood cold and hard inches from my face. Blood continued to rush from my body. Soon I would be lost in the flood. I thought, this could be the last time.

"No," I said.

Each night I'd screamed in the awful darkness, terrified of the aliens' awesome power. My screams had begged them and tried to make them go away. Wounds, sounds of submission defined by the power that came to deny me my life. But that night I didn't scream. Battling myself as much as the agents of darkness, I spoke in a grim but conversational tone. For an instant I felt power surge through me, a sensation I'd not experienced before.

"No, I will not go with you tonight. Not tonight, not any

night." I didn't implore them, I told them. My voice marched the length of my body and met the aliens where they stood. I felt blood return to me. At the same time, I felt something draining from the aliens. How I was able to experience their feelings was a question that, in the moment of struggle, escaped me. The transfusion was not complete by any means. The aliens still had power, but I began to feel mine as well.

"That ain't gonna work," the boy said, shaking his head sadly. "Trust me, it's only gonna be harder on you that way."

"Well," rasped the cadaverous man, "don't this child have some nerve, talkin' back to us. I'm gonna keep his black ass quiet a good long while."

He moved on me. The gaping hole at the end of the gun sucked at my eyes, and the power flowed in reverse once more, from me to them. I was weakening. Drops of sweat burst through my skin. My flesh was about to quiver and jump. I wanted so badly to scream. The new voice had told me right.

"It ain't never easy."

The man's finger curled around the trigger.

"I'm not gonna let you do that," I told him.

It took all my strength to hurl the words at him. It was worth it. The nerves in my skin tingled as blood flowed again. Without effort, I raised my arm. The aliens retreated. My power returned with a jolt. The boy staggered to the foot of the bed before regaining enough strength to stand erect.

"Hey!" I yelled at the man. "I *know* you!"

For months the aliens had gripped me so tightly I could think of no alternative but to run and hide. Night after night they seemed invincible, but for a sliver of time I swore I saw the waxy skin on that man's face begin to tear. In the next second, it reappeared as it had been. The man, who'd retreated to the foot of the bed, advanced toward me again.

"I'm warnin' you," he growled.

"Stop," I said evenly, as if to a friend. "Don't come any closer."

He stopped, puzzlement in his eyes.

"I told you I know you. Understand?"

He wheeled and stalked back to join the boy. He blew out the candle, but I still saw their faces. Perhaps for the very first time in my life, I felt the master of my own destiny. I knew I could control the aliens in my presence.

"Okay, boy, but you ain't seen the last of me," the man said.

"Go on. I'm tired, now leave me alone. Maybe you'll only come back when I want you."

The old man grunted and spat.

"Maybe we will at that," the boy said, and they were gone.

Darkness watched me through the window, but it didn't matter. Alone in the night, I sat in amazement. A profound relief swept through me, as though dawn had arrived. I knew it would remain dark for hours, but it didn't worry me.

Who were the aliens? With astonishing ease, I posed the question to myself. I dared to raise their spirits. They refused the challenge, and I grew stronger. Who were they? I'd always seen them as creatures imposed on me by an outside force, agents sent to punish me for crimes I didn't recognize. I was always under their influence. They were never under mine. They held all the power, I held none. That's the way it always felt. Yet when I fought their attempts to control me, I was able to control them. How could that be? *My* feelings. I began to understand. Maybe the aliens weren't alien at all. The ideas barreled through my being like a runaway train. Maybe they were my own creation. I'd always known they were meant for only me.

I sat motionless in bed, exhausted but alive with new possibilities. Everything was changing, and I wanted to tell the family first and then the world.

"Didn't hear you last night, Rev," Dusty said as the darkness slipped from the room. He awoke suddenly, as if he expected an important surprise under the bed.

"I know," I said excitedly. "I didn't scream and I didn't—"

"—Didn't walk the floor either, did you?"

"Didn't need to. Didn't need to scream, didn't need to walk the floor, didn't need to do no bad things!"

"Rev let his crazy go!" Dusty hollered gleefully.

"See!" Jack exclaimed. "I knew the nigger wasn't crazy! The boy might be a little funny, but the nigger ain't crazy!"

"What happened to those people that was botherin' you, Rev? They gone now?" Bro asked.

"No, they was there. But I stopped them from botherin' me."

As the commotion gained momentum, Mother and Daddy burst into the room.

"Oh my God!" Mother shouted joyfully in a form of prayer. "My Lord, my Lord, my son is better!"

Throwing her arms around me, she kissed my cheeks and rocked me from side to side. The room became a vehicle that elected its own path and traveled at its own chosen speed. When Mother released me, Daddy sat down and put a hand on each of my shoulders. He gazed into my eyes, then pulled me to his chest and held me there.

"I'm so glad, son, and thankful too. Things change sometimes, and sometimes they get better," he said. He laughed and cocked his head to survey the room. "Where's Titter?"

"Here I am."

My sister, six years my senior, stood in the doorway in her nightclothes, her eyes slowly moving across each of our faces, her vision an expression of our chosen commitment to share the moment. More than any of the other children, she could measure the family in terms of its wholeness and thus had the greater capacity to bring the pieces together. She always seemed able to feel what I felt. Tears ran down her face then, but she was laughing too.

"Yes, Lawd!" she shrieked and clapped her hands. "Oh yes!"

"Rev's much better this mornin'," Mother yelled to her above the clamor.

"I know," Titter shouted back. "I can feel it."

The sun had gathered sufficient strength to pour through the window. Titter threw her hands up and led the family in a spontaneous procession throughout the house.

"Rev is better, thank the Lord," she sang. The rest picked up on it, and soon it was a chant reverberating in the hall.

Rev is better, thank the Lord
Rev is better, thank the Lord

I remained in bed, unsure whether my improvement warranted any improvisation on Dr. Wyatt's instructions. As I listened to the joyous parade, I began thinking of my family differently. Perhaps they weren't as powerless as I'd thought them to be.

"Come on, Rev, I think it's all right if you get out of bed for a little while," Mother said, extending her arm to me. The others echoed her encouragement, and led me to the living room, where an old upright piano that Daddy had somehow acquired stood propped against the wall. We gathered around the piano, and Titter began to play. Soon we were singing with an unchained abandon that recreated the old spiritual with every word.

> *There's no hidin' place down here*
> *There's no hidin' place down here*
> *Oh I went to the rock to hide my face*
> *The rock cried out "no hidin' place"*
> *There's no hidin' place down here*

Now, years later, I roll out of bed into the chilly San Francisco darkness. It's Sunday morning, but the first drops of sunlight will not splash against the front window for another hour or more. I will sit and wait for them, as I always do. Each morning for the past thirty-nine years I've risen before dawn. The children lie asleep down the hall. I'm alone in the front of the house, looking down on the silent, empty street. Five hours from now, I must deliver a sermon, if that is truly the correct word, but as a specific task it does not lean too heavily on my mind. I never work out sermons word for word anyway. Perhaps a little later I'll scribble an outline on a single sheet of paper, but even those few words will be signposts, not boundaries.

I don't await the dawn out of fear. When I was a young boy in the clutches of my aliens, I felt the darkness was insurmountable. The light, in turn, became my refuge. It's not that way today. I think the sight of dawn only reaffirms for me, on a daily basis, the contention between darkness and light; not only the contention, but its necessity as well.

Contending with the darkness wasn't a task for a mind at peace but was the product of an emotion we've been taught to deny: anger. In struggling with my aliens, I had to get angry before I could act. Acknowledging my anger was especially difficult because it was in part directed at God. But when the choice became anger or death, I let my anger erupt. It literally saved my life. Anger can be healthy and constructive. The crucial aspect of anger has to do not with the merit of its existence, but with its direction. Anger must be turned toward that which is destructive to human life rather than toward oneself or others. There are people on the street whose anger, because it's misdirected, becomes destructive. There are people in suburbia experiencing the same thing. But it's not the fault of the anger itself, because anger, more so than even love, is the emotion of revolution and the catalyst for change.

I sometimes have dialogues with myself as a ten-year-old in the grip of madness, and I wonder why I didn't meet J.B.'s fate. I think it had very much to do with the supportive community that surrounded me. All of us must battle our own aliens, but to battle them in a vacuum is tempting self-destruction and surrender. I didn't always recognize the power of the supportive community, but after I began to understand who the aliens really were I realized how irresponsible I'd been in expecting the family and community to somehow purge me of my own darkness. The family and community weren't powerless at all. My anger saved my life. The supportive community healed me, and the central element of my community's support, the key to its healing power, was its acceptance of me where I was.

That morning, the night after I said no to the aliens, we sang four or five spirituals, each with more vigor than the last, until we simply had to stop, out of breath but still charged with the spirit of celebration. Mother and Titter went outside to tell everyone the news. Daddy and the brothers walked me back to the bedroom and stayed with me. I knew that as soon as the word spread, community people would come to share in the rejoicing.

Before an hour went by, the people began to arrive, jamming the house full of vibrant sounds. Throughout the day many of them brought food and drink, and by late afternoon the depth of rejoicing surpassed even that of a Sunday after church. It was a special event, more like the birth of a child or the return of a loved one.

I don't think any of us were celebrating a final victory. I know I wasn't. My aliens would try and take me over again, but I was no longer afraid of my feelings. My relationship with the aliens, the world, and myself had changed. That's what we were really celebrating.

The aliens called on me that night. They were strongest when they first appeared, but the longer I engaged them the stronger I became. From the moment of their appearance, I approached them as equals, and as our conversation continued it became clear that they belonged to me more than I belonged to them. I wasn't afraid of them any more, but neither did I hate them. After all, they were part of me. In a sense, we became each other's counsel; I demonstrated my power and set limits with them, and they in turn taught me crucial lessons about myself and the world. We parted that night with a certain mutual respect. I knew they were very dangerous. They knew I was willing to risk. I thought of them as friends of mine.

When they left, I turned to see Mother next to me. She looked at me knowingly, as though she sensed I'd broken through. Darkness persisted outside the window. Daylight was hours away.

"It's all right," I said to her quietly. "You can go to bed now."

The winter began to relax, and so did I. The aliens still visited me, but I remained determined with them. My days weren't clouded with worry about the coming night, and my nights weren't fearful vigils anymore. The aliens no longer spoke to me in threats. They sometimes tried to outwit me, but I always got the best of them. We were adversaries, and yet we were friends. Finally, I was able to say it was all right for the aliens to go to bed too.

In the winter of 1940, three months after they came to me, the aliens began to visit me less and less, and eventually stopped coming altogether. They never said goodbye, because we both knew they'd never be far away. In different forms, they still exist today. By the time their visits ceased, I was permitted to leave my bed as long as I didn't exert myself. It was obvious that I was marching toward recovery. It was just as obvious, at least to me, that I'd become a different person. I was still Cecil Williams, the little Rev marked for the ministry, but something had happened to me in the dead spots of the night. An awakening sense of power driven by a tension I could only feel, not describe, infused my renewed acquaintance with reality. I had no grotesque and overblown delusions of riding out to slay the world's dragons. I was a boy, not a wizard, yet I was sure above all other certainties that I could do things I once believed impossible. If I could rise to fight the aliens, if I could contend with my own evils, then I could rise to fight in other places too. And if I could do it, so could others.

I spent a lot of time in the realm of my imagination, a place of unlimited possibilities that I discovered during the daylight hours of my illness. One of my strongest fantasies involved me and the church. I was angry and disillusioned about many things, and the church stood in the center of my feelings. It was not so much the church itself as the contradiction between what it spoon-fed me and what actually existed. The church promised love and brotherhood, but they were unfulfilled promises.

Rejection by whites had always been my greatest source of pain, great enough to drive me mad. The church promised a certain relief from the pain but was never able to transcend the rejection. Yet I felt a new sense of power that I unleashed in an imagination capable of creating a church powerful enough to withstand and conquer the rejection. I imagined myself a minister before a huge group of all colors, ages, descriptions. I didn't know where this church was, but it certainly wasn't Wesley Methodist in San Angelo. Bright colors were everywhere, streaming down on the people. I stood before them, yet at the same time they were all around me. I don't remember details, but there was something different going on there, unlike anything I'd experienced in the churches of my young life. The whole place was loud, though I couldn't quite identify the sounds, and a sense of power pervaded the scene, the same sensation I felt when I said no to the aliens.

I couldn't wait for the kids to get home from school so I could test out my imaginary sanctuary. Dusty, Jack, and two neighborhood friends, Donnell and Oland, came in together. I immediately dragged all of them into the bedroom.

"Let's play like I'm a preacher and y'all are in church," I said.

"Shit, Rev, you *are* a preacher," Dusty said.

"Sure is," Jack laughed. "Nigger talks his ass off."

"Look," I said, "this ain't no regular church. All kinds of people are there—white folks, too."

Wide-eyed skepticism was all I got for that remark.

"White folks too, huh?" Jack asked.

"Yeah, man, everybody—white folks too."

Jack slid over to me and lowered his voice to a conspiratorial level.

"Rev?"

"Yeah."

"Remember when I said you wasn't crazy."

"Sure."

"I was wrong."

"Okay, okay," I said. "I'm not foolin' here. Are y'all gonna be in my church or not?"

Four heads nodded their agreement.

"I know!" Dusty exclaimed proudly. "You lettin' white folks in 'cause it's some kinda special day, huh?"

"No, there's white folks in my church all the time."

"How come?"

" 'Cause I want 'em there, that's how come."

"Well, don't pass no plate 'cause this is the poorest-ass congregation you ever did see," Donnell said.

"Don't worry, the white folks'll take care of that. Here's the pulpit," I said, patting the bed. "Now y'all just get over there and let the spirit move you."

They shuffled into their places.

"Just one last thing."

"What?" Oland asked.

"Who's gonna be the white folks?"

You could've cut up the silence and sold it by the pound.

"How 'bout you, brother Jack?"

"Me?" he cried. "No, Lord, I ain't been white in so long that I forgot how."

"Dusty?"

"Sorry, Rev, but I holler too much."

"Donnell, Oland?"

They shook their heads in unison.

"I'm too fast," Oland said.

"Yeah, and I can dance," Donnell explained.

But I was not about to be deterred. I'd imagined this church, and, dammit, I wasn't going to let this poor excuse for the faithful stop me from bringing it to life. I wanted a church of all colors, and that's what I was going to get. I wanted to preach before all colors, and that's what I was going to do. The love and brotherhood promised by the world's church was going to be real in mine. Good intentions captivated my awareness, but perhaps it was my youth that kept me from knowing myself too well. I wanted to see all colors together, all right, but I also wanted to avenge myself, my family, my community. I wanted the white folks in *my* church; I didn't want to be showcased in theirs. I wanted the power to be with them. I also wanted the power to be over them. Most of all, I wanted things to change.

"All right, be that way, but I ain't gonna let a raggedy-ass buncha niggers mess me up."

Dusty and Oland giggled. I grabbed an old wooden chair.

"Y'all see this chair?" I asked. It was a rhetorical question. "Well it ain't a chair no more. This chair is now a white person!"

I slammed it down next to Jack, who jumped about a foot.

"Y'know, Rev, this chair *could* be a white person. Know why?"

"No, why?"

"It ain't got no smell to it."

I laughed.

"Well, put the white folks in the back. Then you won't have to think about it. Y'all ready now?"

They got quiet. Church began.

I preached like a railroad train, leaping over mountains and hurtling through valleys trying to reach that place in my imagination. My boy's voice soared, swooped, boomed, and whispered in fervent imitation of those dark men in black robes who set off explosions each Sunday. For the moments I enacted him, I became my own imaginary minister in his strange church. I heard the sound of my words blowing like a hurricane wind, and I knew in the farthest reaches of my heart that all the people heard them, each and every one.

FOUR

THE buffing machine whirred as it slid across the sanctuary floor, leaving a clear shine in its wake. Dusty and I had spent the early afternoon applying the paste wax, and now the machine was buffing it with insulting ease. In defiance of the job's tedious repetition, I let go of the buffer. It jerked spasmodically, lurched off in a new direction, and slammed into a pew with an awful clatter. Dusty looked at the stalled machine, back at me, grinned, and shook his head in mock bewilderment. He asked me if I thought they were through with Mother yet at the hospital. I shrugged and said I didn't know.

It was summertime and terribly hot in the sanctuary of the First Methodist Church of San Angelo, whose all-white congregation was Christian enough to pay blacks as janitors even if we were not permitted to pray there. But it was all right. I was nineteen and growing stronger; everything was working out according to plan. On the road toward fulfilling the family dream, I'd completed my first year at Sam Huston College and already had my Exhorter's License, the first step in a church career. I was going to become a minister, the best they ever saw. Step by step. Four years of college, then seminary, then an appointment to a large black church in a big city like Dallas.

At the rear of the room, framed by sunlight filtering through the church windows, Daddy stood in the open doorway. His shoulders sagged and his body bent forward as if walking into a powerful wind. He came down the aisle with a strangely expressionless face, but when he neared us he straightened up and his eyes came alive.

"Hey, Daddy," Dusty greeted him. He seemed not to hear.

"Cut off the buffer, Rev," he said. "Sit down, sons."

The three of us sat in the middle of the front pew. Daddy gazed at the hands dangling from the end of his thighs.

"Guess there ain't no other way to tell it," he said. "Mother's about to die."

People argue that everything, even death, is the will of God. Life, they plead, is the province of fate. It's easier that way. I've also been told that when people get shot they don't always feel pain right away, that even though they see their flesh rip and blood spurt, their body, mind, and spirit at first refuse to accept what has happened. Eventually, of course, they have no choice. Daddy raised a hand to delay our questions.

"Mother's gonna stay in the hospital a few more days before they let her come on home. They did a lot of testin' down there and the doctor finally told me she has cancer of the colon, down near her stomach. He said there ain't nothin' anyone can do. She's got three to six months—and I want us to make them good months."

I stood and walked to the end of the pew, burning with an angry hurt so powerful it lifted me out of myself. I wanted to scream. In my mind, the sound of my voice crashed against the church walls, although I was only talking aloud to myself. In the sanctuary of the white church with its cross, altar, and velvet, with its decree that I was unworthy of praying in it, I cried out to the God who'd always been presented to me.

"Why? Why Mother? We're not ready, Lord! Why do you make us suffer like this? What have we done?

"Isn't there a plan where you reward the faithful? Mother's a good Christian woman, one of your messengers. She doesn't deserve to die! Not now, Lord. She's not even fifty years old, and she's got a family to care for. If this is your plan, how good can you be?

"You're not bein' fair, Lord! How can I go back to school and become what you want me to become when I know Mother's gonna die? We ain't gone against you. We ain't done anything wrong. It's not fair, Lord. It's just not fair!"

47

His order is something to believe in. He's looking after all of it. He's stern, but he's fair and just, and he looks after all of it. Ain't that the way it is?

"Ain't it, Lord? Ain't it?"

Nothing makes sense.

"God, it's in your hands. Create a miracle! If you are really all powerful, change it! Change it now so we don't have to suffer anymore. Show me a sign, Lord. Show me a sign."

The walls of the white church reflect nothing, the answer to my cry for a miracle. God must be a white man in this church, a white man who doesn't even want us here. How can a white God help me? I'm caught, trapped in a place made for somebody else. Desperate. I need an answer *now.* I must depend on a sacred order whose color is the deepest, purest white. I rush forward to the altar to offer a prayer.

"Lord, I'm appealing to you as one of your children, one of your best. I'm gonna be a great minister for you. Please take this burden from me."

With almost soldierly precision, I slowly backed away. Daddy's hand caught my shoulder and gently turned me around. "I'm goin' home to tell the rest of the family. In a little while I want you two to come on home. There ain't no more work for you here today."

The family sat around the front room, talking quietly. Daddy had rejoined us after going back to finish cleaning up the church. Titter did most of the crying, but it had subsided into a guttural moan. All afternoon long I'd waited for a sign that never came. Now I knew there would be no sign. There would be only death. I wanted to admit it but I didn't know how. What do you say? What can anyone say? I'd called on God but he sent no answer, which was answer enough. It was so hard, because it wasn't supposed to happen the way it had. My lips moved. Words fell out.

"There's no hope," I said. "No hope."

No one disputed me. We talked some more. In the early evening, when the heat retreated and the hard blue sky relaxed, we reached a point of resignation. Mother was dying.

We decided to fix up a room in our auntie's house next door, which happened to be one of the best in the community.

Mother would look her finest there, and we wanted everyone to experience her in a nice place. Daddy said she didn't know she was dying yet. At least no one had told her.

When they brought her home a few days later, I recognized her eyes most of all, green and brown like memories of autumn but still able to see inside me. I could never have deceived her. I loved her more than anything in the world. In my pain and sorrow, I needed her so much then, as we helped walk her up the front steps. She'd grown pale and her body was wasting away with a cruel, incessant regularity. In only a few weeks she'd lost ten or fifteen pounds.

A plastic tube dangled from her lower abdomen and fed into a rubber bag that collected what they called her "waste matter." I sensed the flow of sludge and liquid through the tube and into the bag, and each time the bag was emptied it was as if a little more of her had been thrown out. I knew that what they threw out could never be replaced.

She had pills for the pain, which seemed to work fairly well. We each took turns walking her out the back door of the house, around to the front and back again. She enjoyed the sunshine and talking with the people. Even Reedy, who was only twelve, walked her sometimes, although we all tried to protect him from experiencing her growing weakness. We felt he had been deprived of experiencing Mother's strength, that he had missed something. Because of that, he was somehow apart from the rest of us, and it hurt me. I saw him as a vagabond, and regret that many years passed before I grew close to him.

Late one September afternoon she asked for Daddy and Titter, who along with Daddy had been closest to her since she'd come home. They talked a long time in the bedroom. Finally, as the sun began to set, they emerged and walked with all of us to the front room. Mother had lost close to forty pounds, but her spirit had not diminished. In fact, considering her condition she looked radiant; exhausted but comfortable, as though she'd spent a hard day in the garden and was finally getting her chance to rest. My muscles tensed as I prepared myself for the words I knew would come.

"Children," Mother began, chuckling immediately at her choice of words. "Won't you listen to me! I call you children even when you're almost grown. Now isn't that just a mother's way?"

We smiled with her. Perhaps I should have been embarrassed by her humorous declaration, the attempt to soften the next moment, but I was not.

"Children, I know I've got cancer, and I know I'm not gonna live too much longer. I know I'm dying."

All along I expected her words to come down hard on me. I was a strong young man, but I thought I would burst out crying. And I thought *she* would cry too. I expected the words to knock me down with the force of their truth. Most of all, I thought that somewhere I would refuse to accept them. Instead they were like young trees planted in fertile soil. Sturdy and in a strange way very loving and kind. Like so many words that had parted her lips for those nineteen years. Words from which I drew strength. Yet it was not so much the words as the spirit in which they were spoken.

"It's all right," she said. "It's gonna be all right, and I want all of you to be strong now. You must be strong."

Mother had accepted something I could not: her own death. I'd nearly been depleted by the cruel injustice of it, but Mother, the one who was actually dying, sat in the front room's lone stuffed chair with a strength and wisdom I began to comprehend. She told us what she wanted at her funeral. Nothing too big, fancy, or prolonged.

"And I want you boys to sing 'Precious Lord' for me."

We promised.

"I'm not afraid to die, oh no. You know, I think about a lot of things nowadays, things I've been through and things I've seen. Havin' all you fine children—Lord, the tribulations—seeing you all here with me now. What I mean is, it's been good. I've made my peace and I'm gonna be with the rest of the family over on the other side. I've given it up to the Lord."

Again the rage welled up inside me. God's gonna take care of it? God's already taken care of it! God's taking your life, Mother, and I just can't understand why. Why not me, God? Why not anybody else but her? Why?

I looked at Mother sitting in that chair and came closer in my heart to accepting the fact that soon she would be dead. I didn't realize it then, but that vision of her forced me to accept the existence of chaos. Because that's what death is. Simple, utter chaos; the unplanned, unknown end to everything.

A few days later some people from Sam Huston came and pleaded with me to return to college, but I refused. The family had made a pact to stay together throughout the ordeal. I'd go back to school sooner or later, but, owing to financial realities, it looked as though my brothers would be unable to pursue a college education.

Mother held on through winter, but I saw her slip further and further away. The moments of excruciating pain, when we heard her moan and cry and knew we could do nothing to ease it, were the hardest to bear. When she suffered like that, we had to ask the community people to leave the house. The doctor kept increasing the dosage of her medicine until finally it did no good at all. By mid-January Mother hardly slept, and her daily walks grew progressively shorter. In the beginning, she walked from the back of the house to the front. Then it was from the back to the side. Then it was just out the back door. Soon there would be no walks at all.

The best moments came when we all sat and talked, gathered around her like a brood of younger children. Most of our evenings passed that way, laughing and comforting one another as we'd done on the porch at night when I was a boy. Over and over again, not with her words but her presence and attitude, Mother showed me I had to accept her death as a condition of my own life.

I don't remember the precise moment of my decision, but I finally stopped trying all the prayers, promises, and answers, the things I'd used to deny and stave off death. I'd appealed to the Highest Order to save my mother's life, and it simply hadn't worked. I tried and tried and tried. But death still remained.

Mother, although quite weak, was still strong enough to make her point. She may have been dying physically but her mind was sharp as ever, and she was in especially good humor that February night. We all were. It was nearly midnight and there was lots of joking about how cold it was outside when, with no warning, Mother's head flopped over on its side.

"Baby," Daddy said with the slightest trace of alarm. She

didn't hear him. She lay still, her breathing audible but erratic. We looked at each other, and we knew.

Within the hour her breathing became gasping, the lungs in her unconscious body fighting for the air they needed. It was a horrible, haunting sound of life giving way to death; a sucking, indiscriminate desperation as her chest rose and fell, rose and fell, her mouth all the while open, her body straight and still as though she were sleeping, dreaming, sleeping, dreaming—

I began timing her gasps so I could prepare for them. They absorbed me when they came. I went outside into the night hoping to escape the terrible noise, but I couldn't. I think I could've run for miles and still heard Mother gasping for her last breath.

The clear night was a deep black and full of stars, a mystery that deepened as it grew to full strength. It was so cold that my breath formed puffs of mist that disappeared and reappeared as I heard her choking inside the house. One by one the three older brothers came out too. None of us said much.

Dawn rose about 7 o'clock, a thin band of orange shivering across the plains to the east. Out toward the ranches, columns of smoke spiraled into the sky. Dawn. A symbol of birth, or perhaps rebirth. I jammed my hands deep into my pants pockets.

"I knew Mother'd make it through the night," I declared to no one in particular. Somehow the sounds coming from the house didn't disturb me as much as they had earlier, and I readied myself more for the silence between her gasps than the gasps themselves. The periods of silence lengthened and the gasps weakened, becoming more like hisses. Shortly after 7:30 even the hisses stopped, and there was only silence. For the briefest moment everything stood still. It was as though we'd been frozen in a photograph, as though the earth itself had stopped, as though eternity had come to pass. In the next heartbeat, though, because we'd known it all along, the earth moved again; moving, moving, always moving.

"She's dead," Bro whispered. One after the other the three of us repeated it.

"She's dead."

"She's dead."

"She's dead."

There was a certain majesty in the sound of our voices rolling across the plains to the band of orange and through the charcoal sky until it found the night again, acknowledging the undeniable reality that our mother was dead. Mother was dead, and we were more alive than ever.

"Mother sure fought, didn't she?" Dusty said.

"Yeah, she sure did stand up," Jack agreed.

In all those months, it was the only time I felt like crying, maybe because their words were so true and their meaning somehow so important to me. Maybe it was because in death her fighting hadn't mattered at all. Or maybe it was because in life, the last days of her life, her fighting had mattered so much. A few tears dripped over the rims of my eyes and a bitter wetness burned at the base of my throat, but it passed quickly. She hadn't wanted us to mourn too hard. She told me once, tugging at the tube buried in her side, that she knew her death wouldn't stop me. I swallowed hard at the memory. Whatever she'd given me had become all mine.

The news of Mother's death spread quickly, and by 8:30 the house was packed with grieving neighbors. It was funny, but we consoled them much more than they consoled us. The feeling of community that had always flourished in the black section of San Angelo was present again that morning.

They took her to the funeral home and immediately after her embalming brought her back to the house. All day and much of the night people filed past her body lying in the living room. At one point during the night the minister from First Methodist Church came by. As I saw his solemn expression and heard his mumbled condolences, a rush of contempt surged through me; contempt for him and his God. The truth was I held them both partly responsible. They could've done something, if not about her death then at least about the conditions that had made her life harder than it should have been. I was contemptuous of the white minister, because all he could do was say he was sorry. Even so, I spoke to him so he might know that death would not stop me.

By mid-morning, many adults were preparing for the funeral by getting drunk. It was a short service, but the crowd and procession were impressively large. The quartet sang 'Precious Lord,' and we buried her next to Papa Jack and the rest of the family. Afterward we returned to the house to eat and drink a bit. The choir director from Sam Huston was there, and invited all four of us—not just me, but Dusty, Jack, and Bro, too—to come back to school for the spring semester, which we did. Perhaps Mother's death was in a sense responsible for the college's offer of assistance.

It's difficult to gauge the impact Mother's death had on me as a young man, but I know it helped me change in many ways. It introduced me to the inevitability of chaos, as well as my duty to accept it. From those first moments in the white sanctuary when I learned of her condition, death pointed the finger toward the only method of survival amid chaos: revolt. It was revolt that would give things meaning.

I also began feeling differently about myself. I suppose I'd always felt I was the "chosen one" among us, and I'd always wanted to become a minister. But after the funeral I realized that I'd wanted to do it almost as much to please Mother and others as anything else. With Mother dead, however, the choice had become more my own. A choice that would be revealed only through a search for it.

The search resumed when I returned to Sam Huston, a four-year black college whose job it was to turn out educated Negroes. Getting an education became the most important thing in my life. It had been drummed into me with religious fervor and an almost mathematical certainty that education would open doors of acceptance and success. Getting an education meant I would make it in the mainstream, or as close to the mainstream as they let niggers get.

Sam Huston's very foundation rested on a dilemma. Because it was a black institution, there was always a certain contention with the white world, a sanction of the spirit of revolt. Yet this spirit of revolt was perverted by pressures suffered by every student. We weren't working and studying just to become preachers and teachers, we were working and studying to become acceptable in a world defined and run by white people. I know I was. I yearned to be accepted by whites. I longed to be considered their equal, and in that longing bestowed on them the power to determine my worthiness. Yet I also knew firsthand about the world's ruthlessly dehumanizing forces, and I desperately wished to revolt against them. America was turning the corner toward the 1950s, and I was a very confused young black man.

The quartet sang a lot during those college days, traveling around to schools and churches as Sam Huston emissaries. I even entertained notions of becoming an opera star, but only Marian Anderson and Todd Duncan stood as examples. The white world's stunning rejection of them, despite their obvious talents, was discouraging enough to still my operatic ambitions after a short time.

I was a leader at Sam Huston, the perennial class president and the one most likely to influence student affairs. Invited to all the parties and sought on matters of opinion, I made my way and strutted my stuff. Yet somehow it wasn't fulfilling. As surely as I rode the tide of my popularity I felt I should've been doing more. But more of what? I needed someone who could find and touch the source of my disturbance. I needed someone to disturb *me*. And I found him.

He was the first black to earn a Ph.D. degree in the State of Texas. People said he could have become a bishop in the Methodist Church had he not been so strange and radical. An eccentric who defied traditional order by creating a chaos of his own, he was a man who cared little for appearances and even less for convention. He slept on piles of old newspaper in his room, and on one of their many treks to his sanctuary a group of faculty members discovered a batch of old paychecks he hadn't bothered to cash. He informed his incredulous colleagues that he never cashed any of his checks. The faculty and administration were kept in a continual frenzy trying to decide what to do about him, but his academic credentials were nothing if not impeccable. People said he was crazy.

He was J. Leonard Farmer, whose son James later became a leader of CORE (Congress of Racial Equality) and went on to several high posts in the federal government during America's contemporary Reconstruction in the 1960s. He shocked me. He said that Jesus was not what I'd been taught all my life but that his legacy was one of radical, earthly action rather than heavenly, spiritual peace. He raised questions about the biblical text and railed against the presumed order of theology. He injected chaos into theology and my life. He called on me hard.

The first course I took from him was on the New Testament, and like an unerring marksman J. Leonard Farmer took dead aim against the mythology that formed the basis of my theology. The old man seldom missed and never let up. I was fascinated and terrified. He embodied the crusty rebelliousness of Papa Jack, the horror and courage of surviving my childhood breakdown, the chaos of my mother's recent death. He was a walking revolt who ran so deep that part of me wanted to be just like him. It had been years since I'd felt that way about anyone.

The next semester I took philosophy from him. He trotted out a stable of traditional philosophers such as Spinoza and St. Thomas Aquinas, and then proceeded to tear them down. He didn't necessarily dispute their wisdom but he continually made it clear that the responsibility for philosophy and its resulting actions lay with each of us and not with Spinoza or anybody else. He virtually demanded that we each form philosophies of our own. It was a challenge that scared me to death because I wanted to depend on others for my philosophical ground. I certainly didn't want the responsibility of replacing them with myself.

He disturbed the hell out of me. There was something seething in me that I was afraid to confront, and he touched it every day. Sometimes he affected me so deeply I wished he'd just back off. But the old man wouldn't quit. One day I got into a heated argument with him during class, stormed out, and stayed away two days. At the end of the second day, J. Leonard Farmer knocked on my dormitory door. I was greatly pleased and relieved that he cared enough to come and see me.

"I'm going to tell you something and then I'm leaving," he said. "You may not like what I say or what I teach but you probably have a better grasp of philosophy than anybody else in that class. I think you have something I don't sense in any other student." Then he turned abruptly and left. Until that moment I hadn't realized the depth of my affection and respect for him, and I surely hadn't known of his special affection for me. I'd hoped for his respect but hadn't dared presume it. He never again spoke to me that way; it wasn't really necessary.

I returned to class the next day and eventually earned an A in the course. I completed the final exam in half the time it took the other students, and when I walked out of there I knew I had my stuff. J. Leonard Farmer had given me a sense of pride and confidence. But more than that he'd shown me that one could defy order and still survive.

The old man shook me hard. But not hard enough to tumble me from the rut I was in. Still torn between challenging the world and succumbing to it, I was off balance, unsure about what mattered most to me. I felt the need to revolt and in some way to emulate J. Leonard Farmer. But I wanted even more to make it in the white world.

Six weeks before graduation, Bob Briehan, one of my closest white friends, came to see me at Sam Huston. He brought me a proposition, only it wasn't truly a proposition because there were no sides to it. I had to accept. My entire life had been shaped to receive it, thus its dimension seemed much greater than my own. Like mystery.

Bob was a senior at the Perkins School of Theology on the Southern Methodist University campus in Dallas, where there had been a strong movement to have a small number of blacks admitted. I'd been chosen as one of them. Bob said it with great pleasure and pride, and asked me if I realized the historical import of the proposition. I said I sure did. We both thought it was a rhetorical question. Finally, after so many years, it was happening. The color line was being crossed, and acceptance could be ours. Bob became excited and animated, swept up in the proposition. He began telling me about Perkins; how it looked, how the accommodations were, what instructors to seek and avoid. Except I wasn't listening. Perkins was a *white* seminary. That's all I needed to know.

Make it in a white school and you've got a real chance. Period. All the doubt, rejection, and suffering were being vindicated by my white friend's proposition. Maybe. If only Perkins would let me in, teach me its secrets, give me some of what it had. If only Perkins would accept and transform me. Yes, *transform* me into something acceptable. All my life I'd awaited such a transformation, huddled in the shadows of a world defined by the glint in their blue eyes, the whistle of air between their teeth, the soft curl of their women's hair, the rigidity of their jaws when I came too close. Perkins School of Theology seemed a piece of heaven. Don't laugh. That's how much it meant to me.

On a bright and unusually cold September day, I first set foot on the once forbidden grounds of the Perkins campus. My eyes drank the view of stately buildings squatting among rolling, perfectly maintained lawns. White students scurried along paths that snaked between the buildings. I'd never seen so many white people in my life. And they accepted me! Not only that, they went out of their way to show me and the four other new black students how much they wanted to protect and make things especially easy for us, as though our success meant more to them than us. It was so easy to like them, and we did. In the context of the times, they were decent people. I'm sure of that, even to this day. It's just that none of us realized what was actually at stake. Perkins was a monastery to me, cut off from the outside world, and I was a monk isolated from all I'd ever known. The particular circumstances of my daily routine were immaterial; I was always on an island in the middle of the sea. And from every pulpit, podium, angle, view, the message was clearly written: "Become like them." That's what I was there for. That was my dream.

My first year at Perkins. Here's what was real: The hard wooden chair pressing against my butt. The faces of white ministers and professors peering down at me. Lectures about root words, theological theory, analytical attack. Order, structure, hint of absolutes. A scientific approach to religion. White women. Fresh, creamy, clean, and glowing. The smell of white women swishing past me on their way someplace else. Where? White men. Tall, handsome. Their bones. Thin noses, tight streamlined asses. Their eyes. Green, blue, gray. Their hair. Blond, brown, soft. Their skin. Smooth, pink, tanned, with the peculiar ability to reflect the sun. Their way of looking at things. Confident, temperate, in control. Supreme. Accepting the world as it was. Money, cars, the freedom to go anywhere they pleased. Wanting what they had. They made it so easy to like them and want to be like them. I loved what they had, loved it so madly that at times I would've done just about anything to get some.

Me. Short, unattractive. Nose spilling all over my face. A different smell. Large mouth, uncertain laugh. Brown eyes, which wouldn't have been so bad except they were buried in brown skin. At least I wasn't black, dark like an African with lips like big fat spoons. At least I wasn't black enough for my sweat to shine. At least I wasn't black enough for my teeth to radiate in the darkness. Like some railroad porter. Like the dude on the Cream of Wheat box. My hair. Nappy, springy, tight, strange to the touch. My way of looking at things. Outside, ill at ease but faking it. Anxious, eager, hopeful, trying their world on, hoping for a fit. At their mercy.

I was always smiling.

I hated them. I despised their power to reject me. I despised their power to ignore me. I hated their control, and I hated myself for wanting it so much. I hated myself for not being like them. I hated myself for wanting to be like them and knowing I couldn't but wanting it anyway, wanting to become a learned Negro to impress them so that, even though I was black and would always be black, maybe somehow they could overlook it, because being black wasn't my fault, and if I could only get them to understand then maybe it would be all right. But they *did* accept me. Not all the way, of course, but some. No one called me "nigger." No one treated me like a "boy." Lots of the married students invited me into their homes to share their food. Me more than the other blacks, in fact. Maybe you don't realize how often I had dreamed of precisely such a scene as a youth. Invited into a white person's home just like anybody else. Sit anywhere I want. Tell a joke, stretch out after dinner, and talk a while. And it was happening on the Perkins campus. It was like a piece of heaven, the one I'd imagined all my life. It couldn't have worked out any better had I the power to plan it all myself. So why wasn't I satisfied?

There are different realities. Trust me here. They aren't separate, just different. I guess you could say they all roll into one at the end, but they each come at you in different ways, and they say so many different things.

My second year at Perkins. One reality: Seminary. Buildings.

More hard work. Reading, approval, acceptance. Making it. Becoming like them.

When I was able to choose this reality, I did.

Cruel deceit. Dark skin, blacker in the night. White roommate sleeping, sighing, grunting, spitting. Look at him. Not love. Not hate. Just knowing he's white and I'm black, and something's wrong with wanting him to accept me. What?

Realizing he never will because I can never be what I think he wants me to be. I can't be like him, not exactly like him. I can't become them, not exactly become them. All I can do is try. Learn what they learn, talk what they talk, see what they see, believe what they believe, act like they act. I can. But it won't be the same. No matter what, it won't. Dark skin, blacker in the night. Always and forever.

"Our son in the ministry." The small clique of black ministers who clung to limited and tenuous power in the Methodist Church called me that. They never tired of predicting great things for me. I was their choice, the one to carry forth the great tradition on which their own lives and careers rested. Products of the church's Glory Trail, they didn't dream of the same kind of transformation I did. They didn't want to be accepted as much as tolerated, so they didn't want to shake things up. That was their idea of making it, and they had. They wanted me to make it too. I was almost one of them.

Despite its most lofty and Christian pronouncements, the Methodist Church was split down the middle solely on the basis of color. There was a white bishop and a white conference, and there was a black bishop and a black conference. The racist split was becoming more than hypocritical to me, it was growing into a bitter, painful absurdity. On Sundays I worked as a student pastor in the church of I. B. Loud, one of the most powerful black ministers in Dallas. Because he had no theological training he would never be elected bishop in the Methodist Church, but he *acted* like the bishop anyway, and he commanded a widespread respect in the church community. I greatly admired his ability to move an audience.

As student pastors in I. B. Loud's church, we led the worship service, attended church meetings, and visited the sick. On many Sundays, I. B. Loud let his student pastors preach. I'd begin reasonably enough, true to the middle-class standards of the seminary and the strict conservatism of the black ministers. Like this:

Start. First reality. Reason, intellect, analysis. Soothe the people. Make them comfortable. Don't shake things up. Make it. Remember that you're speaking to a black audience. Vocabulary, pacing, style, structure of argument. Things like that. Watch it. Remember who you want to be. I see Perkins in the back of my brain. I see a paper I wrote. An analysis of the Exodus based on root words, theological derivatives. Who the writers were, who their audience was. Scientific. Not the story itself. No, not that at all. I see the professor's scrawl skitter up the margin. It says "good." I must remember that. Good—

Way down in Egypt land.

—What?

More first reality. Hold on to it, man. Don't let it get away from you now. Because . . . because they'll *see* it. They'll *know.* Sweat now. Hard thin lines carved in forehead. Concentrate, nigger. Push it back. I see I. B. Loud pulling me to the side after one of my short sermons a few Sundays ago. And he says to me, "That was real good . . . real good." I must remember that. Real good.

Headache. Shiver. Not so they can tell, though. Just a little shiver scurrying up your back. Nothing you can't handle if you just keep on talking to them like you're doing now about the love of Jesus and how he can help see us through our tribulations because he died—

Mother.

—for each of us. Tell them somebody loves them, somebody accepts them even if it's somebody who died—

Where is Jesus?

—before they were born into suffering—

and who can't do anything about it now.

—Stop! Jesus, that's not it. Not what I meant to think. You gotta believe that. Can anyone tell? Forget it, they can't. You're trying to make it, nigger. Make it, you hear! See Perkins again. See *the special place in the cafeteria where we usually sit.*

61

All of us are soldiers and travelers whose faith will free us and lead us to the mountaintop. And the church is our refuge and sanctuary. And the church—

is racist to its very core.

—No, not now!—

and you don't have to go to college or seminary to know it, either

—I can't stop it because—

'cause all you have to do is look around you!

—it's greater than I am.—

Look at a church that rejects people based on color. You know it's true, don't you? We're all black, aren't we? Try to go into a white church. You know what I'm talkin' about. They won't let us in. They've never let us in. And if by chance they do let us in, they'll think hard about the quickest way to get rid of us. I know. I'm a witness before you. And you're a witness too. Now we must ask ourselves: What kind of Christianity is that? I say to you right here and right now that the church must change its racist policies if it is to be what it says it is. Not somewhere else. Not some other time. Right here! Now!

—Let my people go.

I can't explain it but sometimes it happened that way. A different reality took hold of me as I stood in the pulpit and became like a man running through the woods under the cover of night. My struggle overtook me, and *I became the struggle.* When a certain reality won that struggle, I shocked and disturbed people. I did it in I. B. Loud's church, and I did it in the white churches too. The white ministers often approached me afterward and confessed I'd said things they wanted to say but either couldn't or wouldn't. I made some whites feel guilty. And they loved it. I made some blacks feel proud and righteous. And they loved that. Sometimes, out of the corner of my eye, I caught I. B. Loud watching me. His face revealed nothing.

The white churches began asking for me more and more. They wanted me for Race Relations Sunday, Brotherhood Month, and a variety of other special occasions at which I pricked their guilt and at the same time assuaged it with my very presence. I was a gesture, nothing more. A racist gesture intended, in the finest Perkins tradition, to soothe. A specialist who held claim to only the most special and restricted place. They accepted me in my special place, but one look at them and I knew better than to hope for anything more. I was still the same: unacceptable.

Between the white church and the black church, I hung like a carcass in the noonday sun. The white church would never fully accept me no matter who I became, and the black church would accept me only so long as I allowed it the power to define me.

Realities. They changed up on me all the time, drifting like clouds passing before the sun, shifting like sands in the desert, flowing one into the other and back again. Maybe you think I was crazy. I almost was. That's what saved me.

My third and final year. One reality: Perkins again. Tangible. Diploma soon. Minister. Proof that I'd made it. Proof you could see, touch, feel, read. Secret dream: becoming the first black minister named to pastor a white church in Texas. Still longing for acceptance. Still yearning to make it. Knowing I never would be accepted in the white church, white world.

Another reality: Knowing I could never be what the black ministers wanted me to be.

White world, black church. What must I do to gain their acceptance? *Be what they want me to be.* Simple. I could do it too. See me at Perkins, being accepted. See me study. See me eat dinner in white homes. Or see me with the black ministers. Hear me get praised. Hear them call me "their son." See them flock around me. I told you I could do it. In either place, I'm capable of doing it. So why do I know something's gone wrong?

Because in doing it I am in collusion with them. In order to become acceptable, I must fit their definition of acceptability. I must do, say, be certain things. For them, not me. All these long years, I thought everything would be all right once they accepted me. But that was another reality, and now I realize how poorly I understood the reality of my desire. When you long for someone else to accept you, it's not they who must accept the most.

It's you.

If you're desperate to be accepted (as I am in other realities), then you must accept their definition of you. You must accept what they think of you, what they want from you. And they only want it all. So here, in this reality of all realities—

—I have no reality. I am nothing, nowhere. Here I don't exist because here there is nothing. Nothing to stand on, nothing to grab, nothing to call my own. Feel me

alone

no reality

nothing.

Sometimes I feel I'm going mad again.

They never told me, but they knew. They never saw it as you see a rash or the gleam of madness in another's eye. But they felt it flow from me. It's something you can't conceal. Whenever I found a reality in which I perceived them differently—the seminary instructors, the students, the black ministers—they felt it. And so they began to perceive me differently as well. It wasn't that I did anything irrational, it was only that every once in a while I rebelled. You've heard what sometimes happened in the pulpit when one reality outfought another. Things like that let them know that I wasn't quite like them. What made it so strange was that in other realities I was a perfect model of what they wanted. Something was out of focus. Something didn't quite fit. It was me, of course, and they saw it. Better, perhaps, than I saw it myself.

The last half of my final year was a nightmare. On the strength of my childhood breakdown, I'd learned a few things, so the nightmares didn't command and control me as the aliens had. I knew they were only voices of a certain reality trying to speak to me, and the knowledge had a stabilizing effect. Nevertheless, the nightmares managed to do one thing well: terrify me. The strongest one repeated itself over and over again.

In this nightmare, it's night outside, and I'm standing at my half-open dorm room window. Springtime. Flowers blooming. The urges of a young man. I'm always dressed for bed. A warm, mellow breeze plays at seducing me, caressing my skin and making my white T-shirt slowly dance. The world is so quiet and peaceful. Sparkling lights bob above the still campus lawns. I hear people talking on the paths far below. Their voices are whispers. The effect is soothing.

I never hear him come. Or her, I'm not sure which. Maybe they simply materialize behind me rather than creep soundlessly across the dorm room floor. Anyway, I never hear them come. I'm straining to make out the whispering voices when suddenly their hands, hard and sure of themselves, latch onto my shoulders.

I never get a chance to turn and see who they are. It happens too quickly. There is the crinkle of broken glass. I don't ever see the window break but I hear it shatter the instant before their hands push my body through the window and out into the night, high above the ground.

First it's nice because it's so slow. I hover, almost like a bird, drifting through the clear spring darkness as though made to fly. All is calm, tranquil, and nearly quiet enough to hear the noise of my dreams taking flight. I extend my arms and float.

In the middle of my reverie, something makes me look down, and then I see the earth rising so terribly fast, coming to get me. Charging with rage. I fall, slowly at first but soon faster and faster as I see the cruel hardness, so merciless and impersonal, rushing to collide with my body hurtling toward it at a speed that streaks my eyes with tears and blurs everything and makes the night air whistle. My blood sings. Splatter. I can almost hear and feel it. Flesh, blood, bone, brain. Faster, faster, faster—the ground opens like a huge pit and swallows me. I never crash into it. Instead I pass through it until I'm back in the night air again, falling fast.

It's not the same this time. No room, no window. I never see my assailants again. What I see now are faces. Near me, beside me, hanging there. White faces. Minister faces. They watch me, hard like rocks, fall. The ground opens and I speed through it, back into the night. More faces. Black ones. Minister faces. Through the ground, up again, falling. Black faces. Family faces. But they have bodies too. They can help. Hands reach for me. I call to them: "Save me!" Fingertips brush my body but can't hold on. Falling, falling, falling through the ground. Earth swallows me. Falling faster even than before. More faces, all mine. I watch myself plunge toward the murderous earth. I see myself watching. The ground rushes to slam into my body. It won't open up this time, I know it won't. As the earth rises to smash my body into jelly, I scream my silent scream.

Drained of all energy by this nightmare, and shivering with a cold sweat, I always woke up just before I hit the ground for the last time. My initial response was, I suppose, quite human: I sat still and hoped the dream would go away. It didn't. So I did what any self-respecting graduate student would do; I engaged in research.

Starting with Freud, I dabbled in different schools of thought. Each of them, of course, had their own predilections and priorities, and as I immersed myself in the analysis of dreams I found myself wedded to no particular camp. I did, however, discern an overall message that served to verify what I'd felt all along: that in the dreams I was sending word to myself. The dreams represented a conflict that I was afraid to confront in a conscious way. That bit of information fell short of revelation, but it was apparently enough to steady my subconscious. The dreams stopped.

Perhaps as a result of the dreams, my behavior changed. Perhaps the dreams strengthened certain realities and weakened others. In any case, I became more open about expressing my anger. I stopped smiling all the time. When I didn't want to do something, I simply refused to do it. When I disagreed with something, I said so. You might say I was starting to come out of the closet. Different realities swirled around me, each attempting to pull me to it, and just as always I kept bouncing from one to the other. The reality that told me to make it in the white world was still the one I chose the most. More than anything else, that's what I wanted—to be recognized as a successful minister.

Toward the end of my third year, I got word that the black bishop planned to send me to El Paso, an impressive appointment indeed for a man fresh out of seminary. I was their son, about to get what he deserved. On the heels of the El Paso rumor, which at times bordered on a guarantee, the actual assignment I received sent me reeling. I was ordered to Hobbs, New Mexico. Sent to the hinterlands. Before leaving for Hobbs

I became engaged to a schoolteacher named Evelyn Robinson. We were married three weeks after my arrival in Hobbs, but the wedding was in Marshall, Texas.

From the schoolhouse steps in Hobbs, I could see the outline of the mountains like deep purple humps in the western sky. I hadn't even inherited a church; I was supposed to start one for a handful of blacks in the middle of nowhere.

Hobbs, New Mexico, was as much a Wild West town as 1956 could fashion. Its population of nearly 10,000 was in constant flux because few people actually lived there. The town was split between transient redneck oil drillers and poor black migratory agricultural workers, a combustible mixture that never ignited but stayed near the flash point at all times.

There was a proper, traditional Methodist Church as well as an African Methodist Episcopal Church for blacks. A small number of blacks, however, desired the dubious benefits of mainline Methodism and thus had taken to attending services in the white Methodist Church. I didn't know it then, but the black district superintendent of the church conference had made a deal with the white ministers of Hobbs to import a black Methodist minister who would relieve the white church of any racial embarrassment. I was chosen. Taking into account my mad desire to make it in the mainstream, it was ruthlessly ironic that my true purpose in Hobbs was to prevent blacks from attending the white church. Our Sunday services were held in the schoolhouse. The rest of the week I spent working with the people and wondering what I was doing in Hobbs, New Mexico.

My congregation began with only six blacks, all misfits who'd been a problem to the other churches, not to mention the community at large. In time the congregation swelled to about forty-five, including one very poor white family who was so uncomfortable at the white church that they came to ours. I chose the father as my unpaid assistant.

The seminary had certainly left its mark on me: I had one great missionary attitude when I preached to my flock. I knew I possessed all this wonderful knowledge and had only to impart it to those poor, ignorant worshippers. The problem was they always fell asleep on me. Each week I faithfully typed a manuscript of the coming Sunday's sermon and then read it to them in a dry, inhuman, and obviously sleep-inducing monotone. Their reaction outraged me; I believed it was all *their* fault. After all, I'd been educated. In a white seminary! I had it, they didn't; and if they didn't get it that was their problem, not mine. I was so immersed in order that it was difficult to relate to chaos, and Hobbs was sheer chaos. Something was wrong. I knew it. I just couldn't tell what it was.

Reddish-brown in skin color, she had short, pressed hair and wore clothes of wild, piercing colors that never even considered matching one another. She was the craziest one in the congregation, an old woman who babbled endlessly. A bedrock sincerity radiating from her eyes made her strange conversations all the more disconcerting. She believed deeply in her visions, and when no one was around to listen to them she talked with voices of her own. Everyone tried to avoid her because once she got started she wore out a day pretty fast. They'd talk to her and move away quickly, or sometimes just talk over or around her. I know because I treated her that way myself.

Unlike almost everyone else, she never gossiped. And gossip was the main form of recreation on the black side of Hobbs. In naked contrast to San Angelo, blacks in Hobbs had no sense of community at all. In her own way, the old madwoman talked about that a lot. An ancient scarlet shawl was her most valued possession, and sometimes she went on for hours about how people in the community wanted to steal it.

She came each Sunday and listened to me read. Quietly she sat, her head nodding from side to side, her brown eyes either wide open and fixed on the wall behind me, or moving up and down my robed body as if measuring me for something.

On that Sunday when she spoke to me I finished my sermon and stared at the congregation, hoping against hope that they'd finally gotten it. After an appropriate moment of silence, long enough to indicate I had no more to say that morning, there came the rustle of stiff bodies rising from their chairs, the stretch of aching muscles that had seen their duty and obediently endured. They weren't ever going to get it. Ever. As the rest of them shuffled wearily for the door, she marched toward me. I cringed inside, afraid I was in for one of her unstructured conversations that could only make a bad day worse. In the front of her eyes was a sincere concern, as when one good friend approaches another in time of need. But in the back of her eyes lay an unimpeachable anger like distant, glowing embers. I stood there clutching my manuscript.

"Son," she said in the raspy voice of the elderly. "I just got to be truthful with you. I don't mean you no offense, but you oughta get up off that paper. You ain't preachin' like you s'posed to, son, and you oughta get up off that paper."

I didn't have to question her; I knew precisely what she meant. When she realized I had no answer for her she nodded, as if she hadn't expected one anyway, turned and walked back up the aisle. She left the building alone, her body hunched slightly and surrounded by the sunlit doorway. I stood at the head of the classroom and after a few moments let the manuscript fall from my hands and float to the floor.

Because she talked out of her head, because I knew she was so very near the edge, she reached me as no one else in Hobbs could've reached me. Had anyone else offered her advice, I'm sure I would've maintained the position that it was their failure rather than my own. But there was a bond between the old woman and me, the experience of madness, the most profound knowledge of chaos amid order, the desperate, simultaneous quest for and realization of truths that run along the fine line between the cliff and the canyon. It was as if she'd shown me a door, a crack in the wall the seminary had helped erect around my authenticity. I still have the feeling that she was the real messenger.

I remained in Hobbs another six months, bringing my total tenure there to a full year. I never used a manuscript again, and the people never went to sleep on me again either. At the end of the year, I received an invitation to return to Sam Huston, which had since merged with Tillotson College to become Huston-Tillotson, as an instructor and as dean of men. I grabbed at the chance, because I'd had my fill of Hobbs and still longed for the blessings of the black ministers who ran the West Texas Conference of the Central

Jurisdiction of the United Methodist Church, the men who'd shipped me to New Mexico.

Back in Austin, I knew I was in a strategically good position that spoke well for my moving up the ladder later on. Shortly after my arrival, I was also appointed campus chaplain. The black ministers hailed the return of their son, welcoming me with open arms and chanting praise in my ears. I loved it. They had not forsaken me. Still, I felt an undeniable shiftiness in their embrace. They were waiting for something from me, waiting to see if I'd learned my lesson, waiting to see if Hobbs had revealed to me their determination to wield their power. Curled beneath the slick surface of their approbations were the cold words of admonition:

"There can always be another Hobbs. And another and another and another."

Something had been revealed to me in Hobbs. It was not the revelation the black ministers had hoped for.

From the moment of my return to Huston-Tillotson, I thrust myself into the midst of a challenge to the campus order. Students had banded together to protest their lack of decision making power, focusing their indignation on J. J. Seabrook, the college president. I not only joined the protest, I helped organize it, and thus became one of Seabrook's strongest adversaries. Late one fall afternoon Seabrook called for me. When I entered his office, his eyes met me with a crystal contempt. I waited. A few moments would disclose the true object of that contempt. He began by confessing his desires. He said he wanted my resignation or, failing that, he wanted to dismiss me. I waited some more. Then he admitted that neither alternative was possible because I was too well respected in the white church. Power. It always came down to that. Self-contempt was what hung in his eyes, even though he aimed it at me. The following week the college board of trustees in effect overruled Seabrook and acceded to many of the student demands.

Because it was essentially restricted to an academic institution, my work on the campus posed no direct threat to the security of the black ministers. Even so, I was still an ordained minister. What would I do next? Campus or no campus, it was all about power. And choosing sides. Capitulation or nothing? On the most instinctive, visceral level, I was beginning to rewrite the question.

During the campus unrest, which the following decade would've surely classified as mild, the black ministers issued a unanimous opinion that I was especially effective in working with young people. I should have recognized that opinion for what it was, but I was too busy moving to catch on. What the black ministers were actually saying, of course, was that until I calmed down it would be far better to divert me from the mainstream and toward those best suited for the growing radicalism reflected in my conduct. They certainly didn't want to bestow on a rabble rouser any claim to the larger church community.

A week before the annual conference, Seabrook invited me to his home to meet the black bishop, who told me I would be appointed minister of Wesley Methodist Church in Austin. Seabrook beamed; he wanted to get rid of me any way he could. And I was delighted because Wesley would be a real plum, even better than El Paso. I remembered El Paso with vivid pain, anger, and bitterness, but this time the bishop himself had extended the promise. Surely the black ministers who voted on appointments would not refute him.

In mid-afternoon on the day of the vote, I got the word: I was not going to Wesley after all. The black ministers had blocked the appointment. Blocked it!

"You ain't learned your lesson yet, boy."

That was the message. Painfully loud and relentlessly clear.

Why? Maybe if they were white you'd understand it—but they're not, dammit! Rejected by your own—your own—son in the ministry. Why? What did you do that was so wrong?

How can you see your own as an enemy, those who are supposed to support and nurture you? They're too close to what you are. They've always been a part of you, Rev. Can you see them as evil?

The white church had all the money, all the power. J. J. Seabrook knew it. That's why he didn't fire me even though he must've dreamt about doing it.

Can you dare break away from them—'cause it'd be like

tearing your flesh. They hate you, man. Hate and fear you. They don't want anything to do with you right now because—why?

Something in you won't let them control you. You ain't no mediocre nigger!

They can't stop you because—I don't know, it's just that you're not white and you're not like them either. Now, finally, you hear it. All that time, all those years you saw nothin' but them and they wanted to create you in their image. Speak for yourself, man!

"Lord, I'm so messed up."

Tears. A storm of tears. Soothing and violent. Tears of hurt, rage, joy, loneliness, fear.

"But I'm gonna move away from here. Yes, I'm gonna move. I ain't runnin' away, I'm just movin' on."

Capitulation or nothing? There was more to the question than that. I never did pastor a church in Texas.

In 1963, while pastoring a church in Kansas City, I was offered a position as director of community involvement at the Glide Urban Center, a program of Glide Memorial United Methodist Church in San Francisco. I accepted. In 1966, in a move that shook the church's white, middle-class, and basically traditional congregation, Bishop Donald H. Tippett appointed me minister of Glide Church.

FIVE

SEPTEMBER 1967. A huge cross is fastened to the sterile white wall of the Glide Church sanctuary. The workers all wear denim coveralls. Sharp instruments hang from their tool belts. Sturdy metal tubes and long wooden planks litter the floor. Soon the workers will climb the face of the wall and begin.

It's burial time.

The Glide Church congregation is tired, all white, and hostile. They know what I'm about to do, and all week long they've come to me with the desperation of strangers longing to go back home. They warned, pleaded, threatened, and argued; they said I could do anything but what I was about to do, then vowed recrimination for my planned act. The cross, they said, had always been there; the actual source, they seemed to say, of their very lives. In its absence, then, their lives would have no meaning. They simply couldn't live without it. As they spoke with me, their bodies seemed rigid, involuntarily inflexible, as if rigor mortis had already begun setting in. They accused me of arrogance and blasphemy, of equating myself with the power of all they held to be divine. I was killing them, they said.

They may have been right.

Something was being killed. Perhaps it was they. But it was also a symbol of death that was dying.

In taking down the cross, I was killing myself as well. Something in *me* had to die. Did I have the power to take down the cross? Do people have such power? And, if we do, can we accept our power, or must we continue to rely on the power of God?

The foreman looks at me. I nod. He nods back, then signals his fellow workers to begin the climb. The scaffold they've erected looks so fragile, as though at any moment it could collapse.

They scale the wall like commandoes, quickly passing the bottom of the gigantic cross on their path to its summit. The foreman holds a large black metal drill with a thin bit sticking from its mouth.

I am afraid.

What must replace the cross? I'm not asking that Jesus be replaced with me. Although members of the church have implied as much, Jesus and I are not the issue. Now, up on the wall, the cross means worship and deference. A blank wall will not ask as much, yet will require so much more. That's it, the seed of my fear. With the cross gone, the wall will be *bare.*

The drill's high whine cuts like a scream. Its sharp bit seems aimed straight for my eyes. Reaching a climax, it screeches to a halt. Fine white dust hovers in the air. A second worker tightropes along the highest board, a chisel in his grasp. He jams the chisel blade between the corner of the cross and the wall.

I feel the pain. There are many reasons for leaving the cross untouched, reasons to which my life has long been anchored. People want and need the cross on the wall because it removes from them the weight of responsibility. How ironic that in taking responsibility for Jesus' death they surrender the same for their lives. And it is the minister, a man of God, who inherits their reverence. I am a minister. You might say I've always been a minister, but I will no longer be defined by the profession. I will define my ministry. I am tearing the old reasons from myself. I am starting all over again. That's what hurts.

The head of a hammer plummets toward the chisel handle and meets it with a muted crack. The blade forges deeper into the widening gap behind the cross.

My heart pumps. My flesh throbs. A minister is dying.

I hear a rhythmic pounding like the heartbeat of someone near death. Or waking from an empty sleep. Pleasure and pain.

Joy and anguish. Freedom and fear. Hope and despair. Just like Freedom Path in San Angelo. The cross loosens, the pounding quickens. Strong, relentless, eternal.

As pieces of the cross are pried free, patches of wall are revealed. The wall is especially white in these spots, much whiter than the rest of the wall, which has been exposed to air, dirt, and dust raised by the presence of people. It's as though the cross was a suit of armor shielding its territory from any signs of life.

White, pure, and holy. Free from dirt and tears and sweat and the juices of sex. Free from bloodshed, because up there the only blood shed is his, not ours. Free to be nailed behind a cross where everything is pure, still, forever white. In that arctic whiteness, the cross itself becomes the cause. An answer to death, a feeble attempt to ward off the inevitable blow. A replacement for living. But do people have the power to take it down? The answer, yes, seems written on the wall. Do people have the power to bear their own crosses, and *is it worth it?* Clearly, yes. But it is not an easy answer. Chunk by chunk, the cross comes down, and every time the workers pull a piece free they rip away a part of me.

The job is nearly done. I see the imprint of the cross on the wall and feel the imprint of its removal on me. Gripped by a great sense of loss, I'm overwhelmed by the sensation that now is the end. The minister is dead. But with every end there is also a beginning. I feel that too, and hear the words of a spiritual we once sang.

> *I feel like my time ain't long*
> *Went to the graveyard the other day*
> *Looked at the place where my mother lay*
> *Mind out, my brother, how you walk the cross*
> *Your foot might slip and your soul get lost*
> *I feel like my time ain't long*

The workers take a short break and weave their conversation through clouds of cigarette smoke. A single five-foot section is all that remains on the wall.

I haven't eaten anything all day, yet am not the least bit hungry. I'm also very tired but not in need of sleep. It's late, and

I should be heading home. But I must wait here, until all of it is gone.

There are some who say that I'm committing the gravest sin, but I'm not sure what sin is anymore. Is it sinful to look away from symbols and toward myself and others? Is that arrogant, or is it being responsible? Is it sinful to cast my own shadow, or is it sinful to live in the shadow of the cross? Is there any such thing as sin, or is there only irresponsibility? Is there any such thing as repentance, or is there only change?

There's no hidin' place down here

The church and I agree on the words but not their meaning. Do they mean we can't hide from God, or do they mean we can't hide from ourselves? As long as the cross is up there, we are not free to dramatize the bearing of the cross, for ourselves.

It's completely gone now, buried in the bowels of this building. The wall is bare. Even as I stand here all alone, air, dust, and dirt work to erase the outline of the cross.

I feel as though something has been torn from my body in a gruesome surgery with nothing to kill the pain. I know I bleed, yet I also feel as though an enormous and oppressive weight has been lifted from me. Breathing comes easier now. Maybe the cross is finally free. And maybe I am free as well.

The blank wall stares at me, offering neither condolences nor congratulations. It says to me,

You have removed the cross. Tell me, what will hang here now?

"Why did you take down the cross?"

The first words of my sermon come freely because they are mine. Now, on this winter morning in 1978, I will tell my story. And if I tell it with authenticity, if I feel it as I tell it, some people will recognize their story in mine. It's always best when it happens that way.

"It's been twelve years since I took it down, and the one question more people have asked me than any other is, 'Why did you take down the cross?'"

The sanctuary is full, 1,500 people of all colors, ages, and appearances. They are wealthy, and they are down and out.

They are kinky, straight, and gay. They are clean, and they are ragged. They come from the corner, and they come from the suburbs. A motley group. Perhaps they are the people I imagined them to be when I was a little boy, reaching back across time to China, Ethiopia, Athens, Peru. Today they are worlds apart yet share the same room. What's the connection?

"I'm gonna answer that question this morning."

A baby yells.

"It was very difficult for me to take down that cross. As I watched them chisel away, my old programming said, 'God's gonna strike you dead.' But I came here to tell you that I had to have a funeral. I had to bury the minister in me, the part of me that needed to control people. It wasn't easy, but I took the cross down anyway."

"All right!" A lone voice soars above the silence.

"Lemme tell you why."

The answers well up inside me. No time to *think* about it. This is no dissertation, it's only what I feel at this moment coming so swiftly from beneath my skin and flesh where time, thought, feeling, and action collide.

The cross once hung there, right behind me, above the stage where you see the guitar and bass propped against their amps, where the electric piano and drums sit waiting to be played. I feel the cross hanging over me, looking down on us all, and I know I've got to take it down. All over again.

"The first reason I took down the cross was because I found the same old God here, the God that people want to give all the power to. They said God's power would save the world—but God's got her power! God's got his power! God gave up the world, and we need to accept the world. It's time for us to have some power to create in the world!"

There's a hum and a buzz, a flow I can't measure or define. Irreversible, like the current of a river carrying us beyond the church walls.

In the midst of it all, I see four of them five or six rows back on the right side. Rigid, unbending, appalled, perhaps even frightened. Young, white, and proper, they unleash waves of rejection with their stern expressions and hands clasped tightly in their laps. I need them to push me on. Perhaps against their

77

wishes they move me. I want them to hear me, but they don't have to. I don't need to convert anyone. When I tell my story, I don't need to win.

"I took that cross down because I decided it was a way to kill this church. Now, a lotta people said, 'Oh, Lawd, please don't kill this church.' "

Peals of laughter. Some of them know my story because they've been in it too; in fearful, misused passions, we all have clung to institutions to verify ourselves.

"I took that cross down because it symbolized a living death, a resistance to life. Everybody here was getting ready for real death—but they were already dead and didn't know it! They were looking for rest, but *ain't no rest while you're here!*

"There's no rest while people starve, while there is injustice and war, while power is defined by money and property, while peace of mind is purchased in drugs, weekend encounters and paperback books. A lot of people are always looking for peace of mind. But the very moment you find it, you're dead. There will be no rest. There will be no death. For this is a life and death situation, and you've got the choice."

Yes, the choice.

The hum is fed by cheers. The four on the right look extremely uncomfortable, as though their minds are not at peace.

"I took down the cross because the people inside this church had entered into a conspiracy to keep everybody else out."

When we were kids, they'd let us go to the white churches on special days.

"This church did not want to take responsibility for its actions, and so they agreed, 'We are the special ones and none of them are like us.' "

They herded us through a side door and kept us in a corner until our turn arrived.

"There are too many self-righteous people who conspire to use religion as a means of standing far off from the world and not getting involved in it."

When we were finally put before them, we sang with a furious abandon, fired by anger, humiliation, and a transcendent desire to show them who we were. But all of it was on their terms. From a safe and comfortable distance, they ate us up.

"But if religion means anything at all it means you put your life where you say you're gonna put it and do what you have to do instead of just talking about it all the time. Because if your doing doesn't dance with your saying, you haven't chosen life."

Sometimes I get the feeling the whole world, in all its diversity, is in this room. I think people from every single country have passed through here. Black, brown, red, yellow, and white. Men, women, and children. Glide is a Methodist church, but what does that really mean?

"We broke apart the conspiracy, you and I. I never thought it would be like this, but I felt the walls of the church cry out, 'Shout your name!'"

There's a young black woman in a knitted cap and an old white man with a stubbled chin.

"I felt the cross cry out, 'Is death the only way?'"

There's a white woman with a baby in her lap and a Chicano dude in a brown leather jacket.

"I felt the worship services in this church cry out, 'Make a joyful noise!'"

There are two gay men in pastel shirts and white coveralls and an old black woman in her Sunday best.

"I felt the people say, 'Let's do it like we've always wanted to do it.'"

It's not my imagination any longer. All of them are here. They are the river and the message. You are the river and the message.

"I took that cross down because I saw Jesus hanging on it, and the people in the church were still screaming, 'Crucify him.'"

Three weeks ago, the wino caught me in front of the church office building.

"As long as we continue to crucify Jesus, we don't have to face our crucifixion of others, our crucifixion of ourselves."

I looked past him and saw my reflection in the window. The impulse to turn away grew stronger, but I fought it off. He was wretched and filthy, surviving on wine. It was killing him. He asked me for a quarter. I refused. He spat near my shoes, then grinned and said he knew all along I wasn't going to give him money. His hand crawled into his greasy overcoat and returned in a gnarled fist.

"They're still arguing about who really crucified him. But the real question is, 'Who's being crucified now!'"

His grubby fingers slowly unfolded. In his soiled palm lay a plain silver cross, which he pressed into my hand. I accepted it.

"We stay on the Jesus symbol so we don't have to confront how we always crucify those folks 'over there,' those poor folks or ugly folks or lame folks or deformed folks or those folks who aren't like us. Crucify them all!"

He winked and said the cross was worth $25 but hadn't cost him anything. It was a stolen cross.

"Blame *them* so you don't have to face yourselves. Blame *them* for being poor and unemployed when you control who makes it and who doesn't. Blame *them* for violence when it is your indifference that is the most violent act. Crucify them!

"Well, I've got something to say to you: Face up to your own crucifixion. And who do *you* crucify? I took the cross down so we can stop crucifying Jesus and begin to understand how we destroy ourselves, others, the world. We must love where love has never taken us, and take action where action threatens those who would control us."

Some of the people spring to their feet. The tumult feels good. It speaks of a connection.

I took the cross down, and twelve years later it returned to me in the palm of a wino. But it wasn't the same cross. Out on the street, resting against the wino's flesh, the cross was alive, crouched in that terrible void between responsibility and irresponsibility, both his and mine. That is the cross's only place. The cross on the sanctuary wall was an instrument of control. It was dead.

"I took the cross down because when I came here *this church was a slavemaster.*"

"All right!" shouts the voice.

"And slavery is over!"

"Yes, it is!"

"So good to be an exslave, because I've walked the dusty roads of racism and sexism and exploitation. I've walked the dusty paths among the imprints of the dead. I took down the cross because it kept getting in the way of the power of people, people who have freedom to choose. The cross must be among you because you are responsible for your life and the world. *You are the cross.*"

Flashing on the white wall where the cross once hung are

pictures of people in protest, moving to change their lives.

"I took down the cross because I am convinced that the cross will not save humanity—humanity will redeem the cross.

"But in order to accept and extend your humanity you must always acknowledge the evil within *you!* Without such acknowledgment, you deceive the source, the essence of which is the choice between good and evil. To deny the evil is to deny the choice. To deny the evil is to give it strength. To deny evil is to deny God."

From behind me storms the band, bass and drums grabbing people by their feet, keyboards and guitar flying above in clean but frenzied flight. We always end this way, with "We Shall Overcome." But at Glide Church it's raucous, not plaintive; and it's no longer "We shall overcome *someday*" but "We shall overcome *today.*" I sing, move, clap. Fifteen hundred others sing, move, clap.

I hand off the mike and sprint down the center aisle, racing past pew after pew and down the stairs to embrace each member of the congregation as they come down. Upstairs, the band plays on, and the people up there still clap and dance. The people descending the stairs embrace me.

Right away I notice him, as soon as he rounds the last corner of the tiled stairwell and has a straight path toward my waiting arms. He inches slowly down the stairs with the rest of the crowd, but it's hard for me not to look at him alone. It's the mountain that won't let go of me. His spine is curved, his body hunched. Out of the middle of his back grows a huge and grotesque hump. Bent as a man with a heavy load, he looks as if his mountain is his oppressor. And all I'm supposed to do is *touch* it. The very thought disorients me. I see much the same anxiety in those around him, their faces torn between staring at the hump and studiously ignoring it. The moment, then, is framed by the deformity, controlled by the mountain rising from the man's slumped and rounded back. In a curious way, the hump belongs to each of us because we define ourselves by our reaction to it. Do we feel pity? Revulsion? Superiority? And what does he want from us?

Philosophical garbage. Legitimate, perhaps, but garbage nonetheless. Because now he stands before me. Waiting, looking, knowing human fingers recoil at the possibility of rubbing across his deformity and feeling the lumpy contour of his back through his shirt and jacket. There aren't enough jackets in the world to deceive either one of us. And here I am, the minister who spouts words of acceptance and backs them up by embracing everyone. In the deepest part of my being, I'm afraid to touch this man. And he knows it.

For seconds that lurch along like hours he stands there, then places his mottled hands around my neck. Nothing matters but the hunchback and me. My arms curl around his trunk on their way to meet his mountain.

It's hard. Like a boulder. Like an actual mountain. My hands are less than tentative. As if the hump could, I feel, be my own. My hands touch but refuse to embrace it. He is aware. His arms hold me tighter, tight until I sense blood flowing through them. He has no trouble accepting and embracing me. When each of his hands pats a shoulder, my own hands grow more certain. From the lower regions of his hooked spine, they climb ever more forcefully over knobby mounds of vertebrae until they reach the slope that begins the hump. They don't hesitate. They move on, feeling the gristle and rocky flesh, the peaks and indentations, the man's back round and full as a pregnant belly. In the instant I touch the hump, the hunchback becomes the messenger. Regardless of his deformities, he is whole, human. There is the startling realization that it is the deformity that deepens his wholeness, his humanity. And unless I accept him for what he is I will not receive and become his message. In grasping the hump, I recognize the message and messenger within me. His deformity is achingly visible, but I am deformed as well. Both of us are human, both of us the message. My hands move further across his mountain, feeling all the empty smiles and sidelong glances and mumbled excuses and special favors. And all the days this man with a mountain rising from his back has stood before me.

Touch for touch and moment for moment, he returns me. Once we know and share the message, we hold on briefly, then let each other go. Neither of us says a word. I watch him as he moves away from me, making his way through the open iron gates and out into the street.

SIX

THOSE white kids filled me with admiration and disgust. *Hippies.* The media hung that label on them to somehow make them simpler to understand. Hippies. Bare feet, ragged clothing, stringy long hair, unwashed bodies. Their contrived embrace of conditions I'd fought all my life to eradicate angered and insulted me. I envisioned their pipeline hooked to the throbbing checkbook of the American Dream, just as I saw them fan out across the streets near Golden Gate Park and beg for "spare change" in a society where "spare change" is such a cruel contradiction in terms for so many. Hipness through poverty. Artificial risk. Mock the poor. Hippies.

They could always go back, you see. Get a haircut, take a bath. Maybe it wasn't their fault, but they could always go back.

Still, they realized the Dream had aborted. Stillborn in the shadow of the atom bomb, the only generation in history weaned on real apocalypse. The only generation in history not left wanting for material comforts. It was their bomb, their luxury.

By any contemporary American standards, they had it made. Nothing to struggle for, nothing to risk, nothing to change. It was all theirs. But something had ruptured inside them, leaving only an emptiness their parents could neither feel nor appreciate. They'd been promised so much, given so much. But it was hollow at its center. They'd been betrayed and left with nothing, not even a cause to follow.

Nevertheless, there was something to recommend them, points with which I could connect. I'd been betrayed and left with nothing too. They were rebelling, and so was I. They were exiles, and so was I. They were exposing and challenging so much of what I wanted to expose and challenge, and I valued them for it. Sons and daughters of white America who knew its emptiness and were daring enough to admit it. Because it was their emptiness also, because they needed something with which to fill it. Sons and daughters who could tell me things I'd never heard before, things they couldn't tell their parents. They had the power to reject the white American world. What were they going to do with it?

At night along Haight Street, compressed in the half mile between Masonic Avenue and the mouth of Golden Gate Park, hung a nearly tangible sense of anticipation and excitement, as if the hippies felt in their marrow that they were onto something. I saw it in the eyes of the barefoot man sidestepping the dog shit and skipping through the milling throng, the assurance that since the battle was fun its outcome could never be in serious doubt. The dance of victory was performed nightly on Haight Street. It cost no money to watch.

A knot of young black men bathed in the pool of light spilling from Uganda Liquors on the corner of Haight and Masonic. They too were part of the scene; first because they'd grown up in the Haight long before the hippies came, and secondly because overt racism was definitely not a groove as far as the hippies were concerned. The postures of the young black men spoke of survival in the midst of chaos, an awareness, perhaps, that those crazy hippies weren't really all *that* different. The Haight sped to the hum of an underground engine revved up as high as it could go, but the young blacks only cruised and idled as if they knew much more than the hippies just how long the ride was. At some unspoken signal, they vanished into the crowd flowing upstream toward the park.

The movement was spreading north to Chicago and other urban centers. Ghettoes were exploding in flames and gunfire. People were being killed. Black power was as real as my own pulsebeat. And, purposely or not, the hippies were drawing energy away from all of it. I was angry at them for that, and angry with myself for being diverted from the struggle of my own people. Our struggle always had direction, our cause never in doubt. No, the hippies weren't like us at all. Their enemy was anyone over thirty, anyone in a suit and tie. "Anyone" became almost everyone not like them. It was a time of extremes, true enough, but their extremism had no focus. I championed their sense of revolt yet saw no place for me among them. But they sure were disturbing the order, and that needed to be done.

It was 1967, and the much trumpeted "Summer of Love" was careening toward San Francisco, completely out of control. All spring long the papers had predicted a deluge of more than 100,000 young people crashing into the city. The feeling on the street was that for once the papers had the story straight. The city officialdom took a hard line against the coming invasion, but Glide Church was among those solidly aligned with the hippies.

The Glide Church senior staff was composed of me and three white men, Ted McIlvenna, Louis Durham, and Don Kuhn. Although I spoke in support of the hippies a number of times before the San Francisco Board of Supervisors, the other senior staff members had much more to do with them than I did. They brought food to the hippies and helped establish a house for runaways. Hippies. White led and white fed. In early spring, Glide helped sponsor the Artists' Liberation Front, an art-oriented event held in the church building parking lot. I had nothing to do with it. Organized by a seminary student named Larry Mamiya, a Glide secretary named Janice Mirikitani, and a number of people from the Haight, the event was so successful that soon afterwards I began hearing talk among the hippies about something called the "Invisible Circus." I had no idea what an Invisible Circus was.

In late May, Ted and Louis told me the hippies wanted to have a three-day "happening," a word that had yet to become a cliché, at Glide. Because I felt no solid identification with the hippies, I didn't much care whether they had their Invisible Circus or not, but an admiration for their sense of revolt outfought misgivings I had about their style. In early June, we informed the Glide Board of Trustees that the Invisible Circus was going to take place. A few hippie organizers came with us and announced that Glide Church was the only place where the happening could happen. I don't recall what they said about the Invisible Circus itself except that it would last from 4 P.M. on Friday, June 18, to late afternoon on Sunday, June 20, that it was supposed to "bring the tribes together," and that it would create a new direction for San Francisco and the nation. I thought that last statement was perhaps a little too grand, but it didn't sound to me like they were kidding, either. Louis, Ted, Don, and I devised a work schedule where I didn't have to come down until midnight on Friday. They would work the swing shift from four to midnight. There was really nothing else to plan. No patterns, no connections, no specific areas of responsibility. Whatever an Invisible Circus was would be revealed on June 18.

The first call came at 8:15 P.M. Friday as I lay on the bed trying to marshal my strength for the long night ahead. I knew there would be calls but hadn't expected them to start so early. On the other end of the line, Louis' voice sounded a bit frantic. He said Glide Church was already bulging at the seams, and the walls seemed to move with the force of the crowd. He wasn't sure if they could handle it, because there were just too many people. We agreed to let it ride a while. I sat up and wondered how many people made too many people. I knew it wasn't simply a question of numbers. In the far corners of Louis' voice had echoed the hollow sound of fear. Unmistakable, like a ringing bell.

The second call came shortly after nine. They told me the hippies had set up a free press on the second floor and were printing leaflets for anyone who thought they had a message. People on the street, alarmed at the words on the flyers being shoved at them, were complaining. The messages were evidently short and to the point. One of them just said "FUCK."

Over the next ninety minutes, the phone kept ringing. I gave up trying to rest. They told me that eighteen belly dancers were in Fellowship Hall, a large ground-floor meeting room, and the police had already stuck their heads in once. They said the second-floor sanctuary was so full you couldn't even see the red carpet on the floor. The game room in the basement was half stuffed with confetti and plastic strips. Strobe lights and black lights fed the frenzy. People, rolling on and under the paper and plastic, were doing all sorts of things to each other. A group of Hell's Angels, working as "security," had already gotten into one fight.

"Uh, I don't think this is quite what we expected," the last caller said. "Why don't you come down a little early?" It was nearly eleven when I stepped out into the night. An uncommonly hot wind coasted through the muggy air. Everything felt so uncomfortably still. Earthquake weather, I'd heard it called. I got in the car and drove.

The sidewalk in front of Glide Church was jammed with bodies. I had to force my way through them. They were neither hostile nor belligerent, but there was something unnerving about them. There were quite a few straight curiosity seekers but most of the people were young, white, and long haired. What I felt emanating from them bothered me: a boundless hunger and an ecstatic, desperate determination to have it fed. Their sense of raw vengeance, as if they had nothing left to lose but their appetites, left me uneasy. What am I doing here? The question wouldn't leave me alone. Nearly everything about them was alien to me except their anger, and I had the feeling that no one knew its object or direction. It took me half an hour to plow fifty feet to the building's front door. Once inside I wedged my way up the stairs to the sanctuary.

The callers had been right. The wall-to-wall red carpet was buried beneath wall-to-wall bodies. A woman clad only in a G-string danced wildly on top of the church organ. Sweat dribbled down her breasts, and her hair whipped back and forth across her face, which was contorted in a grimace of pain. Oblivious to the disorder bursting forth on the floor below, her eyes were vacuous. Nothing mattered to her but her gyrations. They pulled her down long before I could reach her. It was like the sidewalk, only worse. A huge mass of humanity, flesh against flesh. I could barely move. Someone was always breathing down my neck. There must have been 2,000 people crammed into the room, pushing, shoving, clashing, merging. All limits had been broken down, afire, sending chaos through the sanctuary. Yet there was an eerie lack of tension. Light and darkness. Good and evil. There was no tension between them because they were absent. Moral considerations lay in ashes on the floor. The urgency, however, was contained in a single question: How far were they going to go? And burning through my mind was another question: How much could I do about it? I raised my arms above my head and forced my way into the hall, searching for Ted, Louis, and Don.

We met in a second-floor office. Their faces were drawn and haggard, and I sensed them being consumed by a fear I didn't share. I was alarmed at the immensity of what was happening, the sheer magnitude of thousands of people turned loose on themselves with no direction, no purpose, no cause. But I wasn't frightened. There was no place for me there, nothing with which to identify. Maybe there was for them. Maybe that's what frightened them. They said people were all over the building, even on the four upper floors of rental offices whose tenants had nothing to do with the Invisible Circus. We agreed that the uproar should be confined to the basement and first two floors. I volunteered to start at the top and work down.

I struggled to the elevator, stepping over bodies as I went. Except for a rumpled pair of jeans in the corner, the elevator was surprisingly empty. The sixth-floor hallway was wadded full of people. A young man's unconscious body lay on the floor near the elevator door. The crowd made an effort to avoid him, but the corridor was so stuffed that some people had to step on him anyway. With the help of another young man, I dragged the body to the side and left it there. I wanted to help him but there was so much else to do. The hallway was a battlefield where you couldn't always tell the casualties from the survivors. I couldn't see three feet in front of me, the pack was so thick, and I knew that if I stood still for even a moment I'd be pinned to the back of somebody else. I had to keep moving. Behind me I heard mad laughter and turned to see a woman giggling uncontrollably, tears streaming down her cheeks. Her hands were crumpled into fists jammed into her mouth. From each of her wrists hung a bracelet of bells. Blood trickled down the heel of one hand. I waded on through the flesh pulsating around my feet, keeping one eye on the floor and the other straight ahead. A hand reached out and grabbed my sleeve. I jerked my head around. I couldn't tell whose hand it had been.

The relentless artificial light gave the scene a harsh, infernal quality. It seemed to magnify everything; it had no subtlety. Smoke hung in the air like a pale blue shroud. Smells of sweat and desperation. I heard grunts, groans, and shrieks, but it was impossible to tell where they came from. Someone clutched at my trouser leg. I shook off the touch and forged ahead. As I neared the top of the stairs at the far end of the hall, I saw a girl with auburn hair and blank green eyes plopped on the highest step. With trembling hands, she was trying to light a cigarette dangling precariously from her pale lips. Her smooth, pallid face was the picture of bliss; her eyes were half shut, and the lips gripping the cigarette had worked themselves into the betrayal of a smile. She looked horribly at peace. Her fingers were on fire.

I grabbed the silver lighter from her and pressed my flesh against her hands. The heat was sharp but not unbearable. Her fingertips were raw and red but the flames had not eaten any deeper than the outer layer of skin. I plucked the cigarette from her mouth and dropped it and the lighter into my pocket. She gazed up at me. Her face was a mask failing to conceal the emptiness I felt growing all around me. In the deepest recesses of her eyes crouched the faintest shock of recognition, as if she'd just remembered something important. It got swallowed in the sound of her voice.

"Where is Jesus?" she mumbled. "Where is Jesus?" Yeah, I wondered, where is he? In anger and sorrow I looked back at her. I couldn't think of anything to say, which only made me angrier and sorrier.

A few of them were willing to help me, and together we managed to herd the crowd down the stairs. No resistance. They didn't seem to care what floor they were on as long as they could work on losing their appetites. I swept down, down, down toward the pit of the building. Dope was plentiful, and its most bizarre apostles were scattered all over the place. Medical volunteers in baggy white smocks tried to keep track of them. The lower I descended, the more frenetic the atmosphere became. I wasn't becoming inured to the destruction I witnessed, but by the time I reached the third floor I began to wonder why

I was even bothering. I glanced at my watch. It was nearly 1 A.M. Through the floor I heard music blaring from the sanctuary one flight below.

It was much like combat. I waded through the corridors of flesh, stopping only to address what I judged to be the most severe cases. I had to pass a lot of others by. Bodies were everywhere, and all I could do was give them a quick look and keep right on moving, never daring to wonder whatever became of them. I couldn't get away from what was happening. Nobody could. It came at me in every way, the freakouts and laughter and crying jags and rubbing and grabbing and slumped piles of young flesh in faded fabrics fit for a summer's night. It was like quicksand or a tidal wave rolling and roaring with an energy nothing but time could stop. Glide was a dam on the verge of busting open, and I felt like every moment and any moment could be the one when the walls crumbled and sent thousands spilling back into the night.

All those from the upper floors flooded the second-floor hall. Walking became impossible. The only way to move was to turn sideways and sort of shimmy through the mass of bodies. An older woman sat on the edge of a bench near the sanctuary. I recognized her immediately as one of the holdover fundamental Methodists who still regarded Glide Church as their private domain. They wanted to keep Glide in a death grip, as if they were a match for the history igniting around them. I was astonished to see her there because she was neither a thrill seeker nor voyeur. She wore a plain gray two-piece suit. Her face was empty, but I was certain she wasn't a dope case. The ocean of flesh had marooned her on that bench. Her fingers, like tentacles, darted in and out of the sea, tugging at the arms of young men floating by.

"Will you fuck me?" she said quietly to each and every one of them. "Please take me home and fuck me."

I offered to help get her out of there. She didn't even recognize me. Her hands moved mechanically to push me away, as if I were an intruder whose ignorance of her private mission made me most unwelcome. The tide swept me up and sucked me down the hall. I never saw her again that night. Something had been ripped loose within her and she was drowning, another victim of the tidal wave that knocked down all in its path.

Some of those things needed to be knocked down. I was aware of that. Maybe the woman needed to be touched, but it was all so indiscriminate, arrogantly disrespecting the border between liberation and destruction. One of the men who'd worked with us from the early stages suddenly appeared beside me, wide eyes flashing.

"Isn't this beautiful?" he screamed above the roar of other voices. "It's really happening, huh? I mean, it's really fucking happening. And we gotta keep making it happen, right? This is a New Age, Cecil. A brand new age . . ."

His voice dove beneath the waves. Seconds later it broke the surface. All I heard was,

". . . right?"

He disappeared before I could answer him, but he didn't really want to hear me anyway. He only wanted to justify what was happening. Like the Vietnam War—destruction equals salvation. I thought to myself, I wonder if they're going to inflate the body count. An overwhelming urge to get out of there burst inside me, but other bodies strapped my hands to my thighs. My legs felt as if they were encased in cement. I couldn't move. There was no way out. The brutal delusion revealed in the young man's question made me bitterly angry. Beautiful? Bodies everywhere. People destroyed, especially by the drugs. Any sense of community had been bludgeoned to death. Even the bonds of pain and emptiness had been slashed. I felt profoundly sorry for all of them. What made these white kids go this far to say what they had to say? What horrible thing had been done to them? Why did they have to destroy themselves this way? What for?

Yes, that was the question. What did it matter? Something had to happen to make it matter, but nothing was. No direction, no purpose, no cause. Trapped by it, sinking in it, surrounded by it, the truth came to me as clearly as my own name: It didn't matter. People were destroying themselves for nothing. It didn't matter. And I didn't matter either. Nothing mattered but the chaos and destruction. I saw myself suspended in the center of a dark abyss. The walls of cliffs beyond my reach were made of human bodies. It made no difference. I hung there, alone.

It didn't matter. Chaos was in complete control. The hippies had manufactured their own freedom and chaos in the labs of the acid kings, in the minds of people so beaten down they needed colored pills to free their imaginations. Defined by the chaos. What for? That was the question.

About 3 A.M. things began to subside. More people were leaving than arriving, and the hard-edged frenzy softened up a bit. It continued that way for another three hours. At 6 A.M. I stood before a window on the second floor, staring at the parking lot across the street. Above the skyline of grimy hotels with "low monthly rates" rose the dawn, quarreling with my conviction that it didn't matter, that there was no place for me among these people and their Invisible Circus. A voice inside me said,

Something's gotta happen to make it matter.

"You offering a guarantee?" I asked.

The voice chuckled.

You know better than that.

"It's pointless," I said. "You saw it, didn't you? It was pointless."

Yeah, you could say that. Hard for you to understand?

"Damned hard."

They feel like they've got nothing of their own. Hell, they don't even know what it is they're looking for. Those are good grounds for suicide. But every moment contains a revelation.

"Spare me the philosophy, brother."

Okay. But the girl, the one with her hands on fire?

"What about her?"

Remember her.

I grunted and ran my fingers across the ridges of my chin. I wanted to ask the voice "What for?" but that would've been too much an inside joke, even for him.

"They were pretty desperate, weren't they?" I said. "You know what I think? I think they were trying to fill a kind of void and so they did all those crazy things, broke all the rules."

It felt that way.

"But if it had no direction, I guess it didn't matter."

Only to those it destroyed.

"But if it had a direction it would, wouldn't it?"

Madness, chaos, destruction. Chances. They're always gonna be there. Nowhere to run. But that doesn't mean it doesn't matter. It's all right as long as you don't let it define you.

I waved my hand as if to encompass the night that had just passed.

"But what's all this have to do with me?"

You don't need me to answer that. Look, it's getting lighter outside.

The voice was right. Sunlight was replacing the first gray blotches of dawn. It was going to be another hot day. Down on the street, people were already beginning to gather. All night long the radio had broadcast reports about the Invisible Circus. Apparently, lots of people had been listening. Footsteps beat their way up the hall. I wheeled and saw three long-haired young men who'd appeared with us before Glide's Board of Trustees.

"Cecil, we'd like to talk with you," one of them said.

"Sure," I replied. We ducked into a vacant office.

All of us were dead tired, our eyes streaked with red, our mouths dry and tasting like sweatshirts, our ears starting to buzz with fatigue. And it was only the beginning. The radio had estimated the Friday night crowd at 8,000. We guessed that at least 15,000 people would descend on the building before noon. The three young men spoke haltingly, all the bravura of the night drained from them. They gestured toward the crowd in the street below and said we would really be in for it over the next twenty-four hours. They weren't telling me anything I didn't already know.

"What do you think we should do?" one of them asked me.

The words hovered in the stale air. Maybe they understood, I thought to myself. Maybe they realized how they were being defined by the chaos, and how that only meant destruction. More than that, I saw a place for me in their midst. Direction, purpose, and perhaps at the far end of the road a cause.

I didn't want to be a cop and I didn't want to be their daddy. I didn't want to try and control the chaos because that would've been just as destructive as anything else. Chaos was life. I'd learned that much in my thirty-eight years. But they saw the need for direction, a definition that would give the Invisible

Circus a purpose. For over an hour we talked about different possibilities, but none of them felt right. It seemed that even though we understood the necessity for direction, we were at the mercy of the chaos that had already been set in motion. The outlook was grim. Around eight I stepped out to hunt us up some coffee. As I emerged from the office, two police captains rounded the corner and marched toward me. They said they'd been looking for me.

My relationship with the San Francisco Police Department had been touchy almost from my arrival at Glide Church. I'd already organized a number of groups and protests aimed at combating police brutality, particularly brutality against blacks and gays, and I knew that in some quarters of the San Francisco Hall of Justice I was castigated as a cross between a bandit and a lunatic. But I also knew I'd gained a measure of respect from some of them. In any event, they knew better than to force an issue with me, and so, with the obvious exception of undercover agents and informers, rarely entered Glide Church without first securing my approval. Because of that, the sight of the captains surprised me. I waited for them to make their move.

All the talking was done by the older of the pair. He said he'd heard we'd had a "real ball-breaker" during the night, and that from the looks of things it was bound to get worse.

"Somebody could get badly hurt, and we don't wanna see that happen," the captain said. I searched him for clues to his feelings and sense of responsibility. Did the police want to seek a rational solution or did they simply want to clear the building, bust a few heads, and get it over with? I had a split second to make up my mind. I decided to trust him.

"Let's go in and talk," I said. I had no time to wonder about the hippies' reaction to my decision, and to tell you the truth I didn't particularly care. It was my decision and I was going to stand by it.

They followed me into the cramped office. The hippies were astonished, but I was startled by their lack of contempt. They seemed genuinely glad to have those captains in there. In a spirit of cooperation, we circled the problem for over an hour. By 8:30 A.M. I knew I'd made the right decision. It took us ninety minutes to hammer out a tentative solution. The older cop ordered the younger one to get on the phone. A few calls later, the younger captain announced the plan was workable.

The solution was to move the Invisible Circus ten miles west to Ocean Beach, where San Francisco meets the Pacific. The next day, Sunday, the event would return to Glide Church. The hippies agreed to confine their activities to a sandy stretch of two miles along the ocean's edge. The captains promised the hippies that they could build fires, and no one would be beaten, harassed, or intimidated. Open lines of communication were being set up, and both sides agreed that neither would take action without consulting the other. We shook hands all around, and word was passed to the free press to start printing directions to Ocean Beach. By noon, people began drifting away from Glide.

Standing at the second-floor window again, I watched them leave. A stream of relief flushed through me: They'd seen the spectre of their own destruction and taken action against it. Maybe they were naive and self-indulgent, but they still valued human life. That's more than I would've given them credit for ten hours earlier. They were struggling with something that I wasn't sure anyone understood, but at least they were struggling. If anything was to make them great, I mused, it was their recognition of struggle's necessity. Sure, they might go out to the beach and do themselves in, but I was buoyed with the hope and confidence that maybe they'd learned something during the night. The morning's evidence certainly supported me there.

We found it everywhere, from the sixth floor all the way down. Trash would be too elegant a word for it. Papers, bottles, cigarette butts, clothing, hunks and crumbs of food, stains of unknown origin, smears of many colors. Walls, floors, windows, doors. Nothing had escaped the filth. It was exactly as though they'd vomited everything inside them, all they'd been fed from birth. The building was seeping in their regurgitation— the food that had not nourished them, the drink that had not quenched their thirst. It lay stagnating in the halls with a stench and power that intimidated many who stayed to clean it up. In every corner were the remains of the night's terrible attempt to fill the void. The hippies had tried to fill the whole building with their bodies, their lives, and now as I walked among the empty halls I heard the echoes of my footsteps and saw pools of vomit huddled like refugees in the lengthening shadows of the afternoon. For the moment, the hippies were gone. The emptiness remained.

"Fuck 'em," I cursed as I leaned against a third-floor wall, a damp mop in my hand. "Fuck 'em all." I'd been made a nigger again, once more responsible for cleaning up after white folks. My body ached. Dried sweat curled around my skin like crust. The white folks' vomit. A nigger's work. I remembered the young blacks lounging in front of the liquor store. They were right, I thought. The hippies really weren't much different. A small group of them volunteered to help clean the building in preparation for Sunday, and they worked as hard as we did. I was grateful for their help, but it wasn't nearly enough to still my rage. We carted out two huge truckloads of garbage. What for? What did it matter? The questions still awaited an answer.

We'd locked the gates and doors to prevent more people from coming in, but even at 4:30 P.M. thousands were massed in front of the church. Volunteers directed them to the beach. By 6:30 the cleaning was done, and I wasn't sure which had the stronger hold on me, anger or fatigue. I sat slumped in a chair in my office when a janitor stuck his head in.

"Found something you might wanna see," he said. I groaned but got up and followed him down into the basement. He led me to the door of the men's room in the bowels of the building, even deeper than I'd journeyed during the night. The pungent smell of ammonia knifed through the air but couldn't totally drown the lingering odors of the night. It was that way all over the building. Smells of what had happened wafted through the corridors like ghosts who refused to leave.

"In there," he said, pointing to the bathroom door. "On the wall."

I pushed the door open and went in. As such things go, it was quite large, covering a one-by-two section of white wall above the urinals. Deep black in color and still a bit damp to the touch, it was the voice of J. Leonard Farmer and the madwoman in Hobbs. All night and all day I'd been searching for it. It said,

Fuck the Church

Alone in the men's room, I stared at the message on the wall. *Fuck the Church.* Profoundly it spoke to me, bringing back the question: What for? What did it matter?

Fuck the Church

Suddenly it did matter to me. It mattered very much. Fuck the Church. What better place for it than in the deepest region of a building defined as holy, pure, and untouchable? What better author than an unseen human being who understood so well, perhaps in a brilliant, bitter, hopeful, momentary flash, the particular purpose of the Invisible Circus? Not *Jesus Saves,* but *Fuck the Church.* The church had been fucked by the Invisible Circus. That had been the direction, purpose, cause. Fuck the Church in slow, rolling, insistent motion. Fuck the Church and bring it life. Fuck the Church and make it feel. Fuck the Church and make it human, fully woman, fully man, fully child. Fuck the Church until it becomes *pregnant,* for its pregnancy is your pregnancy. Become pregnant with a new way of life. Live your courage, your love, your power.

Fuck the Church. The most secular language imaginable, the most sacred message of all. The manmade distinction between the sacred and secular was forever obliterated by that message on the men's-room wall. What happens beyond the church's walls can happen within them. No, it demanded even more. What happens beyond the church's walls *must* happen within them; and despite their self-destruction, the hippies had accomplished precisely that. They'd brought the world inside the church, and the church would never be the same again.

Fuck the Church. In my lifetime, the church had always been a pimp, pimping its worshippers with promises of God, putting blessings and eternity up for sale. Remaking God in the image of a hustler who respects most of all the power of a dollar.

Fuck the Church. In my lifetime, the church had always been a rapist violating those who sought direction from it. Lie still, it ordered them, and you will be saved. Lie still and we will accept you. It had raped and pillaged for centuries, seeking only perpetuation of its power.

The church is a tomb. Make it throb to the beat of the human heart. Make it moist with the drops of tears and sweat. Make it come to life. It is a womb. Make it pregnant.

The door squeaked and the janitor entered, a soiled rag in his hand.

"I just thought you might wanna see it before I wipe it off," he said.

"Don't!" I snapped. "Don't touch a word of it!"

He looked at me strangely, shrugged, and left. I stood pondering the message a few moments longer, climbed slowly up the stairs, and left the building. By then everyone was gone except a small contingent that would stay the night. I drove out to the beach but remained only ten minutes, quickly succumbing to the exhaustion of the last twenty-four hours. I heard a few radio reports describe the beach atmosphere as "joyful but cool." When I arrived home, I suddenly felt that all senior staff members, the men who were supposed to be decision makers and had arranged for the Invisible Circus in the first place, had deserted me during the night and early morning. The fear I'd sensed in them apparently had been real enough. For a while on Saturday night, my anger at them was all I felt, but I lapsed into a deep sleep as the sun went down.

I got to church very early Sunday morning and walked about the first two floors. Although we'd worked feverishly to clean the place, hand prints, foot prints, and body prints remained on the walls, smudges and stains bearing witness to Friday night's eruption. As I stared at them, I realized why they seemed so strange. It was simply their location. They were downtown walls, human murals found in dimly lit, urine-stained hallways. They were Friday night walls, a work of despair and exuberance thrown against the city nights. You could find them almost anyplace, even in posh Pacific Heights, if you knew how to look for them. But you couldn't find them in church. That was their wonder; they didn't belong on the walls of the church. They were both an introduction and a legacy, and I realized the Invisible Circus was far from over.

My contemplation was interrupted by the arrival of the church choir whose members wandered aghast through the lobby and down into the basement to don their robes. They were the vestigial remains of the old Glide Church, rigid in their virtue and wrathful in their fear. I had inherited them from an era in which Glide Church, beneath the cloak of pious commitment to holy exclusion, had locked its doors simply to preserve itself. White, middle-aged, and middle class, they saw themselves as the only embodiment of the Methodist Church, precisely defined by the very self-righteousness of their rage.

A pair of trembling male choir members accosted me in the lobby.

"I must tell you I am utterly shocked," one of them said in a conflicted voice, as though speaking to a handyman who'd inexplicably gotten the better of him.

"Tell me," I replied.

"And I suppose you haven't seen the . . . filth on the wall," the other one snapped.

"Which wall?"

"The lavatory wall."

"You mean *Fuck the Church?*"

"You needn't repeat it in my presence. I demand you have it removed immediately."

"No, it's saying something important to us," I said. "I will not have it removed!"

They looked at one another in astonishment.

"This is consecrated ground. Or have you forgotten your obligations to the ministry?" one of them said in a voice cracking with hatred.

"Don't tell *me* about being a minister!" I snapped.

"Don't you realize the degradation you're causing?" The voice was nearly screaming. "You have no right! This is a Methodist Church. In the Lord's name, a good, clean house of worship!"

"Not anymore," I said.

"This is unspeakable. If you don't have that . . . obscenity . . . removed this instant, I will leave this congregation!"

"I'm not surprised," I said.

One of the two jerked away and marched toward the door. Over his shoulder he yelled at me, "I'm going to spread the word about you!"

It was my most critical confrontation yet as minister of Glide Church, entailing the risk of losing the hard-line congregation to rebellious defection. Somehow, though, I didn't feel the elation and drain that often accompany the enactment of momentous decisions. It was as if the moment had been coming for a long time, and I had been preparing for it.

Within a short while, the hippies began flocking into the building for the celebration, and they soon comprised the majority of the audience. Joining them and the Methodists were hundreds of people from all segments of society who owed their allegiance to neither side. In many ways, it was these who later grew to form the Glide community; their search, although as desperate as that of the hippies and Methodists, in time revealed an honest confrontation with themselves and the world. It felt to me as if everyone in the church that day was searching for something, although truthfully I didn't recognize the strength of those in the middle. I was much too wrapped up in the battle, and it was the hippies who unquestionably commanded the greatest attention. They appeared as they had two nights earlier, unwashed, unkempt, unnecessarily self-satisfied. In overstating their revolt, they had had the principal effect of minimizing it. One of their leaders had changed his name to "Free," as if freedom were a matter of semantics.

"I'm Free now, and if people call my name enough then they will be freed too," he proclaimed.

Had I not cared for direction, purpose, and cause, I would have savored the ironic absurdity of his gesture, for it was uncomfortably the same as a lordly minister invoking the name of God; both claimed ownership of the Word, the key to the secrets of freedom and the grace of God, and preached that repeating the words would make them so. They shared a need to escape what faced them, and it seemed entirely clear to me that the hippies and the hard-line Methodists were on overlapping frequencies. Neither seemed concerned with substance, only with defining themselves in relationship to something else. The hippies yearned to believe themselves the dawn of a new beginning, yet defined themselves only in relationship to their mothers and fathers, while the Methodists, servants of a two-faced morality, defined themselves in relationship to God.

Scared out of their wits by these wild, convulsive young anarchists indiscriminately attacking society's every assumption, the Methodists clung to a self-righteous rage manifested through a stony silence interrupted with barely audible and blindly venomous accusations and retributions. The hippies, mad with a messianic desire to topple order, and perhaps frightened by the responsibilities it implied, adopted an air of indispensable arrogance as if to suggest that they alone had found the magic path. Self-righteous rage, fearful arrogance. And all I could think of was *Fuck the Church.* That's what mattered, and as the celebration began I grew determined that it not be defined by either group.

In those days, the celebration was structured like a play and designed that Sunday with the Invisible Circus in mind. Jazz and soul singer Ann Weldon and poet Lenore Kandel, who'd created something of a sensation by incorporating the word *fuck* into public recitation of her work, had been added to the middle of the program. The opening acts of the drama included a reading from *Death of a Salesman* and a traditional hymn by the choir housed in the loft behind me.

The hippies cheered enthusiastically at the recitation from *Salesman* and sat in silence as the choir rendered "Sanctus: 'St. Cecilia's Mass.'" When not singing, the choir members, the base of the traditionalist camp, remained mostly quiet, although every so often I heard words such as "disgusting" and "abominable" escape their whispering lips. Early on I decided I would not turn to look back at them, so their words became like pebbles tossed against my back.

The celebration's first portions were borderline for both camps: Each found things to praise and condemn but nothing to hold in dire contempt. That all changed when first Lenore and then Ann took the stage. I felt the equivalent of a chill behind me as the assaults from the loft grew bolder.

"I've never seen such blasphemy."

"Revolting!"

"You can be sure I'll speak to the Bishop about this!"

And, throughout:

"Look how dirty they are."

"Vulgar is the word, absolutely vulgar."

"How dare they associate with good Christians!"

The hippies received Ann and Lenore with a chauvinistic enthusiasm, as if to say only they could truly understand and appreciate the significance of the women's message and presence. As if, in fact, only they were entitled to witness them. I felt in the middle of a tremendously bitter clash over who was going to win that day, hippies to my face and Methodists to my back, each in their own way denying the full condition. And still I saw *Fuck the Church* on the bathroom wall. They will not define the condition for me, I vowed. None of them will.

In those days I gave titles to my sermons, and for Invisible Circus Sunday I chose to call my sermon "Born Free." It was my chance to address them all in the spirit of fucking the church, the spirit of pregnancy.

Waving my arms, I said all the hand prints, foot prints, and body prints had given flesh to the walls.

"Face prints that mirror your faces, your lives; hand prints that touch all people; foot prints that have walked the walls to life."

In my mind, I turned to both of them, hippies and Methodists.

"I feel a struggle in this room, but today everybody wins because everybody loses!"

The Methodists had to give up their death grip on the church and themselves. The hippies had to surrender their arrogance. I couldn't make them do it, of course. The best I could do was make them all see it.

"Born free is to stop calling everybody over thirty a phony. Born free is to give up owning the church that was never yours to own. Born free is to embrace and live your freedom so you don't have to prove it all the time."

Fuck the Church. I was losing too; I was giving up the old Glide Church that day, and I knew it.

"These walls have taken on life! Today these walls are crumbling outside so all people can enter here. There are no walls any longer!"

The hippies whistled, cheered, and stomped their feet. The

Methodists, knowing the end had come, sat rigidly silent. And the hundreds of others, caught in the middle much as I, seemed eager for a significantly new experience without the paradoxically rigid anarchy of the hippies. Of them all, it was those in the middle who would return.

"And this church will never be the same again!" I roared.

After it was over, I found a group of reporters waiting for me at the bottom of the stairs, anxious to know what had really happened Friday night. It was as if I'd walked out of the fog and into a cold light. For the first time since I'd been plunged into the eye of chaos, I became aware of the possible repercussions. Dozens of hard thoughts shot through my mind as I confronted the reporters. The possibility that my career was in jeopardy stopped me cold. They hurled questions like live hand grenades, most of them having to do with sex, drugs, and violence. I fought them off with general comments about the necessity of people coming together, but I do remember one statement that applied:

"We took a great risk here, but sometimes risks must be taken."

Finally they left me alone.

I was horribly tired when I went home Sunday afternoon to rest. The past two days were beginning to exact their toll. I made a few calls to staff people, and we agreed that if the press printed an accurate account of Friday night Glide Church could well go under. The situation was that critical, and we weren't fooling ourselves about it. Still, I wasn't sorry about what had happened; we'd agreed beforehand to accept the consequences. The hippies were going to get off scot free, of course, but we'd known that going in. A strange feeling of accomplishment enveloped me. Had the risk been worth it? I wasn't sure how to measure the answer to that one, but my memory kept returning to the words on the wall.

At 3:30, my phone rang. It was a reporter for the *San Francisco Chronicle.*

"I don't know if you're aware of it or not, but I was there on Friday night," he said. This might be it, I thought. "Cecil, I just want to tell you that it was one of the most profound experiences of my life, but if I print what actually happened, most people wouldn't understand. So I'm not going to print it. Hell, I don't think anyone would believe it anyhow." His perception of Friday night surprised me, but perhaps the Invisible Circus had met his needs better than it had mine. I thanked him.

I'm not sure whether anyone would have believed it, but no major paper ran anything about the Invisible Circus. Only the *Berkeley Barb*, an alternative paper, carried a story about Friday night.

As planned, I returned to Glide around 4 o'clock to conclude the Invisible Circus and went straight to the sanctuary. It was empty. I stared at the altar and pulpit. They'd become foreign objects to me.

A few moments later, the hippies filed in. But they didn't go right to the pews and sit. In a long and silent procession, they marched single file in front of the altar. One by one they left money, rings, necklaces, beads, bracelets, scarves, flowers, clothing, food, and scribbled "IOUs" in a heap before the altar. Not a word was spoken. There was no music, no frenzy, no microphones. It was quiet, dignified, almost serene. Only a few people spoke, and their words were soft and brief.

"This has been the one place, the only place for us, and now we come back to share with you," one young woman said. With sunset glinting through the sanctuary's stained glass windows, the hippies departed with as much silent grace as they'd arrived with.

SEVEN

BELOW us, fifteen minutes to the east, stood Atlanta.

They were waiting for me there. I had been invited to address the General Conference of the United Methodist Church. All reports indicated my promised appearance carried the proportions of great controversy, and for some the scintillating allure of the bizarre. Even before I set foot in Atlanta, I was a media event. I was copy. Even before I uttered my first word to them, I was a show.

I could say anything I pleased. Not only at the airport but further on, in the pulpit of the church whose minister had fought so hard to ban my presence. There they all would be, delegates to a quadrennial gathering of international dimension in which the church's institutional power came as close as ever to human form. In my mind it was almost as if I were returning home after years of absence to show those who'd never left the person I had become. The upheaval surrounding this homecoming gladdened me because I knew the church needed to be shaken, yet there were the briefest moments when I felt certain I somehow was missing the point. I could say anything I pleased. But how would they perceive me? The question seemed to conceal an unrecognized horror.

As the plane bore down on Atlanta that spring afternoon in 1972, the wounds slashing across the distance between the church and me were fresh and moist, those on the surface encouraging escape from any more serious lacerations deep within the substance of the flesh. Although opinions varied as to my validity, I was unanimously regarded as a maverick, that designation being a compromise between rebel and freak. Perceived, even in my own view, as a foreign object in their midst.

I'd staked my own ground in San Francisco and, for doing so, had been branded a heretic and worse by some elements in the church. Sex and theology were among the areas in which they cited me, but the strife was being played on the surface. It felt more symbolic than real. Nobody wished to examine the deeper wounds, the substance of my alienation from them, and so my critics remained content to charge that people disrobed at Glide. They decried the language I used and mourned for language I rejected. They accused me of running a nightclub instead of a church. They beat their drums loudly, but only at the most conspicuous manifestations of my breaking away. No crucial questions were under discussion. The battle was being fought over style, not substance.

But only with my permission.

I was front page. I was feature material. I was the evening news. I stood in danger of reducing myself to a gesture.

Perhaps I would come away from Atlanta the name on everyone's lips. And nothing more, my triumph a function of mathematics. Newspaper column inches, radio and TV air time, the number of people who came to hear me. It was all very real to me, the inducements of a measurable fame, the qualities of a tangible success. It's what mattered to them. In any case, a revelation was guaranteed. But why did it cause me such tension and anguish? Was I in some way being set up? When it came down to it, could I deliver? I considered such questions and decided there was something in particular I had to reveal to the church, but I couldn't exactly say what it was. I asked myself yet another question:

What kind of minister was I?

As Atlanta grew nearer, my mind hovered over the answer to my final question and over what Glide Church and I had to bring this huge gathering of Methodists.

There was always a line on Sunday. From the gates of Glide, it stretched a full block up Taylor Street and around the corner onto O'Farrell. A lot of the people were thirty-five and under, and a good majority of them were white. Still, it was a motley group of all colors, ages, and descriptions. Literally thousands of them every Sunday morning. For those impressed by numbers, it was really something. It always impressed me.

Sometimes I emerged from the church building before the celebration and walked along the line greeting people. Just the sight of them crowding the sidewalk for more than a full city block thrilled and encouraged me, for in their massive number lay testimony to a form of triumph. At moments I nearly was seduced into counting them one by one. There beat in me, as there does in every human heart, the superhuman desire to become exalted. And in them surged equally the temptation to worship another and in their choice surrender themselves. Many among them fiercely withstood such temptation, as did part of me. But others, in their fervent desire for a love not burdened with pain, fear, anger, or struggle, cast themselves before me. It seemed so easy to please them. All of us were vulnerable, sharing, in our weakest moments, an unspoken obligation.

I'd started something completely different, sprung from my lifelong conviction that the essence of mystery is revealed in action, not detachment, and that human life is a community of connections fulfilled not by insulated worship but through a struggle that must be continually renewed. I wanted a church that merged with the world, a church so authentic to human life that it neglected no facet of that life. I wanted a church that in its full embodiment of my own experience embodied the experience of others too, not because my experience was innately more profound than theirs but because it was the only thing I had that could connect us together while revealing my authenticity. I was in great danger, for if that revelation did not speak to the lives of others then Glide Church would be just another merciless deception. Even worse, if I shunned the perilous discrimination between the personal and the universal, if I placed my own experience above all others instead of accepting it as uniquely my own, I would become a slave to my conceit.

We had standing room only crowds for both the 9 A.M. and 11 A.M. celebrations each Sunday, maybe 4,000 people in all.

The 9 A.M. celebration was added to keep pace with the demand. We even entertained the possibility of having another celebration on Saturday, but it never came to that. There was an eight-piece band (piano, guitar, bass, drums, congas, and three horns) that played spirituals, freedom songs, Dylan, the Beatles, Stevie Wonder, and more. We had a choir called the Glide Ensemble whose members wore street clothes and shook their bodies like tambourines. A light show shot the wall full of pictures and blending colors. Chugga-chugga *boom*, chugga-chugga *boom* . . . beat, rhythm, tempo. You've heard it before, elsewhere, and reading about it now you may want to dismiss it as primitive or adolescent or cheap or shallow or antiintellectual or antireligious—as *secular*. But it moved people as they had not been moved before.

No doubt some of the people some of the time chose to believe they were at a house party, but for me the music, beat, rhythm, and tempo transcended their particulars to become messages in themselves. My ancestors didn't sing work songs just to make music. We didn't sing those spirituals simply to manifest a faith in God. Lives have sounds. Authentic, indigenous sounds that erupt from the lives themselves and all they contain. Blues, folk songs, jazz, rock and roll; the best of these sounds not only reflect the lives of their creators and community—they also are and become a part of them. Sacred, in the largest meaning of the word. Prayer in the most human terms.

By their very nature, the celebrations encouraged and even challenged people to participate. I asked everyone to turn around and embrace the person next to them, stranger or not. Most did. I asked them to sing the songs. Most did. Others walked out on us, of course, grumbling about "show biz" and insults to Christianity. It was their decision, and I honored it. In speaking—sometimes shouting—of my own struggle and dignity, I spoke of the audience's as well. Some among them wept, some cheered, some smiled, some touched. I didn't want them just to feel good, I wanted them to feel good about themselves. I wanted them to struggle, risk, and become courageous in their own lives. And many of them did. I wanted Sunday to be a hopeful, joyful experience, but it wouldn't have been the same without the touching and affirmation. And it wouldn't

108

have been the same without the music either.

The celebrations refused to withdraw from the world. On the contrary, we attacked issues the larger church either avoided completely or merely patted on the head. People such as Dick Gregory, Jane Fonda, and Angela Davis spoke at Glide, and we worked in behalf of student radicals, the antiwar movement, the Black Panthers, the Farmworkers, the American Indian Movement, and an army of other community groups. We fed people and stood with them in the streets. By 1972, Glide Church had become a haven for radicals and a sanctuary for those in rebellion. It could have gone no other way, because we were in rebellion ourselves, dedicated to the proposition that probing deeply into the world is a path toward probing deeply into oneself.

Look at it as either entertaining, spiritual, or political. Part of the time you'll be right. But what if you look on it as a novelty, a shuck, a glorified concert? Will you still be right?

We had sung "Oh Freedom," "Wade in the Water," and "You've Got a Friend." The band had played "Livin' for the City" while ushers passed the collection baskets. In my sermon, I'd spoken about Angela Davis, incarcerated in Marin County Jail. Now I stood on the lip of the carpeted stage, sweat pouring off my face. In one hand I clutched an Electro-Voice RE-16 microphone with an extra-long wire trailing behind me like an umbilical cord. I heard the *click* of the guitar player plugging in his amp. All I had to do was lead the people in "We Shall Overcome" and the celebration would be over. The people swam before me, ready. Their faces, subtle shadows around each pair of eyes, craggy lines of age and the damp smoothness of youth. Their different colors painting a dream. I wanted each of us to rise and storm the barriers that confined us, to test the limits of our freedom. At the exact same moment, I longed to hear cheers and place my head in the bosom of something larger that would welcome me. Let me tell you something: Important questions often arise when you least expect them.

Why was I doing it *that* way? Was I a joke trying to fool people into applauding an image? What kind of minister was I?

Propelled by the rhythm section, I went ahead and sang the song, bolted down the center aisle, and embraced people at the bottom of the stairs, as I always did. You don't answer questions like those in a flurry of seconds. They grow inside you a while.

I remembered what I'd always liked best about Wesley Methodist Church in San Angelo—it was the natural feeling I so often experienced inside the place. That brick building seemed forever full of familiar black faces and flowered hats and out-of-style suits and shined shoes and the chaotic aroma of potluck suppers; shrieks of joy, tears of hope, unspeakable pain, bottomless grief, and a near-silent rage. Wesley Methodist Church was more than our sanctuary. It was an extension of our lives. We needed a place authentic to our experience, with the ability to inspire life. Our eyes turned to heaven in supplication to the Lord, as if to suggest that his solution was what bound us together. But it was not. The essence of our existence as blacks, as have-nots, was what drew us to that church. Wesley called us all to its bosom where we inspired each other to life. Wesley Methodist Church was there, I tell you, throbbing like a fresh wound in my memory.

I expected such memories, such an example of the church's potential greatness, to be inspirational, and they were. I didn't expect them to cause me pain. I didn't understand why they did.

Sometimes it was so tempting to be hip. "America's only standing-room-only church." That was the media line describing us. We were the "in" place, the hip place, the place to be. Didn't that matter? Something was *happening* at Glide, and soon the thousands of people were joined by guest artists and celebrities. Quincy Jones, Roberta Flack, Marvin Gaye, and Sammy Davis, Jr., Dr. Spock, Leonard Bernstein, and Saul Alinsky—they all came to Glide and later acknowledged that something had happened to them there.

Sammy called it "unbelievable" and said, "We'd have the world everybody wants to build if everyone was like the people here."

Leonard professed that his experience at Glide helped inspire him to complete a work whose ending had frustrated him for months.

While I was driving him to the airport, Saul turned to me and said, "Most church sermons need to be flushed down the toilet, but you relate to poor people like no church I've ever seen."

Comments like those tempted me to conquer my growing discomfort. Because I was becoming one of them, you see. A celebrity. There was a narcotic quality to my newly earned status, and people were forever coming up and complimenting me on the great things I was doing. The artists and celebrities and community people meant what they said, and I valued their support. But more than that, I came to court it, as though I were hoping they might save me. All I had to do was turn it over to the big names, and there would be long lines at the gates of Glide forever.

Doubts or not, I had to pull myself together, get off the plane and meet Atlanta. The "No Smoking" sign began blinking above me. I imagined myself remaining aboard when the plane touched down, or getting off and grabbing the next flight home. Both thoughts passed quickly. The jet hit the ground with a jerk. A mechanical voice thanked the passengers and wished us a pleasant stay in Atlanta. Then I saw the crowd through the window, sequestered behind metal railings at the far end of the tarmac near the mouth of the terminal. They were all I had expected them to be. Something like fear wriggled up my back. But these people have come to support you, I assured myself. Shock troops in the battle the church wages with itself. Some of them hoisted placards hailing my arrival and pledging their alliance with me. Others shifted from foot to foot in swelling anticipation. I took a quick guess at the count: maybe 300 or more, the majority black but some long-haired young whites, too. I was thankful for their presence. I needed them. A void within me began to fill. Something to do with their loving me and my need to keep them.

The speaker system crackled an anonymous request that all passengers remain seated so Reverend Williams and his party could deplane first. The message startled me and filled me with a sense of importance. It somehow justified my desire to confront the church and receive its judgment. I was big enough to do it, I was worthy of its deliberations. Here was proof of that. I nodded and stood up. A woman across the aisle tugged at my sleeve.

"Reverend," she said, "you surely must be a very important man."

My euphoria was boosted by her remark, yet she'd never seen me before. She knew nothing of Glide or what I was trying to do there. So did her compliment mean anything at all? But of course I was important. All these people were waiting for me.

The moment I ducked through the plane doorway I heard applause and a chant erupted from behind the railings.

"Freedom . . . freedom," they shouted in unison.

I grinned and waved. The tide of community support engulfed and renewed me. I needed it.

Two white men awaited me at the bottom of the steps. One of them I didn't recognize but later discovered to be the religious reporter for the *Atlanta Constitution.* The other was a San Francisco religion columnist who regularly attacked me with devotional fervor and was responsible for dubbing Glide "the nation's only Sunday morning nightclub." His face crinkled into a smile of recognition as he greeted me. I suppose he figured his bone-deep contempt entitled him to be familiar. We spoke for a few moments, until a black man broke the circle and gently took my arm.

"Let him go," he said to the journalists. "We want Cecil now; it's our time with him." He was right. My first responsibility was to those who'd come to support me.

The airport reception had been organized with obvious skill by the Black Methodists for Church Renewal, a group of clergy and laypeople who, although more traditional than I, were also calling the church to task. Some of them regarded me with an alarm normally reserved for the most unsettling aberrations, yet they were standing right beside me, accepting me for what I was. They weren't about to let a black man under attack fight it alone. That's how it was back in San Angelo; there were differences you had to accept just as there were commitments you had to keep. As I approached the terminal, the group began singing a freedom song, and a few of the organizers rushed to embrace me. One of them pulled me aside.

"This is no news to you, but it's liable to get a little touchy before it's through," he said. "Some of those folks downtown don't want to do anything but run you out of here. You've really got this place stirred up, brother!"

"Good," I replied. "It needs to be stirred up, and I'm gonna tell everyone that I'm not leaving Atlanta until I do what I came to do."

What did I mean by that?

He smiled broadly and escorted me back to the crowd while my cryptic vow strangled in the Georgia afternoon. I was glad I didn't have to think any more about it.

Standing on a chair, I gave a short talk to the crowd. Reporters stood along the fringes, scribbling notes in their pads.

"Brothers and sisters, I'm so glad to see all of us here fighting and struggling together, and I want all of you to know that the spirit's hit me. I'm really gonna preach tomorrow!"

Afterward I was rushed to an airport press conference, where I immediately felt the rushing heat of the bright television lights. Staring into the unchanging eye of the camera, I spoke directly into a battalion of microphones. I sensed the movement of tape. They were capturing every word I said. It mattered that they were. I remained aware of that.

Appearing with me were the president and members of the Glide Board of Trustees who in their willingness to support me also risked attack. The reporters barraged us with questions about the battle swirling around my scheduled appearance and about the attacks mounted against me and Glide by fundamentalists and others. I told them the attacks didn't bother me.

"I gather strength from crisis. I'm best in crisis situations because the greater the crisis, the greater the possibilities," I said.

In rented cars, the afternoon rolled into dusk, and the sky softened to the appropriate colors of a ripe peach. From the airport, they shuttled me to a caucus of the Black Methodists for Church Renewal, where I stayed only a short while. As darkness scouted the Atlanta suburbs, I finally reached my motel.

Feeling alone, I paced my room and watched the night wash over Atlanta. A galaxy of lights twinkled below. If only for a few moments, I wanted to escape the irrepressible advance of the following day, Thursday, April 20, 1972. For the first time I realized the life-and-death potential of my visit. The brilliant, seductive chance to lay waste. The hard, insistent calling to be genuine. From a distance, the correct choice seems clear, for we should never betray ourselves. But in the hot longing to be welcomed and secured, the desire, in fact, to know our place, death and betrayal become attractive choices indeed. Words from an old song sang in my head: "Rock my soul in the bosom of Abraham."

There had been no one moment when my opposition began to fear and despise me, when they recognized the threat I posed. Yet I understand the demands of historical perspective, so I trace the conflict back to April 1969, when as one of five Methodist ministers I was invited to speak and conduct seminars at a worship convocation for clergy and laypeople in St. Louis. At one point during my seminar, the discussion turned to sex: sex and the family, sex and single people, homosexuality, sex and the church. It was, I thought at the time, an often honest attempt to confront a web of issues that formed a personal and professional mystery for so many people there. The subject was fraught with danger. It frightened and perplexed many of them, because sex was a mystery that could transcend their church with a power they conceded not even to God. And once the door to that experience was jarred open, once the experience inside leaped beyond the artificial confines of its conventional isolation, anything could happen. Still, many at that St. Louis convocation wanted to confront the problem. We talked about sex a lot.

The thrust of my comments had to do with freeing sex from shame and guilt. In other institutions, not a radical concept at all, but the church traditionally has worked to control the sex lives of the faithful precisely because of sex's mysterious power. During the discussion, I noticed a man slip into the room, only to leave about thirty minutes later. I paid him no mind. Perhaps I should have, although it wouldn't have changed anything.

Reports on that seminar soon began appearing in conservative Methodist publications. In part they read like someone's fantasies. Nudity was elevated to the accepted mode of (un)dress at Glide Church, and implications of orgiastic frenzy paraded shamelessly between the lines. These stories, apparently generated by a St. Louis Methodist pastor who'd attended

114

the seminar for half an hour, hung around like corporate lobbyists on Capitol Hill. They refused to go away, and to tell you the truth I didn't spend too much time and energy bothering to refute them.

Planning for the Atlanta General Conference of the United Methodist Church got underway in 1971, including the appointment of seven ministers to conduct worship services. Not totally blind to the social and political climate, the conference commission on programs was aware that a black face among the seven would be to the conference's benefit. The man who nominated me, Reverend Jack Tuell of Vancouver, Washington, knew who I was but I'm not sure anybody else on the commission recognized my name. "One's as good as another" may have been the guiding principle for some of them. At any rate, I could almost feel the shock waves in the seat of my office chair when the commission belatedly discovered exactly which black minister it had selected.

"You mean *that* Cecil Williams!"

Yes. The disclosure immediately signaled the start of combat, and for the better part of a year the Methodist Church and all its disparate factions fought over the question of my appearance at the conference. The commission was hit with furious pressure to cancel my appointment. Conservative and fundamentalist camps oiled their rhetorical weapons and let fly: I was a "heathen," a "dangerous element," a standard bearer for the "Communist threat."

Arising to this challenge were those who defended my right to speak. Tuell and his colleagues refused to bend to the pressure applied against them.

"Although unconventional, this man's ministry is a credit to our church," Tuell declared.

The mere possibility of my presence at the conference was enough to send the church into paroxysms of self-examination, which some welcomed and others sought to disguise or escape. The year-long battle delivered to me a certain power and position. It would be a hard act for me to follow.

When the conference was still in conception, the United First Methodist Church of Atlanta offered itself as the site for all seven worship services. But when the pastor, Robert Ozment, discovered that I was going to preach in his pulpit, he forbade my appearance, objecting to my "style of worship." I was determined not to let him obscure the issue. Reporters at the Atlanta airport asked me what I thought of Ozment's exceptions to my "style."

"It's a blatant lie," I said. "It's racist."

Finally, in a rare invocation of the authority, Atlanta area Bishop John Owen Smith extended me an episcopal invitation, thus overriding the Ozment forces. I don't keep track of such things but I know they don't happen very often. It was a victory, to be sure, but it also had the indisputable effect of raising the stakes. The church had tempted and delivered me. Now it was I who had to deliver.

The entire episode was tinged with black humor, and no one appreciated the ironies more than I. My appointment may have been a grab bag operation pointing up the church's insensitivity to the individuality of black people. Yet there was a bitter aftertaste in my mouth. I was angry—angrier, I think, than I may have admitted to myself. It wasn't the attacks themselves so much as the deception surrounding them. What did "style of worship" actually mean?

Niggers and white folks. It was there, lurking beneath all the surface controversy. Somehow I'd reversed a historical pattern, and it had to do with blacks and whites. There had been other cases of black ministers inheriting white congregations, and in nearly every instance the church had either folded or its congregation had become pretty black pretty fast. But at Glide the church not only survived, it changed and prospered by embracing and including *all* colors. If Glide's congregation had been all black, I'm sure the battle of Atlanta would not have been so turbulent. But I was in *their* domain, contaminating their legacy not only with my presence but also with my revolt. I was embarrassing the church by defying its racial assumptions and by calling forth, in the hallowed space of the temple, all aspects of human experience. I talked about sex. I spoke about birth; not an antiseptic virgin birth but actual human birth with all its blood, slime, pain, and beauty. I wanted to recreate the essence of Wesley Methodist Church through experiences authentic to the lives of people in 1972. In striving to remain true to that mission I reached deep within the pit of the church where its fears and demons dwelled. That was not my primary purpose, but it flowed naturally from what I did.

I know they wondered, afflicted with visions of black studs with the endurance of animals, and virginal white maidens glowing with innocence. But it was not in its essence a sexual question. Sex was but the strongest, most terrifying symbol, one to which some church people may have attached their secret attention, only to miss the point.

At Glide, sex was celebrated as an authentic experience, a revelation, if you please. And if people could be free about their sexuality, they could risk revelation in other arenas too, and they continually confronted assumptions and directives employed by the church to confine experience. In music, language, and perhaps even perspective, there was always present at Glide the indelible stamp of the black style, but it wasn't a matter of guilt-ridden cultural submission, of people merely talking or walking or eating or styling like blacks. Rather, it was the realization and acknowledgment that something was wrong in the larger society, and it wasn't only political or only cultural or only spiritual. It was all of those, something people of all colors at Glide had felt all along creeping into their existence as light beneath a door, a deficiency that the church, school, family, job, money, sex, prayer, and country simply couldn't quite balance. And they had to face it as themselves, whatever their color. It meant survival in the middle of chaos. It meant there was no easy answer. It meant the hope for eternal salvation was a luxurious conceit. It meant the struggle was continuous. It meant revealing mystery through action. And through it all, for some in Atlanta, ran the fear of ghostly blacks chasing down the bodies and souls of whites. The attacks and controversy were not racist just because I was black (that would have been far too simplistic) but because I was black and in revolt and there were people of all colors around me in revolt as well. We *were* a menace. Damn right we were!

Even given my image as a dangerous nigger on the loose I could have done one thing to help defuse the attacks. I could have used Godtalk. Theological jargon meant to define God. An appeal to providence, a faith in divine intervention, a desperate belief in the power of the Lord. An abdication, finally, of human power and responsibility. I could have said, "God loves you." Godtalk would not have placated my most virulent attackers, but with it I would've become barely palatable to lots more people. The church would have more readily accepted my political radicalism as well as the sensational, wide-open style of the celebrations if only I'd used Godtalk. The fact that I eschewed Godtalk was trouble enough, but I went so far as to denounce it as the language of spiritual slavery. That's what threatened them most. The absence of Godtalk was not some low-budget stab at being "relevant," it was an integral part of an evolving philosophical, anthropological, and theological structure. I was not out to discredit God, Jesus Christ, or the Bible. Neither was I determined to prove God's existence or identity. God doesn't need to be authenticated or defined, and those who seek such a definition never define themselves. No, I was bent on revealing the existence of people, and the words handed down by the church had been corrupted to the point where they had little to do with that existence except as a means of controlling and defining it. Godtalk was no longer authentic to me, because for me the words reflected no purpose, sparked no action, and resisted translation into anything beyond the sounds they shaped in the human throat. So I replaced Godtalk with words containing the struggle of life itself, and even though they came in secular dress they held serious theological implications. Maybe I thought they were better words but they still were only words, and unless they danced with action they weren't much better than the Godtalk I rejected. It was up to me to give them life.

I had risen as a threat to the church, and felt, that first night in Atlanta in 1972, that my relationship with the church was about to explode. I imagined it ripping apart, almost as something human and alive, showering the earth with its remnants. What would be left? I had to *know* the answer, but of course there was no way I could. The answer, the revelation, humiliated me with its mystery. In a sense, it was like entering into battle not knowing whether I would survive, struggling to reach into the next sundown, peeking to see if I were alive or dead. But this was a battle of a different sort. I wasn't even sure what *dead* meant. Thus it came as no surprise to me that I couldn't sleep.

Why had I really come to Atlanta?

I realized that as a black man in revolt I would not be accepted by the church as an important influence. It would never draw me to its bosom, and the knowledge intensified my risk, revolt, and revelation. And yet *I longed to be "rocked in the bosom of Abraham"!*

There was a ceiling above me. There always is for outlaws and outsiders. You learn about the ceiling very early, and you try and work through it, around it, not letting it limit or determine your direction. Yet still you cling almost viciously to a thin stalk of hope that just maybe you will be the one to break the cycle. There were moments when I wished for nothing as much as the church's acceptance of me as an insider, and Atlanta was my great opportunity to reach inside and test that wish. I wanted them to crown the outsider. I dreamed of becoming a ceremony even though I knew beyond redemption that it would never happen. The church was like family—it was not of my blood, yet had become my blood, calling home its rebel son. But it was not going to accept what I'd chosen to become.

My spirit was heavy with confusion. I didn't know what I truly wanted, I only knew that the church lay near the heart of it. I loved the church, perhaps as an ally in the shape of Wesley Methodist, perhaps simply as my oppressor, but I loved it enough to yearn for its recognition. Yet I also hated the church for what it did to people, how it misused and made them meek, with no chance at all of inheriting the earth. I desperately wanted to change that. Gripped by contradictory desires, I longed to storm the church and have it welcome me at the same time. Could I accept the fact that they would never respect me as an important influence? I realized I had no choice there, but still there was the gnawing question: *What if they were right?*

What if I were not important? What if I couldn't reach them, ever? The question of my importance was *their* decision, not mine. I stood beyond the church's gates, my power determined by the people inside; either they would change at my insistence, recognize my name, or ignore me. No matter what, it was in their hands. Me against them, and I was an outlaw. I was outside.

I made page 2 of the morning's *Atlanta Constitution.* In a rather long story on my tumultuous arrival and press conference, the very first word was *controversial.* I took that to be a good sign.

Early in the morning, going against the grain of commute traffic, I drove back out to the airport to welcome a planeload of Glide community people and staff who'd come to be with me. It was a joyous scene, and they cut quite a sight. I was particularly proud of their motley composition: There were black street people and middle-class housewives and gays and men whose appearance belonged in an "ordinary" church. They were a microcosm of Glide on display for the church at large, and each of them knew they would have to stand their ground. Throughout the day, I saw them locked in conversation with others about Glide. They couldn't escape the controversy, and I don't think any of them wished to. Their presence meant more to me than I possibly could have told them.

We went straight from the airport to the motel, where everyone agreed that I should be left alone to concentrate. I returned to my room and spent much of the morning in a fog. I felt as if my entire life was building up inside me, struggling to break loose. There would be an explosion. It was inevitable now.

Around 10:30 A.M., I was called to a first-floor room where some of my security people were staying. The place was swarming with state and local police officials who informed us they'd received numerous threats on my life and said they had information that several fundamentalist groups might disrupt the afternoon service at which I was to speak. We talked strategy for a while, and agreed that while I spoke my own security people would remain close to me and act at my direction. The police were relegated to being a backup force, a role they seemed willing to accept.

As I climbed the stairs to my room, images of death flashed through my mind. Assassination. It had been done before, it would be done again. Was the risk worth my life? I thought about it a moment, climbing up those stairs, and decided it probably wasn't. But was there something greater than the beauties and indignities of my own personal life that was worth dying for? There had to be. What kind of minister was I? I had to know the answer. Fragments of a life unfolding with the quickness of heavy rain rushed by me, leading me back to the climb up the stairs. Revelation was worth dying for, because without it there is no life. Before me stood the temptation to desire death; to be Christlike, if not Godlike; to ensure and validate my importance; to beg for the answer. But life was too precious to me. I had no yearning to become a martyr. It was simply the choice between risking one death and living out another, hunched like a beggar with the ceiling beating down on me.

The phone was ringing as I opened the door. When I answered it, I recognized the voice of an old friend from my days on Huston-Tillotson's faculty. He said he'd just passed First Methodist Church and people were already lining up to get in. It was only 1 o'clock in the afternoon, and the service wasn't scheduled to begin until 4.

"You're gonna get a mighty big crowd, Cecil," he said.

I thanked him, hung up, and with a shudder grew increasingly frightened of what the afternoon represented. A mighty big crowd. They were there, inside the walls already, and they were going to call my hand. There was no escape. I felt painfully vulnerable. The presence of all those people made it imperative that I prove I was different. I had to reveal, enact, authenticate that difference. I had to make it count for something. At 2:30, when I walked across the motel lobby and out into the Georgia sun, I was in a million pieces.

First Methodist Church was only half a block from the motel. When I set foot on the church grounds, a few people hurried to embrace me and offer their encouragement. Others looked at me with naked curiosity, while still others stood far back as if I had something they might catch. I had the feeling that the difference, whatever it was, was already in evidence. The impromptu reception on the church lawn was like the first skirmish of the battle, and I had come through it unhurt. Some of them considered me important.

Inside, the sanctuary was packed, not a seat to be had. Not knowing which way to go, I walked down the center aisle, pushed along by the hum of thousands of voices. People touched me and called out my name. As I neared the pulpit, I ducked through a side door and found the church office. In minutes the room was filled with people from Black Methodists for Church Renewal and from the Glide community. Their presence enriched me. The Soul Exposition, an Atlanta band that was to play behind me, arrived and began setting up.

"We have to *do* something."

I looked up and recognized the face of one of the commission members.

"There's far too many people," he said hurriedly. "Do you realize there are thousands of people, *thousands*, out there on the sidewalk? Well, anyway, we called the Civic Auditorium and they said it would be all right if we moved the service there. How do you feel about that?"

His announcement simultaneously unnerved and gladdened me. I was to be, as advertised, an event.

"I want everyone to participate, but I'd like to go out there and ask the people what they want to do," I said.

We rose as a group and made our way down a narrow hall. I heard the buzz of people waiting as the sanctuary opened before me. I walked toward the pulpit. Hard. Determined. Like stepping on bones and hearing them crunch. Booming applause rolled toward me in huge waves.

I stood in the pulpit and looked out at the people, the incarnation of the church. It wasn't pride I felt, nor was it vengeance. It was more that my existence mattered. In that precious instant, one speck among a million others, I felt powerfully free.

"Brothers and sisters, we have a choice to make," I said.

I told them about the thousands outside and presented the possibility of moving three blocks to the Civic Auditorium, where the general conference itself was being held.

"How do you feel? Can we go to the auditorium?"

Cheers formed their answer. My fingers gripped the edge of the pulpit.

"We've made our point," I declared. "We have won my right to speak at First Methodist Church, and now I'm ready to move on to the Civic Auditorium!"

Standing in that pulpit was a great moment for me, representing as it did a certain triumph over the forces of racism and rejection, but it reflected a decision already made, a victory already won. It was the easy part.

They ushered me out the side exit to a waiting state police station wagon. Dusk drew down on Atlanta as we inched out of the parking lot into heavy traffic. I saw the exodus in twilight, thousands marching from the church to the auditorium, shoulder to shoulder, hip to hip, hand to hand. I thought I heard some of them singing.

At the auditorium, they took me to a backstage room where I was to wait while the band tore down its equipment, hauled it from the church to the auditorium, and set it up all over again. I listened to the scuffle of footsteps and the clatter of folding chairs, sounds of the auditorium beginning to fill. A Black Methodist for Church Renewal worker made his way to me. He was beaming.

"Coretta King has just come in," he said with unabashed pleasure and pride.

"Take me to her," I replied, and a group of them led me away. I saw her in the front lobby with Andy Young and a few others. At that time, I wouldn't have called her a close friend, but we'd met a couple of times before. I'd received no word that she planned to come, so her presence was a shock and surprise. We approached one another and embraced. Some of the passers-by stopped to gawk.

"I've come to be with you and support you," she said.

"Thank you," I answered. "I'm so proud that you have." I knew that her presence and support would legitimize me in the eyes of many who'd put me down. I'm sure she knew it, too. Her unsolicited willingness to stand with me at such an important hour would make a difference, and I've never forgotten her for it.

We patterned the service after the Glide celebration. With more than 6,000 people in the auditorium, the Soul Exposition played, and we sang "Go Down Moses" and "Precious Lord." A black woman from the Glide community read a liturgy entitled "The Time for Confronting Our Hang-Ups," which concluded with the line "Judgment Day means to decide!"

We were different. That much had been established, but I wasn't sure it had begun to count for anything. Before the service, Coretta had told me she'd be pleased to speak briefly to the crowd, and so she was called to the platform.

"My husband's movement started fifteen and a half years ago," she said. "Although some people don't realize it, his movement was always a movement of the church. As he often said, 'The church should be a headlight pointing the way for the world, and not a taillight merely reflecting the world.' I am here to participate and support Cecil in the fine work he's doing," she said. The people, many of whom shared the same city with her, responded warmly to her words.

I heard Jack Tuell's voice introduce me, but I couldn't really connect with the words. Slips of notepaper that I clutched grew moist in my hands. It was time. After forty-two years, reaching so far back, past seminary, past my first sermon preached at the age of twelve, past even Papa Jack and Mother to the harsh, cold wetness of birth, now it was time. I mounted the platform and heard the noise rise from the arena floor. I gulped one last breath and prepared to begin.

Out of the corner of my eye, I saw him rush the platform at an oblique angle, moving with the herky-jerk of an enraged puppet. Nothing about him seemed to match. One arm flailed at the air while the elbow of the other remained crooked and twitched back and forth in the antithesis of rhythm. I saw that he wore a cast on the crooked arm. A young white man with reddish-blond hair cut close to his bobbing head, he wore a suit capable of concealing a weapon. Leaping awkwardly onto the stage, he aimed his vacant eyes at me. As he approached, I saw he was shaking all over. Across his face swept a startling mixture of ecstasy and terror.

"I've got to speak, I must speak," he shrieked. My chief security person moved quickly to intercept him, but I knew in my soul that the young man would have none of it. He was wild, past the fear of anything except what throbbed inside him. He

124

was running on sheer instinct. Hands jumped to grab him. I was running on instinct too. Before anyone touched him, I firmly said, "Let him speak." I gave him the microphone. As he took it, he looked in my direction, almost as if he didn't even realize I was there. His hands were trembling nearly as much as his voice.

"My heart is bleeding for the youth of America who are being led to hell by the likes of Cecil Williams," he said, choking on a sob. "I call on you, Brother Cecil Williams, to repent and believe in the Lord Jesus Christ, and to stop your support of the Communist menace. And I call on all of you to turn away from Cecil Williams and eternal hell, and turn to Jesus Christ."

The young man, who was later identified as the director of a fundamentalist youth group, went on for a couple of minutes. I made no effort to interfere. When he finished, a young woman with him also asked to speak, but I told her she'd already been represented. The audience sat through it all in uneasy silence, shaken by the threatening unpredictability of the episode. It was not the young man's words that disturbed the people, for they were about what you'd expect from the fundamentalist faction for which they spoke. No, it was the way the confrontation burst on the auditorium. I'd dealt with many similar outbursts at Glide. But Atlanta wasn't Glide, and never was that more evident than when that young man rushed the platform and I let him speak.

Even before he spoke, I knew instinctively that I'd made a very important decision. I was a man who'd been denied all his life, yet I chose not to deny this frazzled young man whose sole purpose was to destroy me. The entire Glide experience, including the aberrations its openness invited, was being placed before the church in Atlanta, and people squirmed at the sight of it.

They led him away. The incident had drawn me from behind the podium so that nothing stood between the audience and me. The faces, a bit older and much more homogeneous than those at Glide, looked to me with naked expectation. My jury, whether I liked it or not. I had traveled 3,000 miles to place myself before them, and I'd remained awake nearly the entire night wondering what would happen when I spoke to them. In seconds it would begin to happen, and still I didn't know what I would say. I was up against it. All the way. Revelation would wait no longer.

"I've not come here to scare you to death."
The words rang true in the stale air.
"I've come to scare you to life!"
So sweet and pure and painful. The unconscious, spontaneous articulation of my strongest desire. In that sense, then, the truth. It was as if I'd been locked in a special room but had just thrown open the door and now, after so many years, had the freedom to walk outside. For the briefest moment as I hollered those first words, I lost control of myself. Nothing mattered then but the truth as I felt it. I did not perceive the audience as my jury. I did not sense the cameras rolling.

It felt like a good beginning.

But they were the church. In the very next instant, I realized that was as true as anything I could ever say, and the whole thing was about the relationship between the two of us. Me and them. That's why I was standing before 6,000 people, sadly unable to resolve the inner conflict that was rapidly reducing me to someone less than myself. I wanted to rail against them and force them to confront their greatest failure, their fear of the world. But that was neutralized by my longing for them to open their arms to me and recognize my substance. I wanted them to make me an important figure. On my terms or theirs, would they ever let me inside? The question's inherent imbalance of power tortured me as I stood before them. What kind of minister was I? It was no longer my question to answer.

The more anguished I became, the louder my words boomed. My voice thundered against the walls, trying without hope to make up for the deficit within me. I danced and whirled and strutted and yelled. Many of the people appeared astonished and enthralled. I was different from any preacher they'd ever seen or heard. I was fulfilling their expectations, I was becoming their perception. I was a media event, I was a show. They appeared to enjoy me.

I was faking it, a truth that only a few among the Glide

contingent may have recognized, and my knowledge of that deception drove me further toward desperation. Without missing a beat—I had stage presence and "charisma"; the media said so—I glanced at my notes, something I hadn't done since the long summer in Hobbs. Furious capitulation. Trying to get inside. Even though I wrapped them in my own jazzy, extemporaneous style, I advanced the notepaper's polished propositions simply to impress the church. My sermon had a backbeat; otherwise, I was the essence of the clergyman delivering the Word.

I screamed about a "new church" whose most vital concerns would be for people and not money or property. The crowd responded but didn't really hear me. The new church would accept *me!* That's what I was saying. But I could tell it wasn't happening. They were accepting me as something "interesting," perhaps a little strange, but nothing beyond that. I was becoming what they wished me to become.

I am not one of you!

Revenge, the strongest temptation of all. Revenge against the church, revenge against the white folks back in San Angelo, revenge against being denied. Jutting from behind the podium, I screamed at them:

"I used to despise myself!"

All the history that had gathered in my body began to come out. I told them about niggers having big lips and nappy hair and loose joints and their own smell. I told them about all the skin brighteners and hair straighteners. I told them about how it all used to make me feel so ashamed. And I hollered that I wasn't ashamed anymore.

"I've accepted who I am, and I'm so glad. I rejoice in being Cecil Williams!"

In one sense I was making no progress at all, for in embracing my alienation from the church I was still granting it the power to exclude me. Yet screaming the words felt good to me because, for the first time since my sermon's opening moments, I was telling my story and nobody else's. It seemed my only source of power. Hacking through the swirling words, one of my voices reached me like the clap of my hands.

You can only be who you are. That is your only message.

The voice spoke with compassionate assurance. I couldn't hear anything else.

Accept the fact that you will never be what they want you to be. And accept the fact that you cannot make them do what you want them to do. The bosom of Abraham beats within you. Don't reveal them—reveal yourself!

I jumped from behind the podium once more, scattering my notes on the floor. Quickly I strode across the platform, saying nothing, then wheeled to march back the other way. I hadn't said a word yet, but it made no difference. It would come now. Halfway back across the platform, I turned with jarring suddenness, swooped onto the auditorium floor, and began walking among the people.

"I have walked in the valley of the dry bones!"

It came to me as revelation comes, and I was there in the valley. The door to my room squeaked as I opened it for the final time and stepped into a blazing heat strong enough to bleach the earth into a shimmering, oppressive, crystal whiteness. Except for the knotted skeletons of dead trees and the calcified lumps strewn across the ground, the landscape was hopelessly barren.

"And I have seen the people in the valley of the dry bones."

They were as passive and meek as the empty gestures of their lives. Death reeked from their bones.

"The hand of life is upon us to walk through the valley of the dry bones, among the poor, the oppressed, the disenchanted, the sick, the exprisoners, the drug addicts, the alcoholics, the prostitutes, the gays, and—would you believe?—the middle and upper class. I saw *you* in the valley where the message must be: 'We accept you, we have life, now live it!' "

I told the dead there might be a way out. They castigated me. I spoke of their freedom. They grew angry. I told them they could remain in the valley but I was going to move. Some of them stood and recanted their criticism, but others became more vitriolic. I stood my ground and replied that I could only decide for myself. I said to them:

"These bones are gonna walk again!"

The Civic Auditorium spread before me with astonishing clarity.

"These bones are gonna fight again, these bones are gonna love again!"

From every corner of the room, I felt them flow into me. In the context of their own experiences, they felt what I felt.

"I know what it's like to be in the valley of the dry bones but I want you to know I'm not in the valley of the dry bones no more because I'm alive!"

My voice heard me. It yelled back:

I am the church!

I am the church. Yes, and only then can I let it go. Only then is there nothing left to prove.

"You cannot hold me back any longer because I'm alive."

Murmurs grew to cheers. I had them, but that didn't matter any more, because they were not the source of my redemptive freedom.

"The church, any church must begin by accepting people where they are. Your whiteness is important to you, you keep it. I don't want it. My blackness is important to me, and you can't take it away. Hey, people! Hey, United Methodists! Wake up—risk, revolution, revelation are here!"

I am the church.

It was done.

So many people considered it a total victory, for I had said and done so much, darting from side to side, flitting this way and that, shadow-boxing with my own conflict. You might say I'd lived up to my billing. Never had they seen anything quite like me, and they sought me out to proclaim my finest hour.

It seemed that only I knew better.

Beneath the deluge of their pressing flesh and handsome compliments, I was still torn. The condition of life, true enough. But its intensity then was nearly enough to destroy me. *I* knew I hadn't done it all, not as I could have done it. More than that, I knew that nothing had really happened. I'd journeyed all the way across the country wanting to know in advance what was going to happen, and now that it had finally happened, I *still* didn't know. The church wasn't going to change as a result of my sermon, as all along I realized it wouldn't. Neither did the church call my name as one of its own, and neither did it ignore or ostracize me. It was vast enough, amorphous enough to swallow me without a sound. It was powerful enough to do nothing. A monstrous void consumed the pit of my body, deep and eternal like the valley of the dry bones itself. And I was falling through it alone, beyond the touch of the human hand.

At the same time, of course, I was richly exultant at the attention being showered on me. I needed badly to be reassured. I needed reaffirmation of my identity, even if that identity was the creation of others.

I remained on the premises for nearly an hour. Night had fallen by the time I was reminded of an invitation to appear at a Black Methodists for Church Renewal meeting. I'd pledged my presence and so was dumped in yet another car for the ride across town, inhumanly tired and spent (so I thought) of all that I had. I left the Civic Auditorium realizing I had missed the significance of the event. I'd left out something important.

In the mild evening air, I heard clapping and shouting issuing from the church. The meeting had obviously already started, and I felt momentarily uncomfortable at the implied arrogance and insensitivity of my late arrival. They were my own people, and I didn't wish to slight them in any way. With a bit of extra effort, I climbed the few steps and walked into the church. When they saw me in the doorway, everything stopped. One by one they began applauding, cheering, and shouting "Amen," louder and louder, longer and longer, stronger and stronger. It must've gone on for a good five minutes, the kind of acknowledgment I'd never before received from any church group.

They were crowning me. In the most profound sense, they were embracing our differences because they understood so well our common ground. They escorted me to the front of the room just like we used to do with an important visiting preacher back home. In short order, they dispensed with what they'd been doing when I arrived, then called on me to speak. I had no notes, no plan, no need to prove a thing. Although we were not the same, I was one of them.

"Kill the church."

The raucous and emotional "Amens" vanished in an instant. For a moment the room remained utterly silent, but I didn't have to worry. They knew what I meant. I told them how it was when I, a black minister, took over Glide, a white church.

"Glide Church was dying a slow death!" I roared, oblivious to all but what I needed to say. If there were any cameras or reporters there, I didn't notice them. "I killed it, and that's what all of us must do. The churches are dying, and we've got to make sure that in order to live they die all the way.

"And if those folks over at the Civic Auditorium are to live, they must hear this word and enact it!"

We went downtown to eat and unwind, and I seemed the center of all attention. Strangers of all colors stopped me on the street and pumped my hand. Atop the clamor of traffic, I heard my name called over and over as fingers pointed to me across crowded boulevards and through throngs of weeknight celebrants. In the glare of neon and river of gleaming metal, Atlanta revolved around me.

As we entered a restaurant, a large and light-skinned black man was coming out. He introduced himself as Maynard Jackson (who had not yet ascended to the mayor's office) and told me how proud he was that I had come to Atlanta.

Back on the street after dinner, we were pushing through the crowd when a woman grabbed my arm. She was tall, black, and attractive, with straightened hair cascading down around her shoulders.

"Cecil Williams!" she exclaimed. "Don't you remember me?"

I apologized for my failing memory.

"I used to live in San Francisco. Worked the streets downtown."

A murky recollection shaped itself in my mind. The woman had been a prostitute in the Tenderloin. I nodded.

"Yeah, I went to Glide all the time. Came down here to try it out, but I want you to know something. I ain't doin' that no more, and you helped me change," she said. "I just wanted you to know that."

She faded back into the street. I haven't seen her since.

I awoke early the following morning and scoured the motel lobby for a paper. The morning's report of the night before seemed somehow crucial to me. I still nurtured a need, perhaps stronger than ever now, to know how it had turned out. I needed to be verified. It was so early that the night clerk was still on duty.

"Damn paper's late again," he grumbled.

I turned to walk away.

"Wait a minute!" he said suddenly. "You're the one, aren't you?"

He was a white man getting on in years. I didn't know whether I was in for an insult or not.

"Well," he crowed, "it's a pleasure to have you as our guest. Yessir, a real pleasure."

I returned to the lobby three more times with no luck. Around 6 A.M., the paper finally arrived. I was splashed all over the front page. There was a photo of Coretta and me, and a lengthy, very favorable story by Bill Buchanan, the *Constitution* reporter I'd met two days earlier at the airport. The headline read, *6,000 Get Involved with Cecil Williams.* I was the talk of the town. I was success.

It was late morning, after we'd eaten, when the cab came to take us to the airport. To tell you the truth, I was looking forward to getting the hell out of Atlanta. The driver was a very dark black man whose face lit up when he recognized his fare.

"Man," he chortled gleefully, *"everybody's* talkin' 'bout you this morning. I wish you coulda heard the brothers in the yard. You really did us good. Yes, suh."

He was like a radio. Constant noise all the way to the airport. Unlike others who'd complimented me, he didn't make me at all uneasy because he knew what he was saying, and why. He was like an emissary from the world, a world that had not been present in the Civic Auditorium.

"You sure shook up a lotta folks while you were here, and Lord knows this place need to be kicked in the ass. Uh, 'scuse me, Revren."

I chuckled. "Brother, you told it just right."

"Yes, in*deed!* Shook up plenty white folks. And you know one thing? I'm so glad we can shake up white folks too!"

On entering the terminal, I immediately searched for a copy of the *Journal,* Atlanta's afternoon paper. Luckily, the first edition had just hit the streets. I snapped up a copy and sat down in a lounge to read it. I was below the fold but still front-page news, which propped up my spirits in the same rather empty way that the *Constitution*'s front page had heartened me.

The story meandered through the sermon in the auditorium, giving special play to the young man who had jumped onto the stage. As I had expected, the stories in both papers were quite similar, frequently even identical. But toward the end of the *Journal* copy, the scene shifted to the black church meeting. Funny, I hadn't noticed any reporters there. My eyes wandered over the lines of type until, in a moment still strikingly clear to me, they came upon a single paragraph containing a statement I had made.

Kill the church.

The words jumped out at me, just as they had jumped spontaneously from my mouth in the black church. Leaving me no way out. I'd left the black Methodists no escape either, which was why they had grown so suddenly still and silent. It was all becoming clear to me.

Transfixed, I stared at that paragraph, gripped by its implications. It was somewhat like finding *Fuck the Church* on the men's-room wall. Except these were *my* words, as inescapable as my pulse. I couldn't deny them to myself. In desperation I could pretend I hadn't said them, but I could never pretend I didn't hear them. Amounting to a glorious and horrible discovery, a confrontation with myself. The word was out on me.

Kill the church. Words embodied with a power of terrifying dimension. It was not that I alone had the power to accomplish the act, merely that I had the power to say the words and stick by them. And the words themselves were a statement of suicide, because if I didn't die first my declaration would have the hollow sound of hypocrisy. As much as anyone in the Civic Auditorium, I was the church, and I could never demand the church's death until I took responsibility for my own. That was the horror, reviving me with a clean, intense sense of danger that forced me to understand why I had felt so empty and confused in Atlanta. All along I had realized a killing had to be done, but I had surrendered the responsibility for it. I had given it to them because I was horrified at the prospect of killing myself, severing the cord that bound me to the church. Without risking anything, I wanted them to die. *Kill the church.* But it wasn't going to work like that. I had to do the killing, and I had to start with myself.

What kind of minister was I? The question had dogged me to Atlanta and tracked me across the auditorium stage, but as I read and reread the words in the paper, I understood, in a moment of simple transformation, that while the answer mattered, asking the question did not. And part of the horror lay in a single blade of illumination. In Atlanta I had come to know, finally, that the church would never accept me for who I was. But what I hadn't understood was that whether the church accepted me didn't matter.

There was grave horror and danger implicit in killing the church, but it would not be a cold-blooded death—it would be a death with passion. It would not occur in the marbled halls of its structure, in the corners of its ecclesiastical rooms. The church would not die there; it would die in the world. Killing the church meant creating new life in the world, among its people. Death before rebirth, funeral before pregnancy. I had to kill the church; I had to kill myself. These were my responsibilities, and I couldn't escape them any longer.

I had come to Atlanta a rebel son, and I was leaving Atlanta a rebel son. Once and for all I had let the family go, and said to them, "I no longer belong to you, I am now responsible to the world."

EIGHT

I WOKE just before dawn that Sunday morning, but then I always do. Because January 1979 was San Francisco's coldest of the decade, it had been a brittle night, one that had begged for comfort. The kind of icy darkness in which the body curls around itself beneath layers of blanket, and warmth is especially soothing because one knows how cold it is out there. In such uncommon coldness, any warmth is precious. The early morning was that kind of cold.

I remember rolling out of bed with the conviction that something was terribly wrong. Not with me as such, nor with the tranquil, sighing house, nor with my two sleeping children, Kim and Albert (their mother and I had recently divorced). In short, the tremor had nothing to do with my immediate surroundings. It was more like this:

I knew the world was going mad.

Of course I'd known it all my life, but only in a somewhat disjointed fashion, as one forms fleeting impressions of the countryside from the compartment of a moving train. Never had it seized me with the clarity of that Sunday at first light.

Standing barefoot on the hardwood floor of my living room, I saw America as a huge canister of nerve gas rolling haphazardly around the floor of a rambling boxcar. Attached to the top of the canister was a small round gauge with a series of numbers and a lone hypertensive needle. The needle quivered continually. The gauge reminded me of blood pressure apparatus. I stepped back to gain a better look and saw that the boxcar was connected to nothing. The canister slammed with a vengeance against the boxcar walls. Nerve gas. Odorless, colorless, invisible. The boxcar sped crazily down the tracks, clacking with an ever more alarming cadence. A man lay across the tracks some distance ahead, the boxcar careening toward him. In that instant, I knew that when the boxcar crashed into the man's body it would derail and send the canister hurtling through space to explode on the floor of the ravine below.

Maybe the vision is a bit too apocalyptic; it was not meant to be. Poised on the mountainside in the early morning frost, I did not take it literally. It was not, for example, symbolic of the neutron bomb. Actually, the neutron bomb was symbolic of *it*. The vision contained a reality of violence and suppressed anger, a society contaminated with the emotional equivalent of Legionnaire's disease.

You may wish to dismiss it as self-indulgent pessimism and doomsaying, which to compound its foolishness is years behind the times. But what gripped me that Sunday morning was my utter inability to ignore the vision's wholeness.

It is true, the country is not torn with chaos as it was ten years ago. There's no Vietnam, no riots, no "counterculture," no nothing. A recession, sure. A shortage of energy, yes. But we're not talking loudness here, the bullhorn sound of mass protest and tactical repression. This was the end of the 1970s; something else was hissing below the surface. Listen to it:

All across the country, the wintry climate was uncommonly treacherous in 1979. The paper reported an epidemic of cabin fever in the storm battered Midwest; people probing each other's nerves, threatening to blow apart as a simple result of enforced proximity.

I read where a man in Chicago started smashing cars with a snow plow. One person was crushed to death, and when they caught the snow plow man he only screamed, "I hate my life!" and "I want to see my kids!" The same two things over and over. Winter murders. Even in San Francisco, that most pleasant of cities, it felt like winter in 1979.

With winter approaching, a man picked up a teenaged girl, drove her to Lake Tahoe in northern California, and raped her repeatedly. While he had her, the man hacked off both the girl's arms with an ax, then dumped her in a ditch along a lonely stretch of highway slicing through the Central Valley. Summoning incredible courage, the girl managed to climb from the ditch, seek help, and, in a manner of speaking, survive.

A mother lived alone with her two small children in a highrise apartment. A suburb someplace. That's important, I think, but I can't remember exactly where it was. Some details you tend to forget. Anyhow, the mother threw her two kids off the apartment balcony. Imagine them falling now, almost weightless in the crisp winter air, their limbs flailing about as if their panic might somehow enable them to fly. See the concrete barreling toward them with the power, speed, and indestructibility of a locomotive, until it becomes a gigantic gray blot. Imagine the point of impact. It'll only take you a second. Or let's say you're at the scene. What do you hear? Is the first sound a thud or plop like dropping a bag of wet laundry from the roof? Maybe it's a crunch or crack like snapping a tree limb across your knee.

By the way, the mother then killed herself. Does that in any way restore a sense of justice?

Violence and suppressed anger. Hissing. Rape, murder, blood. The land is soaked with it. On a clear day you can see all the way to South Africa, Marcos' Philippines, Pinoche's Chile. Okay, call those political situations. Avoid the connections if you wish, but that doesn't mean they aren't there. Like it or not, they help frame your existence. The violence in the world is the violence in your family, although you may have enough defenses to ignore the bond between them.

Can you avoid those two small children smashing into the pavement? Perhaps. It wasn't me, you say. But it's not a question of literal culpability as much as it's a question of atmosphere, climate, unseen hatred, unspoken anger, unpredictable violence. You could be driving home from work tomorrow and some guy on top of a building with an automatic weapon could blow you away as you sit waiting for the light to change. Perhaps just as horrifying, he could as easily murder the driver behind or ahead of you. For no reason. You want to try avoiding that one? I'll admit it doesn't happen very often, it only happens enough. Hey, I'm not trying to scare you or anything. I'm just presenting evidence. All right, I sense that some of you still aren't convinced that the man and the canister exist, so I'll rest my case by posing one final question:

When you walk down the street, do you ever feel afraid?

Comeback question:

The world *is* going mad, isn't it?

I thought about all these things as the sun rose above the sleepy houses that Sunday morning, and I became extremely angry. Angry at the waste of life, the violence, the destruction. Angry at the contrived and terrifying conceit that things are more or less all right. Angry at the mother for murdering her children and angry at those who could have touched her before that horrible act. Angry at all the distractions that keeps people apart. Staring out my living room window at the lifeless street, under my breath so as not to wake anyone, I whispered, "I will not conspire with madness. I will not concede to a world going mad."

I stood gazing down at the serene street. Not a soul walked along it. The scene's inertia screamed silently about so much. It was as if the entire world had gone to sleep. Anger broke free within me, building to a point of demanding expression. Dressed only in sweat pants, I threw open the French doors, stepped onto the tiny balcony, and screamed as loudly as I could into the bitter stillness.

"Wake up! Wake up! Come alive!"

At church that morning, I shouted at the congregation, "I'm an angry man this morning! I'm angry because there's a crisis in all our lives, and a lot of us don't want to do anything about it. But I came here to let you know something. There is no greater road to freedom than crisis!"

I thought to myself, *Some of them don't want to hear that.* Such avoidance was one of the things that had angered me in the first place. The sanctuary was nearly full, and the morning was cold, not much warmer than when I'd risen.

"But there's a lotta folks who don't want you to know that. They tell you to avoid it if you can. They talk about stayin' away from trouble, but you're *always* in trouble. Don't you know that? And if they can't get you to avoid the crisis then they want you to—"

Mimic them, I thought. Extend them to the absurdity of their message. Make them sound so nice that they become dishonest.

"—ad-*just* to it. You know, be calm, stay cool, don't let yourself go. But that's not the way you feel, is it? You know it isn't, but America is a place where you're not supposed to feel crisis, America is a place where you're not supposed to get concerned. Well, I wanna tell you something: You can't escape it. You can't *escaaaaaape*, and that's why, when you try to escape, it only gets worse.

"What I'm really tryin' to say is that all of us have crisis. It's all around us, in our personal lives and the life of the world. I don't care how much money you got, how many cars you got, what kind of house you got—you still got crisis. And the critical thing is that only in *cri-sis* can you discover who you are! Lemme give you an example. When I was a young boy, I went out of my head. Night after night I saw people and things comin' to get me. I tried everything, man. I called on God and everybody else to take care of *my* crisis, but I only survived when I began to face it myself. I met my aliens, my crisis, and said, 'I know you're mine and I'm not gonna let you control me no more!' I'm sayin' don't run away from it 'cause you can't get away from it anyway. Don't try to hide it and don't try to deny it. I get so angry when people come up to me and say everything's just fine—*'cause everything ain't just fine!* And don't try to adjust to it, either. It's *your* crisis. Take hold of it and make somethin' out of it. Turn it into life! 'Cause that's what it is in the first place."

Most of the people descended the stairs in tight, animated, little clusters. There was the bustle of activity about them even though the cramped stairwell rendered rapid movement impossible. I embraced them all, one to the next. The third person from the end was a comfortably hip-looking white man with an expansive, rather innocuous face. Although his appearance was not terribly distinctive, something about him interested me. He wore a brushed cotton bush jacket, checkered shirt open at the neck, a pair of tactfully wrinkled corduroy trousers, and oxblood boots. The look of devised tolerance and informality. A pair of gold-rimmed glasses straddled the bridge of his nose, and there was something deviously calm in his eyes. His openness felt somehow out of focus; he seemed the kind of good friend who would turn secrets into weapons.

As he reached the bottom step he threw his arms around me and placed his lips near my ear.

"I have an appointment with you," he whispered.

His announcement intrigued me. I'd never seen him before, but I don't memorize my calendar either. I looked at him questioningly.

"Yes," he said. "Tuesday, at three."

"Who are you?"

"Gotta run," he said, shoving a cream-colored business card into my hand. "See you then."

I watched him lope through the crowd and disappear. Not bothering to look at it right away, I slipped the card into my pants pocket. Well, why not? It's not my style to turn people away. Later, sitting in my office, I retrieved the card. Two lines of thin type on beige. They read, *Lucius A. Masters, Doctor of Psychiatry.* Nothing more. I chuckled and muttered to myself:

"Maybe he thinks one of us is crazy."

Moses *is* crazy. At least that's the going diagnosis. It's undoubtedly correct, as far as it goes. Moses (that's what he chooses to call himself) is tall, black, and strong, a tower of a man who divides his time between living in California mental institutions and living in the streets.

America, meet your bogeyman.

Moses has flashlight eyes more powerful than television. Moses plays his guitar and beats people over the head with it. Moses peed in the corner of my office lobby and then bragged about it.

"I want you to remember my smell," he said.

Moses is an emotional vampire. When he talks, it's difficult not to become absorbed. And Moses is always talking. I'll bet you could go down to the Greyhound Bus Depot at three in the morning and Moses would be there, if they let him stay, reciting poetry and raising hell. Moses spends days at a time scribbling poetry in a childlike scrawl. Bright colors sometimes seem best then, reds and greens and yellows, although black is all right too. Moses has conquered time and treats it like a piece of butcher paper. One moment he's a child (he always says he's a child; sometimes you believe him), and the next moment he's an old man, and it all sounds pretty much the same until you really begin to listen. Moses *compels* you to the point where you become him and he becomes you and all you hear is the torrent of words sucking at you like a river current pulling the pair of you as close to his vision as the river goes that day. When he glides between good and evil, reality and fantasy, sanity and insanity, Moses is as naked as the day he was born. Sometimes he makes you feel naked too. Moses is crazy, all right, and when he's on the street he hangs around the office a lot.

Moses met me at the office door wearing his mad, coercive smile. I nodded to him. His hair was clipped short in typical institutional debasement. The hairline crawled halfway up the back of his skull and there were indentations pocketed within the hair. You could tell by his haircut that Moses hadn't been out too long.

"One thing, I just wanna tell you one thing," he implored in his raspy voice.

"Moses," I replied, holding up my hand as if to stop him. Fat chance.

"Just one thing. Really, it's important. It won't take long, okay?"

"What is it, Moses?"

His eyes bulged. The veins running up his neck popped out in evidence of his concentration. That one important thing. His black face melted back into that grin, and his eyes became beams of concern.

"You didn't get much sleep last night, huh?" he asked.

"Moses—"

"Know how I know? 'Cause your eyes ain't clear. There's all this stuff in 'em and you can't see it because they're *your* eyes, but I can see it 'cause—I didn't sleep at all last night—"

"Moses—"

"—I was down on Sixth Street and then they put me outta the BART station and—"

"MOSES!"

The words ceased. Maybe it was because I yelled.

"Moses," I said in exasperation, "I'm busy right now. What is it you want to say to me?"

"Oh," he said wonderingly, as if I'd just reminded him of something. "—Yeah. Well, see, I found out somethin' this morning and I wanna tell you about it 'cause I know you're gonna like it—Okay, okay, here it is. I'm not gonna die today. Wanna know why?"

What can you do?

"Why?"

" 'Cause I'm just a kid, that's why. And you wanna know somethin' else?"

"What?"

"You're my father, nigger!"

His grin exploded into laughter.

"Bet you didn't know that, huh?"

He gave me my chance, and I took it.

"Yeah, nigger, I know it," I replied as sternly as I could. "And now your daddy's telling you to sit down and be quiet or else I'm gonna put you outta here!"

Moses stiffened and his jaws got tight. Up and down his face, muscles protruded. He pretended to be hurt and angry, but the torrent stopped. I turned to walk toward my office. Over my shoulder I heard him holler, "Just one last thing!"

I wheeled around.

"Keep your black ass alive!"

Moses was screaming at the top of his considerable voice, cracking into intermittent fits of booming laughter. Behind him, unnoticed in the storm, stood the silent figure of Lucius A. Masters, Doctor of Psychiatry. Most people are reluctant to challenge Moses' sense of territory, and the strange psychiatrist seemed no exception. I motioned him to come forward. He slid around Moses.

"Come into my office."

The psychiatrist slid around me too and waited in the doorway to the set of inner offices. Moses, uncommonly silent, watched the man traverse the office lobby, his hypnotic eyes fixed on a spot below the psychiatrist's neck.

The psychiatrist sat very correctly on the corner of the spongy brown couch and peered at me from behind the glasses, weighing his opening gambit. There were lines on his forehead I hadn't noticed before. He fetched a small black notebook from his coat pocket and adjusted his glasses.

"Well, this is a switch. I'm on the couch and you're in the chair."

He smiled wanly.

"Cecil." He produced a cardboard packet of European cigarettes and offered me one. I declined. "Is that too informal?"

"No, that's fine."

"You can call me Luke."

I grunted and waited. He shrugged and dropped the packet back into his pocket without taking a cigarette for himself.

"This is a relaxed situation, right?"

"How can I help you?"

His eyes performed like a camera, holding still for a few seconds until they'd seen what they wished to see—click—then moving almost imperceptibly to another region of my face.

"I've got a problem, Cecil."

"What kind of problem?"

"Actually, *we* have a problem."

"We do?"

"Yes."

He flipped through the notebook but I could tell by his eyes that it was only a ploy. I decided that Lucius A. (Luke) Masters, Doctor of Psychiatry, was either very arrogant or quite afraid. Maybe both.

"Cecil, I've got a very respectable private practice going. Nothing elaborate and extravagant, you understand. Quite small as a matter of fact, but each of my patients is an acute sufferer, if you know what I mean. That is, they need a special type and amount of professional service that many of my colleagues are not in a position to offer."

He paused to measure my reaction. I said nothing.

"I suppose you're wondering what all this has to do with you," he said.

"Yes."

"Several of my patients come to your church to, uh, worship. I can't reveal their names, of course. You understand why, I'm sure. But each of them, there are three by the way, is very disturbed. I don't wish to get clinical here, but these people all have long-term problems that require the most delicate care. It almost boils down to a question of balance for them."

"Go on."

"Well, they speak very highly of their experience here, but when I pursue the subject with them they become, ummmmmm, disoriented. What I mean is they show definite indications of resisting the treatment I've prescribed for them. In laymen's terms, if you'll pardon the semantic intrusion, they become restless, agitated and, in the most extreme instances, transparently maladjusted.

"Last week one of my patients, a woman as it happens, jumped up in the middle of an otherwise very productive session and demanded—*demanded,* I tell you—that I turn off my recording device. You know what she said? You won't believe this, but she said I was taping her imagination. Talk about your psychotic symptoms! Anyhow, I'm sure you can see how damaging all this can be to the therapist-patient relationship."

His eyes refocused and shifted to mine. Looking for a sign.

"Cecil, what I'm trying to say is that every time they come here they seem to regress rather than progress. But I want you to know that I'm never one to make snap judgments, so I decided to come to Glide and experience what my patients have experienced."

"And?"

He paused once more, perhaps for effect. The lines in his forehead bunched together. One hand gripped the notebook prop, the other latched onto a knee. His eyes, a calm blue, took snapshots of the coffee table strewn with old magazines, letters, and styrofoam cups. I heard Moses singing in the lobby, the guitar twanging a random collection of notes like some mad game of musical bingo; sooner or later the pattern would be revealed. I couldn't hear the words he sang.

"Cecil, I've got to tell you that henceforth I'm going to forbid my patients from coming here. For their own good."

Forbid. For good.

I jumped from my chair and in two rapid strides was hovering over him. Bending, I jammed my face as close to his as it could come. His pupils dilated and his hands moved reflexively to protect his chest. The notebook slipped silently onto the carpet, and the furrows on his forehead deepened.

"There's no need to get angry, Cecil."

"Why shouldn't I get angry! You come in here, in my place, and tell me all this—"

He scooted down the couch, and, once at the far end, bounced up as if there were somewhere to run to.

"—*bullshit* about how your patients—and they ain't *yours* to begin with—ain't actin' like you want them to act and that I'm the cause of their mal-ad-just-ment. I'm maladjusted my own damn self! And so are you."

"Please, I—"

"Angry? Damn right I'm angry. I ain't afraid to get angry at you or anybody else, and right now I'm angry with you and I'm directing my anger where it needs to go—at you! You play with people, man. You play with the lives of people until they're so weak they can't do anything but gather around your feet. Maladjusted? Is that what you call them when they stand up to you? Maladjusted! Angry? Yeah, I'm angry. But I'm not real angry. You oughta come by here when I'm real angry!"

Again I moved to confront him. We stood face to face, and the one thing I noticed was that he wasn't sweating.

"I didn't want to tell you this, Cecil, because I wasn't sure. But now, with this—outburst, I must tell you. I'm a professional man and in my opinion, and that's a professional opinion, you, Reverend Williams, are a very dangerous man."

"*Dangerous?* I damn sure hope I'm dangerous. I've tried all my life to be dangerous. Thank you for the compliment."

"Look at yourself. Don't you see? You're irrational."

"Don't you ever get angry?"

"Of course I do, but I'm rational about it. I get in touch with it and stay in touch with it. But you are not a rational person."

That was so *American.* I burst out laughing.

"See?" he said. Perplexed. No sense of humor. "Do you see what I mean? There's no rational pattern to your behavior. Oh, but there is a pattern, though. Tendencies. You have tendencies. Sunday you publicly admitted you had a paranoid experience as a child. I ask you to evaluate your life experience, objectively. The pattern is there. Pardon the suggestion, but you really should seek professional advice."

Now that was *really* funny. I thought maybe I should introduce him to Moses, but I rejected it. He'd just think Moses was crazy.

"All right, all right. What makes me so dangerous?"

"You said it yourself. You just confessed you're maladjusted—"

"Compared to what?"

"—and that's reason enough, believe me. But you are a particularly powerful man, and it's your influence over people that makes you especially dangerous. You glorify your maladjustment and connect with and breed that same maladjustment in others. These people come to you for guidance, and you tell them in so many words to be maladjusted. You betray your position by—"

"I tell them to feel and not be afraid."

"—agitating people. You've got the power to control them, and you use it to destroy."

"Life is theirs. That's all I tell them. They can't run from it no matter what they do, and neither can you. Control? That's your game, man."

"Cecil Williams, you're an egomaniac! You give them chaos to distract them from your mania. You connect with something inside them, I'll grant you that, but you and your influence are dangerous."

Moses and Larry came silently into the office. Larry is a hulking white man who usually doesn't say too much. Larry's crazy too. At least that's the going diagnosis. It's undoubtedly correct, as far as it goes. The last time Larry saw his psychiatrist, they called the cops on him. The psychiatrist was taking notes, and Larry just closed the book on the man's hand and wouldn't turn him loose. With his free hand, the psychiatrist fumbled with the telephone and called the cops.

146

Larry and Moses.

Transparently maladjusted. If you know what I mean.

His back to the door, the psychiatrist didn't see them, and they didn't make another move. For the first time, I noticed droplets of sweat on the psychiatrist's upper lip. He hadn't raised his voice yet, and he never would. I was sure of that. Hesitantly, he pointed a finger in my face.

"You know, Cecil Williams, you remind me very much of another man."

She said I was taping her imagination.

There's no need to get angry, Cecil.

It almost boils down to a question of balance.

The psychiatrist measured his words with the force of indictment. A final plea to a jury of his peers.

"You remind me very much of Jim Jones."

His repulsive comparison did not surprise me, because Jim and I had worked in San Francisco at the same time. Guilt by association. It drew from me remembrances, for in those early days of 1979, ink still moist on dispatches from Guyana, Jim's name was a codeword for the most horrible human and spiritual apocalypse. Something so utterly incomprehensible, and yet— and here lies the horror—so frightfully familiar. As I looked across the table at the psychiatrist, his last-ditch attack on me still coiled in the silence, I vividly recalled the last time Jim Jones spoke with me, in early 1978. As my memories formed, the circumstances surrounding that conversation, the apparently disconnected events into which it flowed, grew to form a whole.

When Jim Jones' last call came, I was talking with a woman who'd come to me for counseling.

"My husband never touches me," she said, her fingertips pressing into eyes shut against the soft office light. "In over five years, he hasn't touched me. Not once in all that time, and all I want to know is why. We share the same bed, him and me. No, that's not right. We *occupy* the same bed. We really do sleep together. That's funny, isn't it?"

Her self-conscious smile was neutral, impassive.

"So one thing I do is watch lots of TV. *Police Woman,* that's my favorite. I don't suppose you . . ."

Her voice trailed off in quirky embarrassment. She searched my listening for an indication.

". . . there's just something about that Angie Dickinson."

She was in her late thirties or early forties. I never asked. It didn't seem to matter. When she wasn't holding her face, she had a habit of smoothing her skirt, running her hands down her thighs as if unseen wrinkles were an attack on the remnants of her self-respect. Her face was plain and solidly constructed, her skin a pallid pink. But she was not unattractive. You might see her on Saturday morning in the Safeway checkout line. There might be three rolls of paper towels in her cart, but only if they're on sale. Without fail, the latest *TV Guide* is the last item tossed into her cart. Her actions contain the predictability of American ritual.

"I know it's silly, the thing about Angie Dickinson."

Without warning (except of course there'd been a great deal of warning), she bit off a sob. Words came in gusts, fighting through the tears and phlegm.

"What's the use? He never even touches me!"

"Then what do you do for yourself?"

She bowed her head, escaping my eyes.

"I have to masturbate."

I leaned forward in my chair.

"You hurt, don't you?"

"If only *he* would—"

"You hurt."

"—touch me—"

"You hurt!"

"—make me feel alive—"

"Say it! Say 'I hurt'!"

"—it's like I'm not even there."

"Say it!"

"Yes, *yes*, YES!"

She collapsed, face wet like a child's, murmuring "yes, yes, yes" over and over, softly, wanting to lessen the impact, wanting me to say "Everything's going to be all right," wanting me to replace the pain with something else, wanting to auction it off as though it were something easily parted with. Wanting assurance that the solution was something bold and simple like

Angie Dickinson when the credits come on and the camera freezes as she clutches the tiny black gun in both her hands and *all she has to do is pull the trigger.* Violence as solution. The quick easy answer as solution. The connection between the two.

I did not wish to cause her pain as much as force her to embrace the pain that was hers. She could not escape it, and the only way she would survive it was to first call it her own. In my persistence, my shaking her, I was attempting to be responsible to the woman. She had gotten by too long.

The intercom buzzer was brutally insistent. I grabbed the receiver.

"Jim Jones on three-five," the program director said.

"Can you get a number? I'm into something right now."

"He said it was urgent. It's long distance, I think."

I looked at the woman, her face buried in her hands.

"I'm sorry, this won't take long."

Her face rose from her hands. She nodded stoically.

The first thing I heard was the suggestion of an echo, a comment on distance and perhaps circumstance, hollowness. Long distance, she'd said.

"Cecil?" Jim's voice, the representation of Jim coursing through wire and cable. How many miles?

"Where are you, Jim? Sounds like you're a long way off."

"Los Angeles," he said, trying to make the subject sound unimportant. "L.A. International Airport."

"What's happening?"

"I'm waiting for a plane to Guyana. I think I'm going to leave the country, but I wanted to talk to you first."

He often wanted to talk to me, mostly in the dead of night. It seemed there was something he had to hear from me. Once I told him he was paranoid, and he hung up on me. Seconds later he called back to attack me. "All you do at Glide is have a good time," he snapped. Still later he phoned to apologize for the second call.

"I have a choice," he said from a pay phone at L.A. International. "I can stay or I can leave. I've chosen to leave. What do you think?"

His choice did not surprise me. I'd seen it coming. In recent months he'd had his first real experience with bad press. Defectors from his People's Temple had begun to come forth and denounce the organization as oppressive and totalitarian. There were reports of members turning over all their money and property to the church, and rumors of coercion, violence, and corruption were beginning to swirl around the temple. I felt Jim wanted me to talk him out of leaving the country, yet at the same time he was certain that nothing could make him stay.

"What is it you have to run from, Jim? Isn't it more important to face what you have to face here?"

"But I'm needed in Jonestown."

"Aren't you needed more here?"

"What would you do, Cecil?"

"Stay here and face it."

"Well, I could stay a while and then come back. Listen to me. If I come back, I'll come like King Jesus. These media motherfuckers are trying to do me in, but I'll bring *all* my power down on them. You understand? All my power."

"But Jim, your power is nothing compared with theirs."

"I know the plan, Cecil. They're tryin' to get me for all the good things I'm doing."

Most of the people who followed Jim were poor and black. Many were elderly. You can say they were completely different from you. Say it if you want. Jim gave them food, clothing, shelter, a sense of destiny. So ripe were they to receive a miracle, the blessings of their father (Father), something with which to transcend the grimy array of "social conditions"—racism, poverty, welfare. So it was a sociopolitical issue. You saw that clearly in the bulging ankles of black ladies stepping off the bus. But it went deeper than that, didn't it? You heard it in the perfectly orchestrated, spine-chilling roar of hundreds at the very mention of his name. Like it or not, that lone monolithic voice became yours as well, seeking a place to drown not its sorrows but its pain; a watery grave, not a harbor, in which to sink its choices forever. Something to take up the fight and absorb the pain. Something to believe in.

Give me your tired, your poor,
Your huddled masses yearning to breathe free,
The wretched refuse of your teeming shore,
Send these, the homeless, tempest-tossed to me:
I lift my lamp beside the golden door.

"But you can't fight them from Jonestown, Jim. You'll be isolated, man, and if you leave now it'll look like you're running because you've done something."

Isolated. Running. Jim was not a stupid man. He realized what I was going to say. I was one of the last people he talked with while he remained on American soil, and he *knew* what I would tell him. Don't run. Stay and be accountable. He had a need to hear that. Why?

"It may look like I'm running but I'll fix that."

"I don't think you can, Jim."

He paused. In those few silent moments, a part of him said goodbye. The part that knew all along he was never coming back. Alive.

"Look," he said, "you've given me something to think about. My plane leaves in half an hour, but I'll call you back in fifteen minutes and let you know my final decision. Will you still be there?"

"Yeah, I'll be here."

I never talked with him again.

The woman had absorbed my conversation with Jim. Not the content but the sound of my voice talking to someone else about something else. She clung to that sound in the mistaken belief that it did not concern her. A surface-level exorcism. She sat demurely on the couch and waited.

"How are you feeling?" I asked.

"Much better," she said brightly. "It really felt good to say it."

"Say what?"

She smoothed her skirt again.

"What I said, before your call." For an instant, her eyes avoided mine. She seemed to be rearranging the space between us, reducing the situation to some empirical element as if to force it into something manageable.

"You only said yes. Yes, what?"

She received the question silently. Her eyes, milky once

again, begged me to go no further, as if catharsis could ever be tossed off in a single word—*yes*—connected to nothing on either side of it.

"I want you to say what you *feel.*"

"I . . . I'm not sure."

"No, say what you feel!"

"I guess I'm a little . . . ummmm, upset."

"Say what you *really* feel. Right now!"

Again she stopped looking directly at me and instead looked to a spot near my left shoulder, then at a corner of the room behind me, and finally, in a twitching swerve, toward the door.

"I feel . . ." she made a choking sound. "Oh, it's all such a bunch of crap!"

Her head toppled forward, and she cried softly. I said nothing. She wept continuously for a couple of minutes, each drop an admission of complicity. *It's all a bunch of crap.* When her eyes rediscovered me, they were weary not from the drain of tears but the weighty realization that it was all indeed a bunch of crap, although she wasn't quite sure why. So much waste and loss that she no longer wished to save her life, she merely wished to be saved from it.

"Can you help me?" she asked.

It always comes down to that. The minister's question, pure and simple. The key that will lock the door forever. Posed to ministers, therapists, counselors, friends, lovers, parents, children, God. "I don't want to be this way anymore. Can you help me?" I watched her. In her eyes curled a desperate need to hear the one special answer—yes, I can help you—that would imprison her. Her treachery was all the more cunning and severe because it was so unconscious and instinctive, the lifeblood of her history funneled to this one peculiar circumstance; another chance, perhaps the final chance, to abdicate. That's why she had come.

I moved from my chair and crouched in front of her so that our faces nearly touched. Her shoulders stiffened and her eyes widened. I saw her nostrils widen and shrink with every breath. Blood had fled her face. I said to her, "I will not be your minister, I will not accept your pain. You want some help?"

Quickly, deliberately, her head jerked up and down.

"Then help yourself!"

My sharpness startled her. Her voice became a spasmodic sputter.

"But that's the point. I've been trying to work on it. I haven't told you, but I've been through a lot of therapy and counseling. Maybe it helped, I don't know, but it's not like I've been sitting around doing nothing. I've tried to work through—"

"You've tried to find a way out, that's all. An escape from your pain. It sounds to me like you've been trying to give it away, but you can't do that. And now you want to give it to me. I can't take it, it's yours. With all that therapy and all those programs, you've been trying to run."

"Run from what?"

"From your pain, whatever it is that hurts you. And from your power to do something about it."

"Power? What in God's name are you talking about?"

In *God's* name?

"Tell me where you hurt," I said. "Don't confess to me, just tell it."

She sighed. Her head dropped.

"All right, I'll try."

Her skirt had actually crumpled a bit as she cried. She straightened it before she spoke again.

"I told you he never touched me."

Her inflection shaped the remark into a question. I nodded.

"Well that's not quite true. Last week, Wednesday in fact or maybe it was Thursday. I don't think I want to remember details like that, but, well . . . Like I told you, this has been going on for so long, and last week I decided that maybe it was my fault. Maybe I wasn't desirable enough anymore, you know what I mean? One thing they taught me in therapy was to take responsibility for my actions and so I thought okay, if it is my fault then I should do something about it, right? I know I'm not what you'd call voluptuous, but when I put my mind to it I can look pretty darn good. So that morning I did the housework real quick and then rushed out and got the works—hair, facial, even a pedicure, if you can believe that. Who looks at anybody's toes, you know? But that's how much I wanted it. I wanted everything to be perfect. I almost bought this really sexy nightie, but

I was afraid he'd notice something like that and ask how much it cost, and I didn't want a scene like that so I didn't get it after all. Anyway, I picked up a bottle of wine, went home, and cooked a special dinner for us. I even went to a bakery and bought some eclairs. God, I don't know why I'm telling you all this."

Astonished at what she was saying, she stopped abruptly.

"Does it bother you to tell me?" I said.

"It's not easy. It's so, uh, personal."

"You came to me, and now I'm not going to let you get away. You're really up against it. You hurt, don't you?"

"Very much."

"Then you ought to break loose. You ought to tell it all."

"I want you to realize how important it was for me. I felt like one of those women you see in perfume and shampoo commercials, the ones who dash through a whole day and still look fabulous at night when they meet the guy in front of some fancy restaurant. I really admire that kind of woman."

She paused to make certain I was listening. I was, but even as she told it she was running, postponing the moment of pain, throwing in details to prolong it all so that maybe she could face its climax on some distant afternoon.

"You're avoiding it again. Tell me what really happened," I said.

"I'm trying to. What really happened was that he came home in time for the six o'clock news. He most always does, you know. I thought I looked pretty good, and he seemed to notice me a little more than usual. He sat in his regular chair, and I began massaging his neck. It had been years since I'd touched him like that. I asked if he wanted me to keep doing it, and he said 'Sure' in the most disinterested way. But he seemed to enjoy it. He even said it felt good. Imagine that! We had dinner and didn't ignore each other, and I thought—"

Her fingers pressed deeper into the yielding flesh of her thighs.

"—it was going so well. All this just to be touched by my own husband. It's so ridiculous, isn't it?"

"Tell it."

"So finally we went upstairs to our room and he showered and

I showered. He has this funny thing about me taking a shower before I get in bed. I put on the sexiest thing I could find. Jesus, how I wanted him! I looked at myself in the bathroom mirror and imagined what it was going to be like. His fingers. His hands. Like it used to be. It was going to be so good. Maybe all the bad stuff was only in my mind. At least that's what I kept telling myself. When I came out, he was already in bed, so I climbed in with him. I touched his shoulder and asked him to make love to me. How else was I to do it? And you know what? He smiled. He actually smiled. He told me to take off my nightgown. I did. Then I asked him again to make love to me, and I felt his hands come for me. Touch me! That's all I could think. Touch me, please! And he did. He touched my face, and then his fingers were all over my body, and it was what I'd been waiting for and longing for and needing all day and all night and God knows how long, and when he touched me like that you know what I felt from him? You really want to know what I felt? *Nothing!"*

She yelled with a passion that, if she felt it, had to be frightening.

"I felt nothing from him. Understand? Nothing! Yes, he touched me. But he didn't really *touch* me, if you get what I'm saying. No warmth, no caring, no sensitivity. Just hands. It could've been any man's hands. No, that's not true. It could only have been him. No one else could make me feel so empty. And then he started pawing at me like I was some kind of prostitute or something, and I just couldn't take any more of it. I froze. I've never had that sort of problem before but I couldn't help it. I got all rigid. I . . . I just couldn't do it. He knew it too, but did he care? He cared he wasn't gonna get laid. He didn't care about me! He said, 'What's wrong?' and I said, 'I don't know,' and he said, 'You frigid bitch.' That's what he said. 'You frigid bitch.' I cried. I didn't know what else to do. I had to cry, and he said, 'That's great, that's just great.' Then he jumped out of bed and started throwing some clothes on. He said, 'You couldn't fuck anybody.' I sat there, naked, watching him dress and hearing him say those things about me. When he put on a jacket and reached the door, I asked him where he was going and he said, 'Someplace where the weather's warmer' and slammed the door. He didn't even have the decency to leave me something to hang on to."

"You need him to give you something to hang on to, don't you?"

"Yes, yes! But every time there's a problem, he walks out!"

"Makes you angry, doesn't it?"

"You're damn right it does. That bastard never cares about my feelings."

"Sounds to me like he's afraid to invest himself."

"Invest? What a perfect word! He never invests himself, he only invests his money. Alone in that bed, I was so afraid he'd gone out to buy some woman. Why the hell should I have cared? Tell me that, won't you? Then I thought of something even worse. Maybe he was going to someone I knew. It just got to be too much. I felt so completely worthless, inadequate. There was nothing left, absolutely nothing. I looked at my life, and nothing was there. I just didn't want it any more. Can you possibly understand that? And for the first time in my entire life I decided to *do* something about it. It felt so good. Almost like being drunk except my senses were clearer than they'd been in years. I went straight to the medicine cabinet and read the labels to see which were the strongest. I was lucky; there were more of them than the others. I told myself it was going to be nice and peaceful. I said, 'You're only going to sleep.' I was tired of being worthless and, dammit, I was going to act. I felt almost noble. Can you see that? I poured eleven pills into my hand. I know because I counted them. I must've replayed the whole night in my head. I saw him walk out, leaving me with nothing. I imagined him in bed with somebody else, and that's when I decided to go ahead. I got them all up to my mouth without spilling any. I wanted to swallow every last one, I swear I did, but at the last moment I couldn't go through with it. I stood there staring at myself in the mirror like a lunatic, bawling at what I saw. I took the lousy pills, but only enough to make me sleep."

She sat perfectly still, her face an expressionless mask. I'd heard the story many times before with only a few changes in detail, and I realized that it was somehow horribly representative of a particular state of mind that swept through segments of society with the microscopic invincibility of an unnamed disease. Emotional plague in epidemic proportions. Sexual death and contemplated suicide. As American, you might say, as baseball and violence. In an instant of frightening clarity, I saw her as the crack in the national psyche widening with each fresh edition of the news. In her, and for that moment only in her, I wanted to know why.

"You feel like nothing?" I asked.

"I did that night. I do a lot."

Suddenly, as if a memory had awakened her, her head perked up and her eyebrows arched.

"I remember feeling that way before, like I felt in the bathroom with those pills."

"When?"

"When my father walked out on us. I guess I was about fourteen when it happened. I never really understood why he left like he did, but now I remember how abandoned I felt. Useless. Like I wasn't worth staying around for."

She cocked her head slightly as though marveling at her reconstruction of the past, her capability to summon it at will. I sensed she saw him then, exactly as she remembered him.

"You needed him to give you something to hang on to?"

"Yes, and in his own way he gave me something, too. He was a good man."

She gazed intently at the ceiling as though she could see him most clearly there.

"Come to think of it, I don't remember him touching me much either. Maybe a kiss on my birthday, but that's about all. I wanted him to be closer to me than he was, to show me something. Yes, I remember once when he changed jobs—he was an office manager—and he was really excited about it. In the middle of the day, he rushed home and gave my mother this gorgeous diamond pin. A real diamond. Then he bent down and put this necklace on me that he'd bought, a gold heart on a pretty little chain. I remember running to the bathroom and looking in the mirror, me and the necklace Daddy gave me. I was so proud of it. It was like he was trying to tell me how much he loved me. I didn't take it off for years. Maybe I'm a sentimental fool, but I've never thrown it away."

"You don't like your father, do you?"

For a few small seconds her face hardened, torn between refuting my blasphemy and observing the sacred stillness of her remembrances. A look of inestimable sorrow reshaped her face. Her voice seemed to shrink. She tottered on the brink of tears.

"I loved him very much, but I can accept losing him. I want you to know I'm strong enough to remember his leaving. Do you know what it's like to love someone and not ever be really sure? I only wanted him to care. Is that so much? I wanted him to touch me, show me some affection. And when he left like that —"

Her voice melted to a whimper, assuming the touching vulnerability of the sounds of small, furry animals.

"—I knew neither of us would get another chance. I haven't seen him in at least twenty-five years."

She certainly had been through a lot of analysis. In telling her story, with all its unfulfilling sadness, she touched me with the insolence of her isolation. She began to make me angry.

"Kill him," I said.

"What?"

"Kill your father!"

"What on earth do you mean?"

Her voice grew to a shrill cry. Clearly I'd gone too far. She grabbed her knees and held on.

"Claim your life, that's what I mean!" I hollered. She seemed confused. "Look at your life. You want to know why you're so sick of it? Because your father still controls it by what he never gave you, and I'm telling you to kill it. Let it go! Suicide? You've been committing suicide all your life!"

She shook her head mechanically.

"I don't understand," she mumbled in a voice muffled by fluids. "I love my father—"

"Kill him!" I yelled, bounding toward her. "Kill your need to escape through him. Kill your need to have him control you. Kill your need to have something you never had in the first place. Kill it! Now! Kill your husband too, and make sure he's dead!"

"Stop it, stop it, stop it!" she cried.

"I mean kill the control you've given him. *You* give it to him. Maybe he can't invest himself but you're not investing yourself either. Your investment is in a need for something that never was. Tell me, do you ever compare your husband to your father?"

"In some ways they get more and more alike every day."

"Kill that comparison! You're spending all your time running around trying to find your father's love. Sometimes I think everybody's running around trying to find their father or their mother or somebody—"

"That sounds so common."

"—it is! So what? Kill it, I tell you. Do you need to hang on to it? Is that it? Is it more comfortable that way? You're so worried about what you're not doing and can't get that you never do what you have to do to get what you really need, and now you want to give it to me—"

"No, I don't!"

"—yes you do! You want me to be your father, just like you wanted all those other folks, all those gurus and therapists and whatever they were. But I'm not going to take your need or your pain. I will not be your father. You've got to kill it. You do!"

"I came to you for help," she wailed. "I can't stand any more hassles in my life!"

"Hassles! What do you think your life is right now? Can't you feel even that much?"

"I don't want to feel this way. Sometimes I'm afraid of what I feel."

"But you can't escape it. Run all you want, it'll stay with you. Emptiness, isolation, all that stuff. Kill it!"

"How? What am I supposed to do?"

She slumped into the cushion, face contorted in agony. She sobbed. Her aching loneliness defined her. She was melodrama, the shape of American miracles. There, hunched on the couch with the romantic burden of unrealized love, she enraged me. She had conspired with others to prolong her own suffering, thus reducing her entire existence to a single, pathetically rhetorical question. How long? Face thin with lines of fear, she looked to me.

"All I want is to be touched," she whined.

I jumped straight up and squatted right back down, motion preceding my words with the purity of instinct, anger hooked to the heart of her unspoken question. How long? With each sound, my finger jabbed in her startled face.

"You

don't

want

to be

touched!"

She opened her mouth to protest. I roared right through her.

"You don't want it! You can't be touched by anyone at any time, and it's not because you want your father; it's because you don't want it yourself!"

She squirmed. I slammed my hand on the table.

"You're afraid, aren't you?"

Her head jerked. She wanted to deny it. She couldn't.

"Afraid of what might happen to you. You might get some feelings about yourself. You're afraid of what you might become —if you kill him!"

Tiny noises escaped through her lips. She exploded in tears. She held her moaning head in her hands.

"You're not hearing me!" she wailed.

"I'm not hearing you the way you want me to hear you. I'm not nodding and taking notes. I'm not listening with my ears and my intellect, I'm listening with my life!"

"You don't understand," she cried.

"You're full of shit!" I bellowed. "You come in here wanting my pity, my sympathy because you're so sad, so sorry. Such a pitiful, pitiful woman. You say you only want to be touched? You're full of shit! You hear me? Full of shit!"

She sprang from the couch, her eyes narrow streaks of angry light.

"Don't you say that!" she screamed.

"I'll say it again!" I yelled.

Like something small in a wind storm, she stumbled rounding the coffee table. I shouted:

"You're full of shit! You *want* to be a victim!"

Our words clashed in the air. Her purse slid down her arm. She grabbed it and held it to her chest.

"I came here for help, and all you can do is hassle me!"

Yes, I said to myself. Yes! As a counselor I'm supposed to lift you out of crisis, not push you toward its center. I am not what you expected, and I will not be what you expect. Your expectations cannot define me. She plunged toward the door. I chased after her.

"Go on and leave. Run away, escape. That's what you've always done, go on and do it again."

She kept her eyes trained on the door, not daring to look back at me. Her voice had the integrity of pure rage. She was wholly desperate, stripped of all pretense and defense. Left with only one last weapon.

"Leave me alone!" she shrieked. This was the last chance, the only chance until the next chance. I knew of no other chance to crack it open with the bright pain of revelation. She knew of no other chance but this chance. She screamed again.

"Just leave me alone!"

She shivered.

"You want to be left alone. You *are* frigid!"

"Shut up!"

"Your bullshit makes your whole life frigid!"

"Damn you! Shut up, you . . . you . . ."

"This is the first time in your life you've been touched, isn't it? Something's finally touched you!"

She whirled to face me and threw her purse on the floor. Where was her father and the gold heart? Her husband? *You frigid bitch!* The pills and the pity. Preserved in a bottle; pristine, senses dulled, apart from all that comes near. Can't you take it any more?

You, reading this, I'm talking to you. Don't you feel like screaming? Don't you feel like walking in there and screaming at him or her or them because you can't take another minute of it? And all this time you've felt powerless in their hands when first of all it was really up to you but you checked your screams or screamed at the wrong thing because to scream at the right thing meant possibly losing it all. Yet still you feel like screaming. Don't you?

"Fuck you!" she screamed. Her training tried to stop her. She stood with her fingers around the doorknob, frozen by the terrifying anger in her voice.

"Say it again!" I shouted.

Yes, no. Go on, hold back. Yes, no, yes, no.

"Fuck you!"

"Again!"

"Fuck you!"

"Again!"

"Fuck you, fuck you, fuck you, fuck you! *I'm so goddamn tired of people telling me what to do!*"

"It's about time!" I yelled.

She stood there, shoulders back, bangs pasted to her damp forehead, until she finally heard what I'd said. She glanced at her feet and back again at me. She'd said things she never thought she'd say, only it wasn't the words themselves that renewed her, nor the cheapness of epithet, nor the admission of a universal dissatisfaction; it was the experience of feelings that led to their expression. The cool, determined silence nourished her. A few moments passed before she bent to retrieve her purse. She opened the door.

"Kill my father?" she asked.

"Kill him," I said.

Father, Father.

An instant vanished as I spun through time, simultaneously experiencing Jim and the woman as I watched Luke Masters expecting an answer to his accusation, becoming myself talking long distance and hearing a woman cry. It was no longer memory but had become an integral part of the present, having everything to do with the psychiatrist and me.

January 1979. Jim Jones dead more than a month. The psychiatrist watching me, believing himself apart from Jonestown.

But how many Fathers were there still?

Sensing intrusion, the psychiatrist turned and blanched at the specter of Moses and Larry closing in around him. Giggling deep in his throat, Larry plodded across the floor as though waist deep in mud. Moses had his eyes turned on. They sucked up everything they saw.

"Who are these people?" blurted the psychiatrist, spellbound by Moses' eyes but not blind to their anger. Fear ripped free from the abstract and landed in the pit of his stomach.

"Don't gimme that shit," Moses snapped. "You know who I am!"

The psychiatrist instinctively retreated behind a chair but I was not going to let him be physically harmed. Other than that, Moses and Larry were on their own. So was he.

"I . . . I will not stand here and be threatened," he said, trying with little success to muster some resolve.

Larry guffawed and started talking to himself in a low, mysterious rumble. His droopy face gleamed with a mad grin, the result of a joke so frighteningly, hysterically personal he couldn't possibly relay it to anyone else.

Leaning over the chair, Moses jammed his face within an inch of the psychiatrist's. The psychiatrist backpedaled. Moses pushed aside the chair and pressed forward, his eyes glowing with an incandescent heat. When he spoke, spittle flew from his mouth.

"I ain't threatenin' you!"

With an unsettling suddenness, Larry stopped giggling and talking, and fished a cigarette from the pocket of his denim jacket. His massive body dwarfed the psychiatrist.

"I seen you someplace. I don't remember liking you," Larry told him. "Got a light?"

The psychiatrist appeared to shrivel.

"I don't have to stay here and listen . . . this is insanity!"

"You think I'm crazy?" Moses roared in accusation.

"I couldn't say without—"

"Well, I am! You're crazy too but you don't understand, huh?"

"Just one—"

"I'm talking now! I'm pissed off, and that scares you, don't it? And you wanna know why?"

"No—"

"I'll tell you why. There's something else you don't know. You don't know a lotta things you think you know. This nigger here is my father, and I don't let nobody talk about my father the way you talk about him. He ain't no Jim Jones. He tells us to be free! Jim Jones? Shit! I ain't goin' to threaten you, man. I'm just gonna kick your ass!"

I grabbed Moses' arm on the way up.

"Moses!" I shouted.

"Cecil, this man is the devil—"

"Moses!"

"—I see him all the time—"

"Moses!"

"—I *know* the motherfucker!"

"Moses! Moses! I'm all right, Moses. He doesn't bother me."

I sensed the relaxation flow through him. His arm dropped to his side. His burning eyes swallowed mine.

"You sure?" he asked.

"I'm sure."

Moses smiled.

"And you the devil too, nigger," he said to me.

"I know that."

With no warning, the smile vanished. I saw one jaw working against the other, grinding something invisible into spit. The muscles flanking his broad forehead stood out like cords.

"Did you hear what this motherfucker said about you?"

"I heard him."

"He don't know what the fuck he's talking about," Moses said. He wheeled to overshadow the psychiatrist again. "You hear that? You don't know what the fuck you're talking about!"

Utter bewilderment took root in the psychiatrist's eyes.

"Can't you control them?" he asked, his plea naked as an open wound.

I grinned at the question's inherent absurdity.

"I don't want to control them," I replied. "If they have feelings here, they can express them, and ain't no one gonna judge them or diagnose them or analyze them or any of that stuff. If you're not prepared to deal with them, that's your problem. You've got a problem. Why are you so uncomfortable with them? Nobody's gonna hurt you here, and I'm sure you realize that very well. So you're really not threatened in a physical sense, are you? Then what is it?"

The psychiatrist, buoyed with what he perceived to be a half-rational question, straightened his body and tugged at his coat sleeves.

"I don't feel the slightest need to defend myself because I know where my head is at," he said. "I know perfectly well who I am."

Larry snickered.

"I know who you are too—you're my psychiatrist," he drawled.

The announcement's bizarre mixture of intuitive accuracy and mistaken identity, in a most literal sense, startled the psychiatrist. He smiled as though his sense of reason had caught Larry committing a crime.

"You're right, I am a therapist," he said, adding with a triumphant flourish, "but you've never been my patient."

Larry's eyes went blank but their edges twinkled with mischief and hostility.

"That don't matter," he said.

The psychiatrist's smile drooped to a sickly grin.

"You right, Larry!" Moses hollered in a strange mixture of anger and glee. "The guy's a shrink. I dug it too. You can always tell, can't you?"

And then to me in a delighted whisper of respect for his friend.

"Larry *knows*, don't he? Larry always knows."

Larry grunted or mumbled, I couldn't tell which. Moses put a hand on the psychiatrist's shoulder and stared him in the eye.

"Shrink, I think your shrinkin' stinks. Wow! I could write a *baaaaad* poem about your ass, but I'm not gonna do it. Wanna know why?"

The psychiatrist said nothing.

" 'Cause you're the opposite of poetry, that's why."

The psychiatrist swallowed and addressed Moses.

"I'd like to say something to your, uh, father."

"Say it! You don't see no badge on my chest."

For a moment, I thought the psychiatrist was actually angry. Too bad I was wrong.

"You see what I mean?" he said to me in an aggrieved voice. "You see what I mean about this place? It encourages this sort of bizarre behavior. But let me tell you something based on years of training: You can only deal effectively with these people in a controlled environment. An uncontrolled situation breeds nothing but sheer havoc, as these last few minutes have sufficiently demonstrated. Look, just so you'll know where I'm coming from, I want nothing more than to, uh, help these people. Treat them, you know? But there are limits and dangers, very real dangers in letting, ummmm, certain individuals act out their feelings. Here, this place is . . . dangerous, a defamation, but . . . ah, hell, I finally see that I can't get through to you on the subject. There's no reason for me to stay any longer."

Standing beside the psychiatrist, Larry began mumbling again.

"You never know, you never really know . . ."

The psychiatrist looked at Larry. The psychiatrist thought Larry was speaking to him.

Moses stepped aside, clearing a path to the door. The psychiatrist wasted no time in navigating it. As he neared the door, I called to him.

"Luke, we may not see eye to eye on some things but I want you to know you're welcome back here any time. We accept everybody here."

He shuddered and walked out in silence. Larry followed, muttering to himself.

"The whole world's on a suicide trip," he said.

Moses stood in the precise center of the room, head tilted slightly forward and cocked to the side in a pose of wondering concentration. His hands gesticulated as he spoke.

"Whew! That guy was really crazy. The people who don't know they're crazy are the craziest people there is. You know that, don't you?"

I moved closer to Moses but didn't answer him.

"Motherfucker made me mad! He didn't make you mad?"

"Some."

"I was really gonna kick his ass."

"I know."

"But you stopped me."

"Yes."

Moses went away for a moment. His eyes told me so, their intensity lowered. Cooling.

"Know why I come here?" he asked suddenly.

"I think I do."

" 'Cause you never call the cops on me."

He was floating in an air pocket, momentarily suspended

between visions, fashioning a new block of time that would disappear in the next mile of his mind. His eyes rekindled and flashed. He was back.

"Damn, he pissed me off!"

He began stalking the office, bumping into things I couldn't see. Prowling.

"Jim Jones kills children, man! I wish he was still alive somewhere. I'd go find him and kick his ass! Children! No man has the right to kill *children.*"

Moses bowed his head, an unusual gesture for him. He wiped his eyes, though they weren't moist.

"Those were my kids down there, Cecil. Every one of them. You understand?"

I understood. The glow in his eyes turned inward. I believe I know what those eyes saw. Water. Flowing in the rushes of his memory, his own personal tragedy of betrayal, death, not being there. Then. Water to water, mixing with the gruesome reality of Jonestown, touching it in a way that perhaps only Moses, in his memory and his present, could. Sun glittering a welcome on the waves, beckoning escape. Paradise there. Infants with their pink mouths agape, thirsting for something wet in the humid subtropical heat. The sweet, sugary odor of something familiar, almost ritual. How were they to understand betrayal? Bright daylight glinting off the syringe, pretty and attractive to the infant eye. Thin rod of metal in the infant mouth squirting the soothing, cooling liquid to the back of the throat. It pacified them.

The sound of his memory, lapping like the stream, carried him back to me. Water spilled from his eyes. Without making a sound he wept, standing at the water's edge, poisoned babies at his feet.

"My kid drowned," he said, "and I wasn't even there."

I'd heard him tell the story before. It was real.

"Fell into a stream and drowned. Six years old. They told me he coulda got out if he hadn't been wearing those boots. Damn boots stuck him to the bottom."

He glanced at me. His face glistened with water.

"I shoulda been there," he said.

He clenched his fists and bent his arms as though hoisting a barbell. His eyes ignited.

"Kids ain't s'posed to die, man!" he screamed. "No kids are s'posed to die!"

His anger was as pure as his tears, as marvelous as his madness. He felt it with a natural, unencumbered strength. The fountain of the power he held over others, the shapeless center of his insane courage. He was a dangerous human being capable of almost anything, an irritant to his circumstances, a wired avenging angel living off an incendiary conviction that children should not die. He scared the living hell out of almost everyone. I loved him.

"I'm so mad right now, Cecil! So damn pissed off. You know, I'm a kid myself. A mad kid. That shrink was crazy, man. Jim Jones was crazy too. The whole damn world is crazy. You know what I mean, nobody gives a shit about nothin'. I'm tellin' you, the whole world's crazy!"

We were standing toe to toe. I felt the spray of his saliva beneath my eyes.

"Ain't it?" he asked.

I grabbed my topcoat, draped it over my arm, and led us toward the door.

"You're right," I said.

He smiled broadly. I saw the gap between his two front teeth.

Outside, we stood on the street in the gathering dusk. A hooker entered a phone booth. Three winos lay sprawled on the sidewalk, their backs propped against the plate glass windows of the church office building. The elderly scattered among the area's cheap hotels were already off the street. They wouldn't be back until morning. There were no children or dogs.

"Gotta move," Moses rasped.

"Okay then."

He turned and proceeded up the street, bouncing as he walked, the battered guitar slung over his shoulder like a rifle. Twenty yards away he spun around, eyes blazing.

"Keep your black ass alive!" he hollered. I heard Moses laughing, singing, screaming as he disappeared around the corner.

NINE

I WAS walking toward the parking lot, still thinking of Moses, when I saw the man slice across the middle of Ellis Street, casting a sharp and cocksure look at the phalanx of cars checked by the red light, his head moving only as much as necessary. There was a definite economy to all the man's moves as he crossed the street, some statement about his relationship to the world. Standing at the mouth of the church lot, I waited. He approached me directly, without the slightest hint of evasiveness.

"Revren," he said.

"What say, brother."

"You don't know me, but I know you."

He was a black man, rather short, but with a wiry build that suggested strength. A navy-blue watchman's cap hugged his head, and the smoldering remains of a cigarette protruded between his fingers. His dark brown eyes registered a very selective patience; he seemed willing to spend time with me, but not with things in general. His only erratic motion was a seemingly unnecessary glance back over his shoulder as though he sensed danger. It did not strike me as the gesture of a paranoid but more the playing of percentages, the habitual reaction of a man who'd spent much time looking over his shoulder for a very sound reason. What he told me next I'd already guessed.

"I've been in the penitentiary. Everybody inside knows you, man."

"How's your life now?"

"I need to talk with you."

Two men in a passing car gave us a look, then drove on.

"Things are funny out here," he said.

His eyes never once left mine. He took a drag from the stub of his cigarette. The tip glowed in the gathering twilight.

"How long you been out?"

His teeth flashed a bitter grin.

"About four months now, and it's about to get to me. I need a job, just somethin' to make it on, but these suckers out here ain't givin' up nothin', are they? 'Specially to a brother from the joint."

He took a final hit from the cigarette. The orange glow ate into the filter. He'd obviously learned a main cellblock lesson: waste nothing. He took another look behind him. An unmarked police car cruised the far side of the street. The police were riding four deep.

"Shit," he hissed. "The law."

As if by an unspoken agreement, the street lights lit suddenly. The man stepped closer to me.

"There's only one law out here, Revren. Survival. It ain't about nothin' else, just survival. There's plenty bullshit on these streets, but there ain't no jive. Everything is real. I don't have no job, and that's real. I can work out here if that's what I have to do. I can handle it, but it ain't no good, is it? Nothing's changed out here. It's the same shit it was when I went up, except now I got a record. I'm a desperate nigger, man. I might do any damn thing."

"I might be able to help you about the job, brother."

The anger in his eyes wavered, reflecting caution.

"But that isn't all it is, is it?" I said.

He smiled a full and hearty smile, and shook his head as if someone had whispered a ridiculous joke to him.

"No," he said with quiet confidence, "that's not all."

"Where'd they have you?"

"Quentin."

"How long?"

"Nine and a half years."

"Learn a lot there?"

"Yeah, I learned how to press shirts. I'm the most shirt-pressin' motherfucker you ever saw."

His body jutted forward slightly and he broke into a throaty cackle, enjoying the absurdity of the joke perpetrated on him. Rehabilitation. That was the joke—but he was not a man to laugh at his own demise. His laughter was raw and triumphant, sounding his conviction to not be fooled.

"But we're not talking about that, are we?" I said.

"No, guess we're not."

"What did you really learn in there?"

"Same thing I'm learning out here: survival. In the joint, you learn how to survive or you die, one way or another. Either you're a dog, or you're somebody's punk or you survive. Sounds simple, don't it? But I've seen a lotta dudes inside just give it up. They don't want you bein' a man in the penitentiary. Before I went in they didn't want me to be a man; inside they didn't want me to be a man; and out here they don't want me to be a man, either. Guess you could say it's all the same, but I'm tellin' you it's different out here. Inside, a man knows what to look out for. Out here, shit, it could come from anywhere. But I'll tell you one thing, Revren: I ain't goin' to jail no more."

He leaned on the metal parking lot post and looked into my eyes, his entire manner glistening with a sure awareness of how things really were. I understood him well—he meant he would never again be a prisoner.

"You know what I'm tryin' my damndest to forget?"

"What's that?"

"My number. I'm hip to how those numbers work, man. Every time I went before the board, they had my file jacket on that big table they got, and you know what? My number was bigger than my name. Ain't that somethin'? They sure be downin' a nigger in jail, and I know that as long as I can remember my number I'll still be in there. But I'm an exprisoner now. You hear that *ex*, don't you now? I know how the shit works, man."

"I hear you, brother."

"You know somethin', you're a good dude to talk to. You understand what a nigger be tellin' you. Tell me, you sure *you* never been in jail?"

"Depends on how you meant that, my man."

I thought I saw his eyes twinkle. He nodded slowly, considering what I'd said.

"I heard that. I'm out here. A free country, right? I'm out here, but I'm still in jail. I know what they can do to me any time they want to. Got me spendin' all my time just worrying about stayin' alive, gettin' by. Seems like they done took everything else, and now everything counts. Every damn thing. I wake up in the morning knowin' in my heart it might be the last day. Every day is the last day."

"Yes."

He instinctively turned away from me to pluck a cigarette from his pack. Another impulse of the prison yard. He expertly cupped his hands against a bitter wind and lit up. I moved to touch him lightly on the arm.

"In some ways you're doing a lot better than most folks," I said.

"What do you mean?" he replied, unable to fully bridle his irritation.

"I mean that every day is the last day for all of us, no matter who we are. You and I understand it, but most folks don't. Most folks don't want to understand it. You're right, brother. It's all about survival."

He tugged at the back of his wool cap.

"Come on, man. You gonna tell me that the rich man ain't got what he wants?"

"He's got some things he wants but nothing that he needs. I know him, brother. Every day's the same for him because he can't face the fact that it's the last day. He's desperate, just like you, but he doesn't know why. He ain't surviving either, because he hasn't learned the lesson. I bet there's one more thing you learned in Quentin about survival."

"Yeah, what's that?"

"You can't escape."

His lips flickered into a knowing smile, and he shook his head once more.

"You're somethin' else, Revren. Maybe you ain't never been to jail, but I sure get the idea you know what it's like."

I reached into my pocket for my keys. It was growing late.

"Everybody's got their prison, brother."

172

He flicked the cigarette butt into the street. Sparkling embers leaped and died.

"Everybody's got a prison, huh?" he repeated, more to himself than me. "You came to the joint once and talked to us, remember that?"

I did.

"Soul Day, right?" I said.

"Yeah, Soul Day. You said something then about everybody having a prison, and we, as prisoners, could not allow ourselves to be split up. You said they could lock us up but they couldn't lock up our souls unless we let them. Maybe that's why we called it Soul Day. Anyway, I meant to tell you I remember you for that."

He extended his hand to me. I grabbed and held it.

"I gotta be moving," he said. "Thanks for talkin' with me."

"Survival, brother."

"Survival."

"Come by the office and we'll work on the job thing."

"All right."

He slipped into the near darkness. In the dying light, I stood alone in the parking lot, feeling the night grow stronger around me. A chilly wind snapped at my cuffs and bit at my face. I was cold, hungry, and tired. I wanted to go home, but I couldn't. For some unclear reason, perhaps having to do with all I had experienced during the hectic day, I felt I had to stay in the street a while.

Lines of cars groped westward in search of the freeway and an escape from the city. The faces inside seemed bunched together in a protective ring, eyes pointed straight ahead, both hands tightening their grip around the wheel. They didn't want to see me, so they wouldn't. They didn't want to see the winos and hookers and gangsters, and all the other residents of the Tenderloin, the elderly and the immigrants and the sick, running for cover before night fell. They didn't want to see the rawness, so they wouldn't. They were desperate to avoid it, as desperate in their own way as those who would inherit the street during the night, and there was something dangerous and horrible about their exodus. Street survival. They couldn't face it. Reassuring themselves, through the paths their eyes refused to travel, that they were beyond horror. Reducing it to something they didn't need to feel.

Sensing myself between the street and the cars, the neon and the headlights, I felt as though life were contracting around me. Hard jolts shook me, pressure at uncertain intervals, a force whose existence both included and went beyond me. The contractions would exist even if I didn't acknowledge them, but at the moment I felt them cleanly, without reservation. Willing to receive them. It was what the exprisoner meant by saying survival was the only law. Feeling the contractions, standing in them. Because they are always there. Birth and death as continuous acts.

I began to breath deeply, bringing forth all I had experienced, the struggle, the pain, the joy. Summoning the past, rushing deeper than memory. Because I wasn't going backward to remember experiences, I was bringing them forward, calling on them as resources, making them present in the moment. Facing the contractions of the present by being open to the contractions of the past. Breathing deeply, the sensation of pushing. As if I had stored time internally and, through experiencing it, had earned the right to call it mine. My time, inside, coming forth. Of course I couldn't change the actuality of the events in my time, but I could create them all over again, and, based on a million additional experiences since their birth, I could see them better. They empowered the present.

I was thinking of the exprisoner, still fresh in my mind, when something within me said, "You are not fully present with him." I didn't want merely to remember being with him by traveling backward, I wanted to be with him all over again, fully present, by bringing him forward. My time continued to roll in the parking lot, simultaneously allowing me to experience other moments. As the night grew darker, I never left either one. Both were my time. Both were one.

On Soul Day, 1971, the car jerked and bounced along the raggedy road that swerved and hooked through white, hot, dusty hills. Then, curving around the ultimate bend, I arrived. After parking the car, I climbed a flight of steps to the first gate, a gargantuan work of metal radiating its own force, the sense of being eternally immovable. I wondered what it would sound like when it closed behind me. In any event, I had reached the gates of San Quentin.

Two slack-faced guards in uniforms wrinkled by the heat slid the gate open, checked my name against a list, and waved me on. Another guard station stood some hundred yards away. Behind it rose a second gate. As I walked toward it, I listened to my feet slapping earth in a regimented cadence I'd never noticed before. Things were beginning to change.

When I reached the guard station, I glanced through the gate and saw San Quentin itself on the other side. In the stark summer heat, I shivered. I was told to stand and wait.

I first noticed the five men when they were about eighty yards away. They were an awful vision. Something inside me went cold. All of them were black and dressed in the lifeless, impersonal uniform of the prisoner. My eyes locked on their faces still small but incessantly growing larger, searching for details that might separate them from me and somehow explain their condition. I picked out shades of a grin, skin the color of black coffee, hair cushioning skull, teeth white against the sun. They were just like me, coming to call my name.

As I stared at them closing the ground between us, I experienced a shock of recognition as clear and chilling as the moment of death. *Their condition was my condition,* made manifest only by the walls, gates, guns, and guards. Their hopelessness was my hopelessness, their despair my despair. I felt their breath on my face. I looked into the eyes of the first prisoner.

I am at the gates of San Quentin, back there as if it were now. In the next instant, I will speak to the prisoner and he will answer me.

I said, "What's happenin', brother?"

"I'm just tryin' to survive," he said.

You see? His answer is so much clearer now, its meaning much more explicit. Survival, the horror of survival. He meant he was in a place of horror, one in which there was no escape from danger. He had to face that, and he was telling me I had to face it too. The danger came in very concrete forms, a honed file or the gruff authority of a prison guard, but it was danger he had to embrace. He couldn't get away from it. Later, the exprisoner said the same thing: "In the joint, you learn how to survive or you die." But now, you see, I realize that danger, horror, and survival are not contained solely within the walls of a penitentiary. Danger and horror are around us constantly, in shapes less concrete than prisonmade knives, and the horror of survival is the horror of embracing the danger.

And what is true horror? Earlier that same afternoon, when the psychiatrist had mentioned Jim Jones, he tried to cheat horror, but I can't let him get by with that. Not in my time.

I'm angry with you, Jim Jones, *because you didn't die first.* That is one horror. You had to watch them all, didn't you? There in the jungle (you would like to think it *your* jungle), the illusion of being removed from the contractions of life itself, the compulsion to become history. Exhort them, beckon them one by one to the altar, which was wherever you stood, to the rail, which was a plain and humble table too soon littered with paper cups. A communion, certainly, but whose blood was being poured, Jim? Even then you knew, fearfully denying its significance. You measured each life lost in the sun, absorbing them all as if to prove yourself greater than the sum of their deaths. Your greatness was all that mattered then. It was all that ever mattered. Beginning with the babies, it grew with each moment, bodies piled one on top of each other in a chilling demonstration.

You could have died first, but we both know why you didn't. You could've said, "All who believe follow me"—but you couldn't be sure they would, could you? You had to *know* the answer. Your very existence had been narrowed to that final most pitiful question: Would 900 people die at your command? Death was the only power left. The final, supreme evidence, and my anger with you embraces the cruelest irony to chase you into your grave: *You needed them!* Whose blood, Jim? Their blood! So answer the question for us now:

Where did the true power rest?

You didn't have it, Jim, they did. Even in the grip of poison their power was greater than yours, for without their deaths there would have been no fame, no history. You understood the necessity of their deaths in ensuring your place in history, and so you shaped an ingenious sacrifice, an inspired final hour. But as testimony to your power it was all for nothing! In denying them their power in the most absolute way, you succeeded only in affirming it. In baring their deepest weaknesses, you succeeded only in baring your own. Your existence as a leader was always based on the denial of their power. Then again, leaders lead—but *you* didn't die first.

I saw you speak before your people a few times, you behind the dark glasses, worn not in the defiant, aggressive manner of the militant but as a man who feared what his eyes might betray. There was the weakness of Guyana to conceal, the uncertainty of your very worth. Your appearance at the rostrum provoked deafening cheers among them, you bathing in the sound behind your dark glasses, they roaring at the mere sight of you because you had them believe that nothing else counted. The cheers rolled on, never once wavering, until you cut them off with a flick of the wrist, your arm locked at the elbow, your hand, palm flat, snapping forward from your chest in a gesture of hard, fascistic simplicity. Immediately the cheers stopped. You could hear a baby breathe then. And still you couldn't face it: The power was in their roar, their silence.

I saw your security force shadow you wherever you went, even riding with you in that armored car. They spoke of you in reverential whispers; like all the others, their verbal responses were extreme. Your people either cheered or whispered. There was nothing in between. You denied them their humanity, the power to meet you as an equal and address you as a human being. I saw them with you everywhere, as if the prospect of being alone were the most terrible of all.

They had a need, Jim. A need that cried for a promise. They had a need because they were poor and black. Like the exprisoner told me, they had to spend all their time worrying about staying alive. You exploited that. At their expense, you promoted yourself, first in your own mind and then to the world. You exploited their weaknesses to strengthen your own institution. The poor will always be exploited, because their needs are so great. There will always be room for you, Jim, and I am angry at that.

How badly did you want to be black, Jim? I know you did, and there's no point in denying it now. You used me for that, I realize it now. You traded on my blackness as a calling card to open certain doors in the community, and every once in a while some incredulous person would blurt out to me, "Jim Jones is white!" They couldn't believe it, because you had all these black folks following you and had become a force in the black community. I know it had much to do with whatever you truly loathed about yourself. You wanted to be something you were not and never could become, and that says to me that you hated what you were, hated it so much you would have done anything to change it, hated it so much you would have become a nigger had you the power. And in a clearing in the equatorial jungle the loathing came all the way around, and you came to hate niggers too. Perhaps, in fact, as you always had. Don't argue with me now, Jim! Look what you did to them at your last communion, mounds of black bodies paying homage to the Father, the Great White Father. Hundreds of black corpses on that jungle floor, dead at your insistence. I am not belittling the white people who died in Jonestown. Human life is human life. But you advanced yourself as the champion of the oppressed, and it was all the basest deceit. The best witnesses to that are dead, but I who remain alive am angry with you and with the condition that created you.

You betrayed the cause of freedom and justice for all people. That much is obvious and requires little testimony. You also betrayed me.

People used to like to lump us together, a pair of unorthodox churchmen with radical politics and racially mixed congregations. It wasn't that simple, of course, but we were allies on certain issues. You sometimes said we were alike by virtue of our common struggle, and in a broad sense that was true. We lent our support to identical causes, and you often called me for advice, much of which you never took. I remember your calling me more than once about the bad press you thought was coming. I said, "The press isn't always going to be good."

"Whenever they don't tell the truth about me, I'm going to fight them," you said.

"You've gotta be able to stand the heat," I told you.

"But it really bothers me to read those lies."

"If I fought the press over every bad thing they said about me, I'd never be able to do anything else," I said.

I remember how you used to take that bus and tour the country in the spring trying to enlist converts with your healings and promises, that peculiar blend of bedrock theology and socialistic philosophy that appeared contradictory unless one looked closely at how cleverly you employed it. Each year you brought back at least a hundred people, but the last time out you came back with fewer than fifty.

"I don't know what's happening in these cities, Cecil. The people just aren't coming out," you said.

"People's lives are moving in other directions now," I answered.

"How do you know?"

"You've got to *feel* where they are, that's all. You've got to feel."

I'm angry with Jim Jones, but he was not the greatest horror. Early on the Sunday morning when I first heard the news about the Jonestown suicides, I couldn't believe all those black folks had taken their lives like that. I know from my own experience and the experience of my family that black folks grow up sensing danger, their lives by necessity pointed toward survival. But they didn't survive in Jonestown, and at first I couldn't believe it. Now I can. They couldn't sense the danger, and they couldn't face the horror of admitting that Jim Jones was not God, was not the Father. Isolated in the jungle, they had become the only ones for their cause, believing themselves in touch with the only source. Cause and source soon became one, and when death became his cause, death became *the* cause. They could not face the horror of survival.

I saw them on the front page, lifeless bodies heaped in mounds. America escaped through those photographs, for they let it believe the horror of Jonestown was limited to piles of dead bodies. But the horror drives much deeper than that.

Those people in Jonestown, all of whom had lived with lies and false promises throughout their existence, could not embrace the horror that they themselves had become the lie. They would rather kill or die than admit the lie. They had abdicated themselves to the lie that they had no power, the lie that they could not survive without him. When I saw those photos, I thought for a moment of Vietnam. Rather than admit it had become the lie, America was willing to wipe a race of people from the face of the earth, and in the process condemn many of its own to death.

Death over life. It happens all the time. That is horror. Time after time, people choosing death over life rather than admitting they are living a lie. Condemning themselves to dead marriages or choosing to remain in other situations that will slowly kill them rather than embracing the danger of breaking free. Death over life—and the horror of survival is the horror of embracing the danger.

It was growing much colder on the street, and, if possible, darker. Human figures standing in doorways seemed like shadows. When the figures walked along the street, they stayed close to the grimy buildings and storefronts, as if they needed something to hold on to. As if a mighty wind were blowing. The outbound traffic had all but vanished, and the few cars remaining sped through the damp street in a great hurry to pass. Leaning against my car, I felt the scene around me. I put myself deeply into it.

I am there now. Something will happen to me if I stay here, I'm certain of it. Something has already begun to happen, and it has to do with the wholeness of my experience. Time as blood rather than stone, much more a tool than a barrier. Something I needn't fear. Seeing, feeling, pushing, learning.

I have been taught the lessons of survival because I have lived in the company of some of the greatest survivors. I have seen them choose life over death by embracing the danger and horror, and turning it into opportunity. I have experienced their power. Without so much as speaking to me of profound things, they have helped me fashion my life's work. I am a minister by profession, but a minister is not what I designate myself to be.

I designate myself a midwife, standing in the contractions. Pushing for life.

Nearly all of these great survivors have been black women,

which is not to say they are the only midwives—merely that they have been the midwives in my experience. Each of them survived through "mother wit," an ability to conquer any situation and wring life from it, an instinctive capacity to sense the danger. They perceived things clearly and maintained the awesome human power to reduce what they saw to basic life and death choices.

A midwife puts food on the family table, no matter what the circumstances. A midwife cares for and stands with the sick in the community. She helps birth the young and gives strength to the witnesses of death, all the while pushing for life, demanding that it come.

There is a quality of urgency to her, the knowledge that this moment is the most important moment. She cannot worry about dinner tomorrow, she must worry about dinner today. And this urgency is infused with something else. A midwife never goes beyond caring, and what she cares most about is pushing for life. Thus there is great passion in her urgency. A midwife doesn't giggle, a midwife laughs. She doesn't sniffle, she cries. A midwife doesn't talk of love, a midwife loves. She knows, as the exprisoner knew, that it's all about survival, and so she embraces the danger and the horror. Challenges them, if you please. She pushes for life—and the greater the horror, the greater the push.

In my time I learned to receive their message, with a receptivity that the world seemed structured to deny. Men do not seem to learn easily from women, but a true midwife demands that you push for life because she has learned the lesson of survival herself.

Life over death.

I sense the danger of People's Temple, I embrace the horror of Jonestown. In the jungle far removed, a mirror of ourselves. I will not let you tell me that People's Temple was just a cult and had nothing to do with us. Believe the dead are not like you, but that is not sensing the danger, embracing the horror. Go now to a window and whisper against the glass, *"It had nothing to do with me."*

You have chosen death over life.

Your excuse becomes the condition, and the condition is the

prison. Because I've seen you search for someone, something to heal you, cure you, release you, relieve you—bring you peace of mind. The malaise, the unerring sense of being incomplete (again, I've heard you speak of it) as though something immeasurable and unseen has been lost. Like feeling a relationship die. And wondering why.

The primary American wish: If only everything were all right.

Jim Jones promised them that. He promised he would heal them and create for them a socialist paradise. All they had to do was believe to the point of surrender, and I am angry with the condition—social, economic, spiritual, and psychological—that made his promise so appealing. How badly do you long for an answer that will assume your burdens, absorb your pain, fill your void?

Go to church and listen to the promise. Expect the promise when you say the words.

Say *"Jesus loves me."*

But do *you* love you?

Say *"It's in God's hands."*

But what about *your* hands?

Say the words again and again. They become more and more like advertising—the promise!—as you substitute their sound for experience, attempting to subvert the horror with their emptiness. It is easier to believe in the promise of heaven, flee to Guyana, than to face the world. The promise negates the horror, negates the danger.

There are no promises I need to hear. The world, survival itself, is inescapably around us, and our decision is whether to face it. I've made mine. I live in the world when I oppose the racist regime in South Africa. I also live in the world when I encounter a suburban executive who plays golf on weekends solely to avoid being around his alcoholic wife. Both dangers exist, and all the external promises can neither hide nor change that fact. We are all in the world—but so many promises have been erected to provide us escape. Therapy, counseling, consciousness raising, and all manner of disciplines and "paths." Alcohol, drugs, and television.

South Africa and the suburban couple are connected, you see, because in both situations death is being chosen over life. And a midwife must resist that choice wherever he or she finds it, not because of a questionable do-good mentality but because, and I say it once more, it's all about survival, sensing the danger, embracing the horror, moving into and beyond it.

Living as a midwife is dangerous because I find myself in constant crisis, whether the crisis is mine or the larger world's, but I am alive in the world, the only place for life.

Time and again, I am a midwife. I crush out a cigarette, grinding it into the parking lot asphalt, and stand in the cold. When a midwife pushes for life, it takes everything she has, all the resources at her command. She calls on the past as she experiences the present. A simultaneous act. I feel the contractions in the street. I am also in 1969.

Inside the San Francisco Black Panther office, it looked like war. Sandbag barricades had been piled against every wall. Based on the situation, the undeniable mood of imminence, I didn't doubt that guns were nearby. You could reach out and touch the grimness, the possibility of death in there. You leaned against the sandbags and peered into the street.

Squads of heavily armed police wearing flak jackets and toting automatic weapons had assumed strategic positions up and down the block, listening for the command to move in. You could hear the intermittent squawk of radios and walkie-talkies outside.

On the sidewalk, between the Panthers and the police, we stood in the day's flickering last light. Some 500 community people of all colors had rallied to serve as a human buffer and prevent the threatened shootout if they could. We huddled in the ripening darkness, wondering when we'd hear the first warning (certain they'd give us that) and knowing that even then we'd have to stand our ground.

In Chicago, Fred Hampton, a top Panther official in the Midwest, was dead. Details were sketchy, but still we got the picture: The law had kicked down his door in the middle of the night and had shot him. After Hampton, we knew what was coming next. The stakes were clear. The fury of open war had escalated from the possible to the probable.

I remembered that surly cop on the streets of San Angelo who made us crawl after our groceries. I remembered staring at the wooden handle of his pistol and yearning to avenge his insult to Mother and the rest of us. How much had things really changed since then? It still seemed like open season on all questionable niggers. Blood squeezed from the stroke of J. Edgar Hoover's pen. (We only assumed the federal government's culpability in those days. Now, with the release of volumes of documents, we know the FBI had a systematic program to sabotage, undermine, and ultimately destroy the Panthers.)

Despite the near-inevitability of armed conflict, I still believed that death was not the answer. Nobody had to die.

The official explanation was that a suspect being chased by police had taken refuge in the Panther office on Fillmore Street, the artery through San Francisco's Western Addition ghetto. By mid-afternoon, the Panthers noticed police units roaming the area, apparently preparing for an assault. They called me with a terse and distinct message: It was coming soon.

I had also received a call from the chief of police, a robust Irish Catholic who for an array of personal, political, and professional reasons didn't especially want a bloodbath in his town.

"Please go down there and do whatever you can," he told me.

I saw only one solution: The community itself, on the whole quite sympathetic to the Panthers' position, had to surround the office and stand between the two armed camps.

Now I see that all of us standing there were midwives.

Word was quickly passed through the community grapevine, and by 6:30 P.M. the street in front of the Panther office was jammed with people prepared to chance their lives for the conviction that there should be no Fred Hamptons in San Francisco.

Throughout the tense confrontation, I kept in contact with the police chief. Finally he agreed to evacuate all police units from the area, and by mid-evening they were nowhere to be seen. I stayed at the Panther headquarters until 3 o'clock in the morning. Bloodshed had been averted.

Because I am a black person, my survival, my push for life, takes on a strength sensitive to color. I do not value blackness above whiteness, but I know who my people are. Living life in a society imbedded in racism, I have learned to embrace my blackness (which some would surely call horror) as a resource, an opportunity. If I don't live my blackness, I can't live my humanity. I have had to learn this; it is the first lesson of survival for black people in this country. It is, in fact, the first lesson of survival for anyone: Embrace who you are. Thus I am often a midwife among my own people, those who sense the danger and embrace the horror of living in a world of black and white. Like the Panthers. Like others as well.

George Jackson was dead. On a balmy August Saturday afternoon in 1971, he'd been gunned down behind San Quentin's walls. We knew why, and in the narrowest sense we knew how. But the larger *how* had been kept from us. Georgia Jackson, George's mother, had called San Quentin immediately on hearing the news, but they would only tell her what she already knew: Her son was dead.

The following Monday morning, Georgia and other members of the Jackson family had called a press conference at Glide Church to respond to George's death and the prison system's handling of it. Now it was over, the reporters with their notebooks and cameras were trickling away. We stood around talking, and through the words glowed the anger of a family that had been eviscerated by forces, pressures, fears too vast and ghostly for any of us to fully grasp. There come moments when you wonder if it's ever going to stop, the death, hatred, injustice, suffering, apathy, and in your heart you know it never will. It is then most of all, in the flutter of strongest doubt, that you must feel the reason to struggle. Otherwise you're dead.

Somebody pulled me to the side and advised me to go outside. Quickly. I hurried through the lobby and out into the street.

Squads of heavily armed police had surrounded Glide Church. Another cadre stared at the building from across the street. All of them wore riot gear, and some clutched automatic weapons. For an instant I had visions of them storming the church, guns drawn.

Attempting to short-circuit the order to move in, I hurriedly found the commanding officer, who told me that according to some accounts a person inside Glide Church was armed. I told him that to my knowledge it wasn't true. He eyed me with hooded skepticism and repeated the assertion. At that point, a thin, middle-aged white man approached and announced that a black man inside had pointed a gun at him. I exploded.

"What are you trying to start, man?" I yelled.

On the other side of the glass lobby door, I saw the Jacksons and others glaring. It was for them that the police had come with such naked force; the very mention of their name provoked the helmets and guns. In a sense that was very powerful, but too many had died already. It burned in the eyes of the Jacksons; they were ready. The battle-garbed police were what constituted a riot to me.

The white man repeated his story, but this time I ignored him and spoke only to the captain. I said that somebody could get hurt if he and his men didn't withdraw. I guaranteed safe passage for anyone if the police pulled out, but I couldn't guarantee what might happen if they remained. Their very presence was an affront, the most grievous insult, although I doubt the captain fully understood that. He mulled over my suggestion and for the briefest instant gazed into the lobby. From his standpoint, any action he took entailed risk. In that we were equals, but I'd already made my decision. I think he realized that. From ten feet away, he nodded in my direction and waved his right arm in a semicircle. One by one the police peeled away from the walls of the church. In minutes, they'd all disappeared.

A midwife, pushing for life. But it isn't always life and death in a literal sense. Often the danger is camouflaged, the horror more obscure.

The three vice squad officers stared across the huge table at Ted McIlvenna and me with unabashed consternation, as though we'd just dropped from the sky or perhaps crawled from under a wet rock.

"I really don't understand you fellas," one of them said, shaking his head in bewilderment. "Don't you realize what you're condoning here?"

It was early 1967, and we were helping to sponsor a dance for

186

homosexuals. The meeting with the vice squad had been arranged in hopes of avoiding a confrontation between police and celebrants at the dance.

"I mean, think about it for a second," the same officer groaned. "You guys are *ministers.*"

Precisely the point. As a minister, I was attempting to respond to the needs of a people who'd been defamed, dehumanized, and crucified. If I was condoning anything, it was their right to live their lives as they saw fit, without being harassed or put down. But this was 1967, a time when *queer* was the surest of fighting words, and homosexuality nearly equaled incest in the closet of American sexual prohibitions. It was buried so deep within the national psyche that the vice squad officers couldn't for the life of them understand our absurdly simple request. In their eyes, I saw the possibility dancing: Maybe these ministers are queer themselves! The question never arose, although over the years I've become all too familiar with the phenomenon of guilt by association. Based on my involvement at Glide, I've been called everything from a homosexual to a pimp to a gun-toting Communist. But the vice squadders didn't call me any names. They just thought about it a lot.

We went ahead with the dance because, after all, there was nothing illegal about it. As expected, the vice squad swooped down on the festivities and made some arrests on a batch of patently ridiculous charges. I was there, along with nine other ministers, but they carefully avoided busting any of us. There was no violence. As though peeping through a gummy keyhole, the papers had a wild time with the story, but despite the excesses and blatant misconceptions, the dawn of gay consciousness in San Francisco in some ways dates back to that dance in 1967.

Years later I was in a hotel bar when that same vice squad officer came up to me.

"Reverend, I just want you to know that now we see the gay issue from the same side."

Sex in America. The power to create deep horror, great danger. Which is why it comes in for such ridicule, I suppose, a part of survival we'd rather laugh at than truly embrace. Perhaps it is so full of life that it frightens us. But a midwife cannot be afraid of life.

I am in 1972.

"We'd love to have you come upstairs and welcome us," Margo said.

I looked up from the notepad I was studying.

"You know, say a few words."

Welcome a group of prostitutes? I hadn't thought of that, but now that she'd invited me it seemed the natural thing to do. We were alone in my office, Margo and I. It was early evening, and I was preparing for a speaking engagement elsewhere. She was about to climb the stairs to the sanctuary and officially open the First Annual Hookers Convention.

Hookers in church. The mere announcement had stirred up a storm, and the act itself threatened to ignite a full-scale ecclesiastical scandal. The church deflowered, stripped of its virginal pretensions by Glide, Margo St. James and her fledgling association of professional women parading beneath the banner of COYOTE (Call Off Your Old Tired Ethics), a "loose women's organization." COYOTE and the Hookers Convention had been Margo's idea. Glide's participation had been arranged by the church's business manager, and even though I had nothing to do with the initial decision to offer Glide Church as the site for the convention, I was in full agreement with it.

"I've got to go to another place very soon but I'd be glad to come up and welcome you," I told her.

She let out a quick laugh.

"Oh, that's great," she said.

Neither the irresistible irony nor the underlying substance of our joint appearance was wasted on either one of us. Together we emerged from my office, and as soon as we mounted the stairs to the sanctuary the lights clicked on and the cameras whirred. The Preacher and the Prostitute. Those reporters sure knew hot stuff when they saw it. We were either committing the most heinous blasphemy or assaulting the most shameless hypocrisy. It depended on one's point of view. As for me, there wasn't a doubt in my mind about what we were doing. When we reached the sanctuary door, the reporters, through some strange asexual process, seemed to multiply. The room itself was about half full. A good majority of the people in it were women. Margo and I walked onstage together. I think she said a few words, and then we embraced, right there in front of God and Methodists and everybody. The wire services picked up the photo and shot it all over the world, a black minister embracing a white prostitute on the sacred ground of his own church.

"This is the place you really ought to be," I told the crowd. "I can think of no other place where you should hold your first convention than right here at Glide."

I meant it too. First of all, Glide Church rose from the streets of the Tenderloin where I am standing now, one of the reddest of San Francisco's red light districts. Thus the Hookers Convention was a question of a church's responsibility to its community. Secondly, I recognized many of the women there to be at least semiregular members of my own congregation, and certainly a minister must be responsive to the needs of his or her constituents. Finally, hookers are human beings, in many cases more open about their humanity than those who leap to vilify them. Of course, a lot of people disagreed with me there. I received more hate mail and opposition over my involvement with the hookers than anything I've ever done, as if to suggest that prostitutes in church is a much more crucial issue than war, racism, violence, injustice. But sex will do it every time, won't it? The skeleton hiding under America's bed.

As I was leaving the sanctuary, a woman reporter approached me.

"Reverend," she said, "have *you* ever employed a prostitute?"

I wanted to laugh at her short-sightedness (invoked in the name of good copy) but instead told her she was baiting me and I would not be drawn into that. She represented the feelings of many worried people when she attempted to obscure the real issues raised by the Hookers Convention, for the gathering was not about who buys and sells sex. It was about people being treated as human beings, and the church's responsibility to see that it happens. In the spirit of fear and titillating escape, her sorry question spoke for itself.

It seems I've been in this parking lot for hours, as if Moses and the exprisoner are relics of some distant moment. Yet they are part of the reason I choose to remain on the street. I haven't

189

been here long, but why do I want to stay longer still? I feel that something is coming together inside me. A message, a vision. Not a mystic revelation presented by some higher authority, but a decision grown of my own experience. If there are any authorities at all right now they are in the form of Moses and the exprisoner. Of this world, carrying me further in my experience as the streets wind endlessly through my time. It is life. Something's coming. A new way of seeing things. An understanding. Survival.

A selective interpretation of my time, a pattern there, a lesson. Jim Jones, the Panthers, George Jackson, the gays, the hookers. Standing in the contractions, pushing for life. First horror, then survival. Always danger. Decisions that each time brought me naked into the world; much like birth, if you want to look at it that way. My birth, their birth, the birth of life. The midwife's responsibility, the midwife's risks.

"But where are the assurances?" you ask. That's just it: There are none. But midwives don't require guarantees, and survival cannot depend on them. The decision to push for life, made only in the face of danger and horror, comes only from an understanding of the ground of life, something intrinsic within us all. The decision, the push is ours. No one else can give it to us, no one else can assume responsibility for it. The only thing we've got going for us is our ground—sometimes infirm, often mysterious, always authentic. But if we trust it, it can be enough.

My own push begins with those most in need. The poor, the misfits, the outcasts. My own decisions spring from an awareness of the thread of violence woven through the American fabric, the terrible capacity we seem to possess for self-destruction, the characteristic choice of living the lie, the choice of death over life. Fully in the flow of my time, I understand that all people must experience their power, feel their ground, if you will, and from that come to define themselves. All the rest is a lie, and my midwife's resolve to oppose the lie arises through anger and love. Anger and love must be fused; neither can exist without the other. Fuck the church, kill the church. I feel the anger and love in both these statements, the contractions, the push. I am not a man of cheapshot love, sanguine and beatific, the spiritual leader come to soothe a troubled humanity and lead it from chaos into blissful quietude. I am not a man at the mercy of his anger, bitter, hateful, compelled toward destruction. I am an angry, loving man whose decisions have led him to support the elderly Chinese and Filipinos fighting their eviction from San Francisco's International Hotel, a man whose decisions have led him to actively protest the Vietnam war and the indiscriminate detention of black citizens during the Zebra killings here.

I hear some among you say, "Well, that's all very noble, but it's not as easy as all that." No, the lie is not easy to see and even harder to fight. A matrix of powerful forces impinges on us. Perhaps it is the reality or memory of our parents. Certainly it's the government, corporate giants, and other mammoth institutions bent on reducing us to something impersonal and unremarkable, beyond even our own recognition. They are determined to deny us our power, our humanity. Determined to make us the lie. These forces are part of the condition. But always there is the ground from which life can be demanded.

I see the lie clearly now, as clearly as I've seen it since I set foot in this parking lot tonight. I feel myself sensing the danger and embracing the horror. Unending contractions, a continuous struggle to create life in each moment. I am my survival. Now, and a few years ago. 1974. In my time.

I stood alone in my office at 2 o'clock in the morning listening to the silence. My presence somehow intrusive, an interruption of the nightly order of things. But it had reached the point where I was spending nearly all my nights at the office. Something could break at any time, and I had to stay ready. Patty was still in captivity, although I saw the word from many different points of view. The police and the FBI had thrown everything into the hunt, only to come up embarrassingly empty. The Symbionese Liberation Army was close at hand, perhaps as near as around the corner. And I was in the middle of them all.

In the eerily silent office, I saw Randolph Hearst then, not as an apparition but more as a presence. I saw the understated jacket, the creases that flanked his mouth, the glasses that seemed to square off his face. I felt the barely restrained tension in his vaguely bawdy laugh, which erupted at the most inappropriate times, moments when a scream or honest curse might have served him better. The power broker, the American baron, he'd requested my help in understanding what he would call "the left." In a sense so abstract as to be paradoxically narrow, he was my enemy. I'd come to call him "Randy."

I couldn't see his primary adversaries nearly as well, but I felt the force of the self-styled SLA just the same. Even though I suspected I'd seen each of them at Glide, I had no peculiar faces to remember. I felt their desperate madness, the romance in the stilted military language of their communiqués (the word *communiqué* itself bearing witness), their naked wish for death. More than that, though, I felt something of their lives, the rightness of what they claimed to want. And the lie their wishes had become.

They'd designated Glide as one of the community groups to oversee the free food program that was supposed to ransom Patty Hearst. And they'd designated me an unofficial intermediary simply by sending me a taped message. I was more than willing to ferret through their many obfuscations to reach what truths they espoused, and I didn't want to see any of them die. The issues they raised made them more than a gang of sorry desperadoes to me.

Hearst and the SLA. Both of them were pressure. One had requested, the other had designated. I was in the middle, with, one might think, no decisions of my own to make. I felt jammed inside a dilemma of someone else's construction.

What, indeed, was the issue?

For the press, Patty was the issue. This was understandable. The Hearsts, after all, *were* the press—a fact not lost on the SLA. Miles away, a siren beat hopelessly against the night. Somewhere a young white heiress was being held captive by a crew of revolutionaries with the foolhardy notion of swapping her for some social change. Working toward the young woman's safe return was important, but was it the only issue? If it were, I was trapped between her father and her captors, defined solely by my orders. In short, if Patty were the only question I had precious little ground.

Few people gave a damn about the SLA. I did, though. They

were extortionists with inventive delusions of grandeur, acting out a fantasy that led in only one direction. But human life beat within them, and I saw the push for life as my principal duty. From the first moments of the bizarre caper, I'd tried to organize a community wedge to help avert violence when the moment of truth turned up. To this day, I believe that when they fled San Francisco the SLA members assured their own destruction.

But was that as far as the issue went, Patty and the SLA? If there were no other questions, then I was still caught in someone else's dilemma, reading from a script that wasn't mine. In the drama that struck beneath the soil of America, Patty and the SLA were indeed the headline personalities; but the sensationalistic promotion of the incident obscured the conditions that created it. That was a big part of the lie. Hearst and the SLA. Sometimes they almost mocked the ground I stood on. At others they crowded me relentlessly with their own imprisonments, their participation in the lie.

I walked from my office to an adjoining room. Nothing stirred. In the corner of the room, piled haphazardly against a row of filing cabinets, were three wrinkled bags of clothing donated to Glide. I've never considered Glide a missionary settlement, but we try to meet the basic needs of poor people. Perhaps from idle curiosity I bent to look into the nearest bag. Perched innocently atop the contents was a pair of toddler's tennis shoes. The shoes seemed to speak to me: *Somewhere there's a child.* There was a need for those shoes, alive like the child itself, and it angered me.

Somewhere there was a child with no shoes. *That* was the true issue, that was survival. It wasn't Patty or the SLA or Randy or me. Especially not in a roomful of old clothes, especially not out on the street with its orange peels and broken glass and mothers calling their children home for Monday's dinner leftovers stretched to Thursday. The condition was out there, in the office, among us all. Patty and the SLA and Randy and I were being impacted by the condition. But the question was "Would we impact the condition ourselves?" Everything else was part of the lie. All the headlines were lies. All the agonizing, Patty's name on everyone's tongue, was a lie. The lives of Patty and her kidnappers were significant enough, but they were being used to escape the truth of a shoeless child. Something grew firm beneath me. I knew that as long as I focused on the true condition I would remain on solid ground.

It was nearing 6 A.M. by then, and dawn was lacing the darkness. From the room where the clothes lay, I looked out at the street. A bent and grizzled old man shuffled along the sidewalk, dragging a shopping bag behind him. He bowed to peer into a garbage can, retrieved something, and dropped it into his bag. I thought of Randy once more. Somehow it seemed appropriate. How far apart they were, Randy and the old man, and yet how connected. The condition. Survival. I couldn't blame Randy in a strictly personal sense, but he was who he was. The old man disappeared around the corner. I wondered what went through Randy's mind whenever he saw an old man scrounging in garbage cans. I remembered our first contact.

I was at home. It was shortly after 9 P.M. Patty had been kidnapped the week before, and the SLA had already designated Glide to help with the food program. The phone rang. It was William Coblentz, an attorney and friend of the Hearsts. He asked if it would be all right were Randy to call me himself. I said it would. Less than ten minutes later, the phone rang a second time.

"Cecil Williams? This is Randolph Hearst, ha-ha."

He told me he had a request that he didn't wish to discuss over the phone. I'm sure he figured the FBI had tapped his line. I figured they'd been tapping mine for years. We agreed to meet the following morning at a hotel in downtown San Francisco. I had no idea what he wanted of me, some doubts as to whether I could meet the request, and, most importantly, whether I even *wanted* to meet it. The man represented all I had grown to protest and oppose, the money, the power, the exploitation. Yet that was exactly the advantage. He was a power broker, and perhaps I would be given one chance to influence him.

The next morning I met with him in a hotel suite. Paul Jacobs, journalist and radical activist, now dead, was also there. Randy cut through the formalities and asked me to help him understand the thoughts and actions of leftist radicals. It was ironic, but I think he selected me for the same reason the SLA had, because Glide worked with such a variety of radical groups, communities, and causes. We were well connected. I told him I could put him in touch with a number of people and groups, but only if he were serious about listening to them. He seemed pleased.

I couldn't tell whether he was only interested in gaining an edge on the SLA or, as a result of the suddenly adverse circumstances, he would actually use his power to affect the condition. There was no way to know if he was merely exploiting me, but at that point I was willing to take a chance. Despite the mystery of his motive, I quickly got a sense of the man.

There was about him an attempt to be familiar. He talked as if he sincerely wished he could roll up his sleeves and have a beer and argue about women and baseball, as if somehow there had to be a release for the feelings, the need for passion I sensed within him. But something stopped him. He was a reflection, an embodiment, of the power he had inherited. It was never exercised with passion either. I immediately recognized that he loved his daughter, but he couldn't bring himself to say it, much less scream it.

A second-generation power broker, he appeared in some ways uncomfortable with his position, as though he'd been forced to wear someone else's clothes. He projected neither the greed nor obsessive righteousness of his magnate father, a man who had redefined the press, exploited millions of people, shaped foreign policy with an influence that humbled presidents, and amassed an obscene fortune doing all three. Yet Randy carried the Hearst name, wealth, and privilege. He had no choice there, and that alone seemed partial explanation for his nervous laughter. He was an outsized version of the American drive to become rich and powerful, yet he was imprisoned by something he never made, and I believe he realized it. Still, the awesome power he held at his fingertips was exactly the point. Sitting in that hotel room didn't make me feel bad for Randy. It was his power, and I wanted him to use it.

As morning rose, I paced the floor, charged with the energy I'd found among the old clothes. The situation clutched me in its grasp, and I was prepared to go to the mat with it. A break, a twist, a scrap of information could come at any moment, and it was the SLA itself, unseen and unknown, that made the whole thing so explosively unpredictable. As much as any moment in my time, I felt the contractions, sensed the danger, and experienced the horror of embracing the danger. The potential loss of my life presented an immediate danger, of course. But there was also great danger in saying to the world, "It isn't wholly about Patty at all," in saying what I knew to be the truth.

The week before, I had been driving to the office when I heard a radio report that the SLA had sent a taped message to a Berkeley radio station. I listened to the story's lead with mild interest, but then the reporter said the SLA had designated certain community groups to oversee the free food program it had demanded as a condition of the Hearst girl's release. Glide was the second group named. When I heard my name, a shock rippled through me. My first response was to wonder why we'd been designated, but the answer was both obvious and no longer relevant. The hard truth was that I'd been an observer before; now I was a participant. We held a brief staff meeting at Glide and decided to beef up coverage of our telephones. Little more than a week later, on a Saturday morning, we got a call instructing us to go to a phone booth, where we found a key to a locker in the airport bus terminal. Inside the locker was a tape from the SLA. It was addressed to me, and put me right in the middle.

The memories of all this were still fresh in my mind in the early morning light. To some extent, they frightened me. People's lives were at stake. But they also angered me enough to make me hopeful. I had no difficulty denouncing terrorist tactics. I am not a violent person. But all the hand wringing and castigation only camouflaged the inescapable truth that the SLA's tactics had succeeded in forcing issues where so many other tactics had failed. No one seemed willing to face up to that, and it said more to me about the condition than about the terrorists. America embraces and responds to violence (old man Hearst had known that real well), a truth almost too horrible to risk your sanity on. Choosing death over life—an airtight willingness to kill or die rather than admit the lie.

A number of leftist groups decried the SLA as "counterrevolutionary gangsters" and suggested the group might be a CIA plant. They were correct, of course, even if their fingers pointed in the wrong direction. The SLA *was* a CIA product, but only in the sense that it took root in American soil and rose to reflect a condition framed and fostered by big-time terrorists like the CIA itself. The SLA had indicted America, not through its ridiculously worded manifestos, but through its very existence. The condition was foul enough, desperate enough, to make room for the SLA, not to mention the CIA. That was the lesson of the entire episode, the danger and the horror. It is what we must all survive, even now, and to deny the horror is to live the lie.

The condition's decay, brought to a momentary flashpoint by the SLA, angered me. And in true anger there is always hope. In the SLA, America was coming face to face with itself. I saw great possibilities in that encounter. I didn't want them to go to waste.

By 7 A.M., staff people who'd spent the night in the building began to stir. Soon after, others began trickling in from their homes. Many Glide workers and volunteers had taken up temporary residence in the church, infusing the place with the sensibilities of a frontier outpost.

There were the usual bomb threats, assassination threats, and bogus leads. A few people with overactive imaginations even accused me of being Cinque, the SLA's "General Field Marshal" and apparent ringleader. Some people were convinced I had a pipeline to the SLA, while others were certain I had Randy Hearst's ear in my pocket. The falsity of both beliefs did nothing to stem the flood of "urgent" phone messages and ingenious attempts to hustle me.

Still, despite the darkly comic atmosphere, we all walked with an ever-present sense of real danger. This was neither idle speculation nor trendy paranoia. Every time we looked out the window, there was a guy in the phone booth across the street. Every time we went out to get something to eat, it was like a low-profile parade. We were under the continual surveillance of the FBI, the press, and the SLA itself, which through various means proved it had us covered. It was quite likely that at certain times FBI agents and SLA compatriots stood shoulder to shoulder across the street, each of them watching *us*. It didn't seem at all funny at the time. In the most frightening sense, we were experiencing a moment-to-moment existence. The danger had been pushed to the maximum, and we made each decision under extreme pressure.

As the afternoon sped toward dusk, it occurred to me that I was living in the condition extended to its darkest, most absurd extreme. There seemed something incredibly *American* about the episode, as if the condition, like a lame beast in the jungle, had no place else to go. I do not subscribe to fate, but there was something inevitable about the situation. The poor, as usual, were pawns in somebody else's game, yet their subjugation had led to the kidnap in the first place. Had the condition been more just and equitable, had it been less of a lie, there would've been no need for a free food program. But the condition was neither just nor equitable, despite the predominant American yearning to believe that it was, and so it had come to food as payment for extortion. Criminal acts as corrective force, however wrong and injurious, were bound to break loose sooner or later. Even as America worked hard to dismiss the urban riots of the 1960s as some sort of historical accident, new crimes were in the works. How many options does the condition grant the poor?

And then there were Randy and Patty. It was clear to me that, while he loved her, Randy did not particularly understand his daughter. In his first message to her, once having heard her voice on an SLA tape, he concluded with the pathetic advice to "Hang in there, honey." It wasn't that he didn't care. He was merely unable to expose and proclaim it. Passion suffocated by a sensibility shaped and designed to deny it. I knew already, from my work, that the American family was in a state of decay. Some children, many for the soundest of reasons, were openly reviling their parents. A few carried their resentment all the way to murder. The choice of death over life had displaced caring and freedom (one does not flourish without the other) with expectation, control, emptiness. And now, hurled across the front page of every paper in the world, an American parent and an American child were coming face to face with their own separate realities even before Patty joined her captors. The ring of hollowness there, the desperation without passion, the swallowed conversations and hands dangling short of touching, the unmistakable impression that somewhere along the way each had lost sight of the other, spoke to me.

Around 8 P.M., our shadows absorbed by darkness, a group of us left the office to eat. In the heat of the crisis, my brother Dusty had come from another job in Oakland to work with me. He's still with me today. Another brother, Jack, who, along with Reedy, had relocated to the Bay Area, was with us that night as well. Janice Mirikitani, Glide's program director, was the only woman among us, a point whose importance became clear only later. Before leaving the building, we informed other staff members of our destination and told them to get in touch with us immediately if anything broke. We then drove to a restaurant in the Western Addition. Around 8:30, we got an urgent message to call the office. The SLA had made contact and left precise instructions for us.

We were to go directly to the main branch of the San Francisco Public Library, about a fifteen-minute drive from the restaurant. The library was due to close in twenty minutes, which told me the SLA had been aware of our exact location. Once at the library, Jan was to go into the first-floor women's restroom, where we were told she would find a message taped to the pipe of a sink. The SLA obviously knew a woman was in our party.

There was really no decision to make. We had to go, and there was little time to discuss it. Still, the pressure of the unknown hovered around us. We talked as we ran for the car. The whole thing could be a setup. That didn't make much sense, but then nothing seemed to make much sense any more. We were confident that some SLA members would be in the library vicinity (after all, they'd tracked us to the restaurant), and that raised the possibility of a shootout between them and the police, with us stuck in the crossfire. Given the likelihood of an unoccupied restroom five minutes to closing time, another possibility was that the package contained a bomb, not a message. Images of violent death whirled before us as we raced down the street.

At seven minutes to nine, we lurched to a stop in a bus zone fronting the stone steps climbing to the main library entrance. It seemed as though hordes of people were swarming down those steps. We couldn't help wondering, which ones among them were SLA?

Inside, the library was a murmuring jumble of last-minute activity. People were everywhere, but we were the only ones moving against the grain. Dusty and the others took positions at either end of the restroom hallway, and Jan disappeared behind the wooden door marked "Ladies."

When she entered the room, she saw no one. Quickly her eyes swept beneath each stall. No feet. Completely alone, she strode purposefully toward the sink and, afraid but expectant, looked under the basin. A manila envelope folded to the shape of a cassette was taped in the gooseneck trap. Carefully, she tore it free. The name "Cecil Williams" was lettered across its face. Clutching it tightly, she turned and hurried from the room.

The taped message amounted to Cinque and the SLA's rejection of Randy's $2 million free food offer. Instead, they demanded an additional $4 million. The following day, Randy announced he couldn't come up with $4 million more, and offered a grand total of $4 million instead. In all the bottom-line bickering and slapdash creation of the food giveaway, I saw it happening: The poor were being forgotten again.

For the briefest time, the drama had gravitated toward the condition, and there was no way anyone in America could avoid the recognition of hunger and poverty, the very enactment of the lie. That's where the focus belonged, for it was the only thing that would elevate the case above the level of a real-life movie script, another tawdry melodrama in which America might lose itself. I wanted the drama to expose and impact the lie because the condition, more so than the individual players, was the issue for me. But by the time the food giveaway actually began in late February it was evident to me that both sides were using the poor and exploiting the condition. The moment of opportunity, the chance to embrace the horror, was passing almost without notice. Power exercised without passion for life, for Randy's and the SLA's convictions never went beyond themselves. They had tried to sidestep the lie, and thus had only perpetuated it. Even though he exerted immense influence over politicians, law enforcement, the media, and corporate titans, Randy seemed incapable of deciding to affect the condition. His monstrous power was being unleashed only to save his daughter, which was understandable, but he couldn't face the danger and horror of what such power truly meant. Played against that, the SLA seemed to nurture a passion only for self-destruction and glorified immolation, unable to embrace the horror that they were not who they claimed to be. The issue for them was not survival but martyrdom, as if they lacked the courage to see that their deaths would have all the glory and passion of animals being butchered in a slaughterhouse. The lie was at hand; the lie that life in America was abundant, that power ensured justice, that Cinque and his followers were revolutionaries, that bags of groceries would supplant and remove the hunger. The lie that Patty's safe return would make everything all right. Against such a backdrop, I refused to participate directly in the free food program because I understood it to be a part of the lie. As I'd expected, the program itself was a disaster. Grocery bags were tossed to the poor in the manner of feeding time at the zoo. In the words of the press, the distribution was "marred by confusion and violence." But what did they expect? The entire structure of the program, indeed the SLA's giveaway demand itself, displayed no sensitivity toward the poor, no understanding of the condition. The SLA was using the poor as witnesses to its naive illusions of revolution. In fact, when I began talking to the media about the condition, Cinque sent word that I was getting too much publicity. In this instance, Randy was forced to use the poor to get his daughter back. I was damn tired of seeing the poor used by anybody. All this made me extremely angry, and I despaired at what I saw as a lost opportunity. But I didn't surrender all hope. I worked hard to maintain my ground, pushing for life in any way possible. And there were still lives to be protected.

Not long after the food fiasco came the startling announcement that Patty had renounced her birthright and thrown in with her abductors. Her coming out as "Tania," after Che Guevara's lover, meant much to Randy, of course, but it didn't drastically alter my perspective. For me, the issue had always been preventing violence, the choice of any life over any death. The only difference now was that all the lives appeared to be on the same side.

Sometime in March, by which time all that remained of the free food program was afloat in the sewer system, I received a

secondhand message that the SLA was giving strong considera-
tion to a deal that would ensure them safe passage to another
country. About the same time, through different sources, Randy
got similar information. As we understood it, the deal involved
Randy flying with the SLA to an unnamed country at which
point Patty, her revolutionary conversion notwithstanding,
would be allowed to return home with him. At best it was a risky
proposition, but late one morning Randy contacted me and said
we had to talk. A meeting was arranged for that night at a motel
in the San Francisco suburb of San Mateo.

Randy met me in his shirt sleeves. He looked tired and worn,
as though roused from a particularly fretful sleep. He tested my
knowledge of the exile plan. Our information was basically the
same.

"I'll make arrangements for a plane," he said, leaving his
announcement suspended in silence as though needing to hear
it for himself.

He was properly circumspect about the details but left the
indelible impression that the FBI had sanctioned the plan. In
any event, it would have been extremely difficult without federal approval, because the FBI was sticking so close to him. He
said there was some problem finding a place willing to accept
the fugitives but he didn't seem dismayed by it.

"Cecil, I don't want to go with them alone," he said.

I looked him dead in the eye.

"I want you to come with me."

He was asking for my life, and he was well aware of it. There
was not even the veneer of mirth in his pale eyes.

"Why, Randy?"

"Because you understand the situation a helluva lot better
than I do. They wouldn't hurt you, I'm sure of it. And if you're
there maybe nobody will get hurt."

In the span of a few moments, I weighed the possibilities.
Trapped in a plane with a bunch of twisted, well-armed roman-
tics, anything could happen. Randy wasn't blind to that either.
Among other things, he was asking me to save *his* life. They
could kill us any number of ways, and, aside from the powers
of reason and emotional persuasion, there would be nothing we
could do to stop them. We'd be unarmed and outnumbered.
We'd be their prisoners.

Yet I felt a keen responsibility to human life, the one thing that makes the condition matter. I didn't perceive myself as a savior, but if my presence would in any way lessen the chance for bloodshed and destruction did I then have a moral duty to be there, even if it meant risking my own destruction? Or, put another way, where was life's ground?

There are times when the unknown nearly becomes unbearable, and it is then when our beliefs, feelings, wants, needs, freedoms, our struggle between responsibility and irresponsibility, are most tested. Scattered across a lifetime are pinpoint decisions in which all we have to go on is our ground. By such decisions do we define ourselves.

"If it comes to that, Randy, I'll go with you."

Over the next few days, the exile plan continued to merit serious discussion. Information came through me that a prisoner called Death Row Jeff, incarcerated in the state facility at Vacaville, was the man to see about the SLA. Word had it the SLA was a mutation of a group Jeff had helped shape behind the walls of Vacaville. Death Row Jeff, we were told, could get word to the SLA, and they would listen to what he said. A number of meetings took place between Randy and Jeff, and then I was called in with a few other people. The hope was that Jeff would sign a message advising the SLA to release the Hearst woman and assuring them, through the use of code words, that the exile plan was prepared and workable.

The cast that assembled in the prison that day went almost beyond imagination in capturing so many different strains of America. There was a millionaire, Randy himself. There was a cop, Charles Bates, head of the FBI's San Francisco office. There was a jailer, Raymond Procunier, then chief of California's prison system. There was a white radical lawyer, Vincent Hallinan, who'd been retained by Randy. There were two black prisoners, Jeff and an inmate named Raymond Scott. And there was me. Two things were suitably symbolic and ironic. The whole thing was happening behind prison walls. And it was a black prisoner, Death Row Jeff, who possessed what everybody else wanted. Much more because of his commanding presence than the important position he occupied, Jeff determined what went on. Proud and unshakable, he radiated self-definition. His own ground was harder, more solid, than the walls that enclosed him. He knew how to survive. Before the meeting, Randy told me he deeply respected Jeff. I could see why.

The negotiations wore on through late morning. Jeff's position was quite simple: He was reluctant to become personally involved for fear that repercussions might be visited on the prison population, particularly if things on the outside went awry. He was experienced enough to realize how easily he and his companions could be made scapegoats if, for example, Patty were to be murdered. His credibility behind the walls, the only credibility that mattered to him under the circumstances, hung in the balance. He also implied that, far from being his own creation, the SLA was nothing but an offshoot of a black prisoners' group over which he held much influence. Things being what they were, you would expect him to say something like that. But his implication nevertheless rang true for me. Imprisoned by the condition in the most literal fashion, Jeff seemed far too wise and strong to misrepresent the struggle by kidnapping some frail white heiress.

Shortly after noon, Jeff demanded the room be cleared so that he and Scott could discuss things privately. Outside in the hall, with its odor of floor wax and the impassive suggestion of endless years, I was overwhelmed by the numbing atmosphere of the prison. The guards and walls seemed much less a threat than the blank neutrality of time in there. I became angry and a little bit sad, but not because of the sterile environment. I realized that when we returned to the room we wouldn't be addressing the condition, the lie. That's what upset me most.

Why had we been reduced to investing ourselves in the lives of maybe a dozen people instead of thousands, maybe millions? In some ways, I laid the responsibility on the SLA, the self-proclaimed army of "the people." Despite their naiveté and brutal tactics, at least they began by exposing the lie with such instant clarity and alarming suddenness that it actually became a topic of brief national discussion. But now they'd allowed the lie to escape, and had become, simply, another distraction for the nation.

I also recalled the thinly concealed self-righteousness of so many leftist groups who rushed to denounce the SLA as some form of political plague. The criticism fell like rain, all the way from armchair revolutionaries to cadres of underground bombers. The *revolution*. Sometimes I didn't know whether to laugh or scream at its sacred invocation. Waiting in the hall, I realized that, like the surveillance and the guns, the SLA was merely the lie extended to its most absurd yet revealing extreme. The SLA, saviors of the working class. The SLA, pirouetting for a media splash. The SLA, summoning imported doctrine and rhetoric. The SLA, turning from life for the sake of their own egos. The SLA, determining themselves the needs of the people. The SLA, finally and probably from the beginning, betraying the cause of survival.

I tell you now, especially some of you who believe yourselves "radical," that revolution *is* sacred to me. A revolution that ensures human dignity, equity, justice, and freedom. A revolution that endures because it is and will be continual. But most of all a revolution determined by those whom it must serve most. Self-determination is at the heart of my revolution, and I know that before it is anything else revolution must be a personal, individual act. It's not, at its root, a political question, it is a human question. It is a question of survival, the act of a midwife pushing for life. Theory is relevant. Socialism promises more than capitalism, for example. But the fires of revolution don't feed on theory, they feed on human needs.

True revolutionaries are not political evangelists, but many of you abandon the cause because you see yourselves as saviors, the only ones with the solution. Your doctrine becomes the cause, you become missionaries, and "the people" you claim to revere become the secretly inferior object of your politics. They are weak to you, sadly barbaric until brought your light. Many of you don't even come from the communities on which you arrogantly and religiously impose your dogma. Argue the point if you wish, but I've seen it happen time and again, college students armed with slogans and abstractions descending on a poor community with the fervor of the "born again." But the people don't listen, do they? Is it because they've been brainwashed by the lie that they lack the power to change their lives? Partly so. But isn't it more because you fail to recognize the lie at the base of your righteousness? The poor are not only the "masses." They are *human beings.* They can't eat your slogans. Your theories may have legitimate applications, but your actions so often ignore the actual human needs, the push for life. Understand this well: Unless you meet their needs, there can be no revolution. Relinquish your control to them, for that is where it rests. Sense the danger in doing otherwise, embrace the horror of admitting that you are not above them.

Perhaps you do not meet their needs because you do not meet your own. So gripped are you by your cause, your need to be "the ones," that you cannot confront yourselves. Maybe that's the way you want it, but if you fail to confront yourselves then revolution is an illusion. You promote change in society, sweeping social and political reform, but you will not accept change among yourselves. You become as rigid as those you accuse of being inflexible. There is always the struggle between self and the world, and a midwife understands that both must be attended. The push for life is never limited; in each decision we make, it applies. The revolution of the 1960s, if you'll pardon the forced grandeur, failed in part because the revolutionaries, swept up in the storm of political protest and social change, didn't take care of themselves. All the lies were "out there," and none of them were your own. In Atlanta, I placed all the burden on the church because I couldn't face the horror of killing and changing a part of myself. But we as individual human beings are never separate from social activism. As much as we must change the world, we must change ourselves. That is horror; thus many political groups tend to dismiss human growth as a bourgeois invention. And yet it is not enough to want to change ourselves beyond the context of the world. It cannot be done. Our survival in every sense depends on what happens to the world, and knowing the world is as horrifying as knowing ourselves. Thus many "human growth" groups shun issues of the world as a troublesome, often contemptuous distraction from the quest for inner peace. Neither group will change anything. Moving and being. The being people won't move, and the movement people won't be.

Political evangelism. Personal and organizational rigidity. The race is on to see who is most revolutionary. The condition becomes totally irrelevant, because the enemy is no longer the system but other radical groups rushing to claim the revolution as their own personal territory. The system need not worry about fighting you. You'll ego yourselves to death, echoing words of a different time, a different place. Your revolution, its rhetoric, theory, heroes, and foundation, is imported and in many ways does not apply. No revolution can succeed unless it is indigenous. If it isn't, it can grow into a lie.

Was the SLA so inconceivable? Awaiting the resumption of the meeting, I saw the answer clearly. People would rather kill or die than admit the lie. Gazing down the hall, I noticed Randy leaning against a door frame, conferring with Bates, the FBI man. As a power broker, Randy seemed even more responsible than the SLA for the narrow scope of our negotiations, for it is the power brokers who have most fashioned the condition. Because they have the wealth and means to perpetuate their condition and ours, power brokers see their world as the only way. In the name of free enterprise, their "solution" continues to exploit and misuse people. Worst of all, power brokers are indifferent. They have no passion. They don't even hate the poor, which at least would be a form of passion. In hate, there is the hope for change. There is no hope in indifference. Thus the outcome is always the same, regardless of appearance. For the sake of expediency, they bend to absorb public pressure, knowing full well that the limits are wholly determined by their own self-interest.

Power brokers, you are the vision America secretly cherishes. You are the end, the pinnacle, the envy of your nation. With the stroke of a pen, a long-distance call, you can change history. And there's nothing you need that you can't have. Your power is real, we see it every day. We know you exist but we never see you. Who took us to Vietnam? You are obscure, you are a vision. A sentiment, a network of desires. You are success in America.

But you have no experience.

You see yourselves in a certain light, the way in which America likes to see itself. You consider yourself ruthless at times, but never evil. You believe in fair play, goodness, honor. An embrace of moral principles. You have families of your own, and you care for them. There is a soft spot in your heart for the notion of children, and you take pity on wounded animals. You are not the traditional concept of evil.

But you kill without experiencing the act.

That is your horror. You may have moral principles, but you are beyond morality because you have no passion. Even at the moment of death, you have no passion. Especially when others are dying and not your own. Death as an acceptable way of life. It is your indifference that is murderous.

I sometimes meet with you in your top-floor conference rooms, but only to confront you, to break through your isolation. I don't come because you want me to come. I don't make appointments with you. I come because certain circumstances demand a response from you, and I want you to face the horror of your power. In your rooms high above the city, it's as though you are literally attempting the climb to the castle, determined to escape the realities of the earth. You live to be isolated and insulated. Much of America lives this way also, but you have the wealth and tools to erect your skyscrapers and your elegant mansions in the woods. Even if you care about the condition, and I know some of you who do, your own structures prevent you from touching it. When forced to address the condition, you deny the participation of those most affected by it. The greed and oppression inherent in your solution have trapped you. What is a huge and opulent house ringed with electrified fencing and stone walls, and patrolled by a private security force? What is that, if not a prison?

You trust no one unlike you. I'm not sure you even trust yourselves. You trust only power. Invisible, omnipotent, nearly divine. Its perpetuation is your only cause. Your position depends on maintenance of the lie, your profits depend on the exploitation of the poor, your power is dependent on the powerlessness of us all. Our powerlessness. *That* is the lie you need the most, but life will survive you.

The Vacaville meeting room door squeaked open, and Jeff appeared in the hall, motioning for me to come. He stepped aside for me to enter but kept the rest from coming in. Once the two prisoners and I were alone, Jeff asked me whether in my opinion he could trust the situation. I said I couldn't make any guarantees but that given the gravity of the circumstances

I didn't think anyone would renege on concessions they made. Jeff nodded and said they'd decided to give it a try.

The final document called on the SLA to release Patty. In a code that only Jeff and the SLA understood, it also promised a flight to exile. I was hopeful that the message might bring the episode to a safe end, but I despaired because even then nothing would truly change. Despite the despondency, however, I felt renewed by the conviction that I would push for life again and again. Hope and despair. The fugue, the rhythm of life below my melody.

Beneath the darkening afternoon sky, we stepped from the building into a courtyard. The others marched across it chatting among themselves, but I stood still a moment and stared at the prison walls rising around me. Silent, inescapable, everlasting.

Prison walls spread before me in the church parking lot, the contractions growing even more forceful as I stand alone in full darkness. I feel it is not time to leave yet. Breaths much deeper now, disturbing the silence with the sound of life, the hope and despair of Vacaville, but especially the hope, coming forth as the hope of this very moment at the end of the 1970s. A new decade coming down the street, fresh and unstoppable. The 1980s. An arbitrary accident of time, but still the suggestion of another beginning. The contractions of the present rising from the contractions of all my experience, the contractions of the 1980s soon to come, pushing for life. My time bursts forth in defined chunks, proposing a lesson in its shape and form. The 1980s. This is why I have waited here tonight. At this moment in 1979, how did the 1970s begin? In San Quentin, on Soul Day.

I remained face to face with the five San Quentin prisoners, the steel bars of the gate still between us. The gate opened with a metallic sigh, and the prisoners' hands were instantly on me. Excepting a certain supportive insistence—I did not feel unwelcome then—they were no different from yours or mine. Human voices bid emphatic greetings, and I followed the prisoners inside the walls and across a vast yard toward the auditorium.

In every direction were stone walls and catwalks and uniformed guards who were frightening in their anonymity, their identities absorbed by their uniforms and the assumption of power. From the viewpoint of the hot yard, they were the enemy. One sensed that clearly. Yet I supposed that from their perch above the yard the guards perceived the prisoners in much the same fashion, indistinguishable as human beings, defined by their uniforms and the verdicts that imprisoned them. The nature of their crimes hardly mattered in the long run. The verdict was what counted. The prison seemed to possess the power to render everyone invisible, guards and inmates alike.

The prisoners were celebrating the day with an easy jocularity, glad, it seemed to me, at the small connection with the outside world. And for all of us it was exactly as though I'd come from another world. I began to sense their inexorable, almost overpowering isolation. For them, the rest of the world in a sense did not exist. Out there beyond the impenetrable walls was a reality in which they played no part. Their lone reality was inside, among themselves. Invisible, forgotten, locked into categories, victimized by a sense of motionless time in which moments existed only to be counted. Alienation would be too cerebral a word for what I felt in there. At that moment, I liked burial a lot better.

"We better get inside," one of them said to me.

"Yes."

"Then follow me."

Why was I there? In the instant before I entered the auditorium, that was the only question that seemed to contain substance.

When they call you on Soul Day, you go. In a sense so temporal it embraces the spiritual, Soul Day means Judgment Day to me. But it does not imply the end, because it comes more than once. It comes time after time.

Some 1,600 prisoners were inside the hall, each assigned a designated seat. Guards ambled up and down the aisles spot-checking seats and the bodies that occupied them. I saw a few men being ordered out of one seat and into another. There was no freedom of movement.

A collection of community dignitaries was spread across the stage. Since I was the main speaker, I waited through the preliminaries. The prisoners were a good audience, attentive and responsive, but there remained the aura of unequivocal confinement.

What does one say to a roomful of prisoners?

I was powerless to affect the structure of their imprisonment. They would remain incarcerated after I departed, their survival reduced to the most basic terms. Gazing at the men, who were invisible to all but themselves and perhaps a handful of people on the outside, I realized that even in its degradation and embittering loneliness it was the prison that bonded them together.

Finally I was introduced. As I approached the microphone and removed it from the stand, the prisoners gave me a warm and boisterous welcome.

"All of you know what prison is because you are imprisoned here," I said. "But let me tell you about the prisons of a lot of other people. The prison of those who feel no power."

Looks of recognition there.

"Those who feel no love. Those who feel no courage, no pride, no dignity. Those who feel nothing. They have no community, you see. They pretend, they are indecisive, they are not involved. They've given up all hope."

I saw their lips move. I heard their voices then, but not as clearly as I heard my own, inside: *I am the prisoner.* All along, from San Angelo to San Quentin (all the way to now), I have been a prisoner. There will always be the prison. So where is the hope?

"Because you are locked up together, you have a better chance to move beyond control by, first of all, not letting them fragment you. The prison system wants you fragmented. But as long as you are, you'll never have the power that is yours, the power to be who you must be and do what you must do."

In all their colors and disparities, the prisoners erupted in cheers and applause. There was the ripple of something beneath the sound. The nature of power. The core of survival. Papa Jack had said to me, *"You all be exslaves too."*

"People on the outside are always being set up just like you. Set up so they can be apart from self, apart from community, apart from the world. They're made to feel isolated. They're made to feel they can't do anything for themselves. They are inside too, my brothers."

The lights flickered, a visible gasp. I thought it was my imagination.

"That's why institutions and systems depend on your weakness. They can control you when you're weak, fragmented, isolated. And the weaker you get, the stronger they grow. But you, each and every one of you, have a great opportunity because you're in the hole together. Now is the time for you to organize. Then your voice will be heard. When you come together, your rhetoric changes to action. When you organize, you don't have to put each other down and feel put down. You begin to feel your power. I say to you, Walk your power, talk your power, live your power!"

Suddenly, with no sound or warning, the lights died, plunging the entire auditorium into pitch darkness. Confusion, the sudden emergence of chaos and mystery. I struggled to find the shadowy definition of my own hand lost in the blackness. Everything was invisible. In the absence of light, only the prison itself gained strength. I grew fearful. Voices spoke to me: *Go on, man. Say it. Don't be afraid.*

Even rational thought, memories of the precise circumstances before the lights went out, brought me no comfort. I was trapped in a dark room with 1,600 convicted prisoners, many of whom had nothing to lose. Would they come and get me? In a frenzy of violent destruction, would they turn on each other? Darkness has such power.

The voices increased in volume and frequency. They were human yet alien, disembodied in the blackness, hovering near, their intentions masked by darkness. For a moment, I allowed the darkness to define the voices, as if it were more worthy than they of my fractured attention. Should I trust them? Voices in the dark. Do you hear me? Wherever you are, do you hear me now?

Don't be afraid, brother. Keep on rappin'.

What was I to say to them?

We're with you.

Fear fed my indecision. In the darkness, I was more than ever just like them. And what of the guards and guns and violence and isolation? I felt their presence keenly, like things sensed in

212

the night. Anything could happen, and no one would ever know for sure. In the end, who could tell us apart? The darkness played no favorites; it treated each of us equally. I *was* just like them. That was the point, but fear kept me from accepting it. Not the fear of death but the fear of the darkness.

Talk to us, brother.

It's never the darkness that matters, is it? That's only part of the condition we share. Horror is never the darkness, it's only what is done within it. Could I trust the voices? I yelled at them,

"Keep talkin' to me. Keep tellin' me. Step with me, stay with me."

Right now I can calm the prisoners, can't I? As long as I advance myself as someone important and suggest they defer their power to me, I can tell them to remain in their special seats until the lights come back on. But then I will be one with those who have the power to turn the lights on and off at their will. I don't want them to have that power. I must have it. The prisoners must have it. *You* must have it. Will you dare to use it?

I wasn't going to let them determine for me the power of light and darkness.

"There is no escape!" I screamed into the pit.

Do you hear me?

There's no escape for us. If you believe in escape, then *you* are the prisoner, a prisoner within your escape. The stench and filth and dirt and beauty will stay with you no matter what you do or where you go. You can cover up all you want, but you will never escape the darkness, the prison, the life. The coverup is the prison, and still I hear you say,

"I am condemned for the rest of my life."

And I say to you, "The greater danger is not in being condemned, but in breaking out." Escaping is living the lie. Breaking out is killing the lie and pulling life from its death.

"It's dark in here!"

Amen.

"I said it's dark in here!"

Amen!

"But that doesn't bother me because we're going to walk in the darkness and talk in the darkness and move in the darkness and do in the darkness. No, that don't bother me."

You say, "I can't take it." And I say, *"Embrace your horror!"* The greater danger is not in escaping horror, but in embracing horror. Where there is great horror, there is great hope. There's always the light. Hope means struggle, and the struggle never truly leaves any of us. Face it, confront it, walk into it, do battle with it. There is the hope.

Push for life. The greater the contractions, the greater the push. The greater danger is not in taking life, but in giving life. I am a midwife, pushing for life. Between the pain and the breath, between death and life, between darkness and light, I push for survival. Breath pushes through pain, life pushes through death, light pushes through darkness.

Light and darkness have a way of breaking through each other. The light becomes so strong that the darkness erupts with all its power. Yet still there is the light. Even then.

Voices of prisoners in the dark.
Stand up.
We're with you.
We'll walk with you.
We are together.
I roared, "Yes! In the darkness they will not claim us. In the darkness they can't destroy us. We will survive!"

In silent mystery, the lights came back on. All the prisoners had moved from their designated seats. They stood with their arms locked together, filling me with an inexpressible hope.

It is what the night has been building toward, the reason I could not leave. The 1980s, time itself coming toward me down the street, that moment in San Quentin filled with so much more meaning now. The contractions then, the contractions now becoming a single powerful experience. We must all become midwives if we are to survive. On the edge of the 1980s, I see them rising before me on Ellis Street. All prisoners standing, one arm locked to the next.

Each day we survive is Soul Day. Yes, I'm alive.